Disruptive Voices

Critical Perspectives on Women and Gender

Critical Perspectives on Women and Gender brings books on timely issues and controversies to an interdisciplinary audience. The series explores gender-related topics and illuminates the issues involved in current debates in feminist scholarship and across the disciplines.

Series Editorial Board

Ruth Behar
Müge Göçek
Anne Herrmann
Patricia Simons
Domna Stanton
Abigail Stewart
Christina Brooks Whitman

Titles in the series

Michelle Fine
Disruptive Voices: The Possibilities of Feminist Research

Susan D. Clayton and Faye J. Crosby
Justice, Gender, and Affirmative Action

Janice Doane and Devon Hodges
From Klein to Kristeva: Psychoanalytic Feminism and the Search for the "Good Enough" Mother

Disruptive Voices
The Possibilities
of Feminist Research

Michelle Fine

Ann Arbor

THE UNIVERSITY OF MICHIGAN PRESS

Copyright © by the University of Michigan 1992
All rights reserved
Published in the United States of America by
The University of Michigan Press
Manufactured in the United States of America

1995   1994   1993   4   3   2

Library of Congress Cataloging-in-Publication Data

Fine, Michelle.
    Disruptive voices : the possibilities of feminist research /
Michelle Fine.
        p.   cm. — (Critical perspectives on women and gender)
    Includes bibliographical references and index.
    ISBN 0-472-09465-3 (alk. paper). — ISBN 0-472-06465-7 (pbk. :
alk. paper)
    1. Women—Psychology. 2. Feminist psychology. 3. Women—
Research. I. Title. II. Series.
HQ1206.F464   1992
305.4'072—dc20   92-7620
                                                    CIP

Acknowledgments

Many of the essays in this text have been previously published, if in somewhat revised form. I gratefully acknowledge the publishers and editors of the following texts for their support in putting together this volume:

Asch, A., and Fine, M. 1988. Beyond pedestals: An introduction. In *Women with disabilities: Essays in psychology, culture, and politics,* ed. M. Fine and A. Asch. Philadelphia: Temple University Press.

Brodkey, L., and Fine, M. 1988. Presence of mind in the absence of body. *Journal of Education* 170, no. 3:84–99.

Fine, M. 1988. Sexuality, schooling, and adolescent females: The missing discourse of desire. *Harvard Educational Review* 58, no. 1 (February): 29–53.

Fine, M. 1989. Coping with rape: Critical perspectives on consciousness. In *Representations: Social constructions of gender,* ed. R. Unger. Amityville, N.Y.: Baywood Press.

Fine, M. 1989. Silencing and nurturing voice in an improbable context: Urban adolescents in public schools. In *Critical pedagogy, the state, and cultural struggle,* ed. H. Giroux and P. McLaren. Albany: SUNY Press.

Fine, M., and Gordon, S. 1989. Feminist transformations of/despite psychology. In *Gender and thought: Psychological perspectives,* ed. M. Crawford and M. Gentry. New York: Springer-Verlag.

Fine, M. 1990. The "public" in public schools: The social constriction/construction of a moral community. *Journal of Social Issues* 46, no. 1:107–19.

Fine, M., and Macpherson, P. Forthcoming. Over dinner: Feminism and adolescent female bodies. In *Gender and education.,* ed. S. Biklen and D. Pollard. National Society for Secondary Education Yearbook.

Preface

I remember as a child watching my mother cry on the kitchen table. Most would say she had a difficult childhood. The youngest of eighteen, from an impoverished and oppressive household. She worried always about her aged, widowed mother's health and felt responsible always for everyone. I remember her mid-adulthood, her late thirties and early forties. These years, tears saturated her daily existence. I decided, probably before age five, that my life would be different. And so it was, nourished with love and strength she and my father gave me. Second-wave feminist outrage was undoubtedly well nourished, for so many of us witnessed, from under or beyond the kitchen table, the swelling of maternal depression across the 1940s and 1950s.

Most profoundly, I remember the ways in which my mother harbored secrets, from her friends, kin, and maybe herself, as if her not telling would somehow render her experiences untrue. Her secrets could not have differed much from what most women struggled with during the 1950s—their marriages, loneliness and isolation, finances, children, disappointments, worries about health, and probably even their passions. But my mother told me her secrets. Then I carried her silences. And, since adolescence, I have voiced our outrage. As a child, I must have vowed that I would tell and invite other women to tell. So unfolds this collection of essays, on the stories women tell and don't, about their passions, pains, and collective possibilities.

This text collects stories that I, and others, have gathered and narrated through the methods of feminist psychology invented over the past several decades. Today, or maybe always, it seems desperately important for feminist researchers to see ourselves centrally as activists—to press, provoke, and unbalance social inequities that choreograph relations of gender, race, class, disability, and sexuality. But such work, as scholarship, bears serious consequences—resentment and resistance—as Rachel Hare-Mustin and Jeanne Marecek have written:

Drawing attention to inequality in male-female relations arouses considerable cultural resistance. In American society, egalitarianism is a primary value. Americans are thus strongly disposed to deny relations of inequality. Moreover, those who have power in such an "egalitarian society" have a vested interest in either denying their privileged position or legitimizing it as natural, moral or right. (1990, 185)

The essays in this text construct feminist psychology as a social change strategy. Three particular instances of "mother wit" signify how radically such a feminist psychology departs from traditional psychology. First, as it evolves across this text, feminist psychology presumes that social activism is the project within which we conduct our work. In so doing, our audiences, tasks, assumptions, ethical concerns, and our interest in collaboration are profoundly transformed. Second, within feminist psychology, personal passions and collective politics fundamentally ground our critical scholarship. The mystified space yawning between "objectivity" and "politics" is exposed as an illusion, justifying and laminating existing forms of social privilege in the name of objectivity. Third, unlike traditional psychology, which presumes a fair playing field for all, feminist psychology rests upon the assumption that deep and sustained power asymmetries construct our conceptions and relations of gender, race, class, disability, and sexuality.

In these essays, I try to resurface those contradictions within women's lives which have been suffocated by structured social silences; to reframe those dimensions of "difference" which have been represented as natural and inevitable; to imagine what "could be" for very diverse groups of women; and to provoke feminist strategies for change. The task is to incite a feminist psychology that takes the politics of race/ethnicity, class, sexuality, and disability as seriously as we take gender and not reproduce what critical legal theorist Angela Harris calls feminist essentialism:

In a racist society, like this one, the storytellers are usually white, and so "woman" turns out to be "white woman."

Why, in the face of challenges from "different" women and from feminist method itself, is feminist essentialism so persistent and pervasive? . . . In my view, as long as feminists, like theorists in the dominant culture, continue to search for gender and racial essences, black women will never be anything more than a crossroads between two kinds of domination, or at the bottom of a hierarchy of oppressions; we will always be required to choose pieces of ourselves to present as wholeness. (Harris 1990, 589)

By braiding gender with race, class, disability, and sexuality, feminist psychology can expose critically the multiple and contradictory silences that women have long preserved and transgress creatively at the negotiated boundaries of "what's possible."

For inspiration, we retreat for a moment to the Heterodoxy Club, early 1900s. Historians Kathy Peiss, Judith Schwarz, and Christina Simmons have woven a powerful narrative and photographic documentary about this "little band of willful women, the most unruly and individualistic you ever fell upon." The club, founded in 1912 by suffrage leader Marie Jenney Howe,

explored women's intellectual and psychological repression, their desire for self-fulfillment and the historic opening of new experiences and opportunities. . . . They countered dominant ideas of women's physical and intellectual inferiority and dependency in their work as physicians, lawyers, college teachers and political activists. (1989, 120)

Leta Hollingworth was an early feminist educational psychologist who joined the Heterodites. In her writings, she captured much of what we can only imagine to be their collective passions and politics:

SALUTATION

Het'rodites, Yuletide greetings!
At this season of gifts.
Shall I tell you the gifts you bestow on me,
As we sit at the long tables,
And the years slip along?
Gifts intangible and imponderable—
Yet bright with reality?

For there is no subtler pleasure—
than to know minds capable
Of performing the complete act of thought.

There is no keener joy than to see
Clear cut human faces,
Faces like those men choose—
For coins and cameos.
(Leta S. Hollingworth [in Peiss, Schwarz, and Simmons
1990, 137])

Almost four generations since Hollingworth, feminist psychologists today still hesitate to assert self-consciously the politics and passions that season our scholarship so deeply. And yet we continue to accumulate unprecedented evidence of women's oppression, outrages, and pleasures. So most feminist psychologists simply dangle there as we legitimate, in the constructed space between a discourse of objectivity and politics, denying our politics even as our texts are drenched in them.

This collection of essays seeks to explode the objectivity/politics dichotomy by insisting that feminist researchers, like the Heterodoxy women, use research to expose and dislodge psychological notions deployed to comfort, justify, and "make science" of social inequities. Psychology, probably more than any other social science, has been relied upon to "explain" the origins of gender, race, class, and sexual- and disability-based inequities and to situate the origins squarely within individual personalities. In the face of this, we, echoing the women of Heterodoxy, need to resituate our political struggles and our personal passions at the very center of our work, exploring, rather than denying, the nexus of activism and scholarship.

Following an introductory analysis of the historical relationship of feminism and psychology, "Feminist Transformations of/despite Psychology," the chapters of this book are organized around three layers of feminist work. Part 1 focuses on women's bodies, with particular attention paid to the discourses that have surrounded sexual representations of women and women's own reflections on themselves as objects and subjects of sex and violence. Part 2 enters explicitly the social silences and shadows to which women's lives and stories have been relegated and in which women's resistances have fermented. Part 3, to conclude, pries open feminist talk as a space for creative, activist research, with essays that move toward "what could be" a deeply feminist psychology, unraveling social secrets while provoking feminist activism.

This book grows out of the lived politics of women before me: those who somehow resisted, like the Heterodoxy women, and those who somehow didn't—women who lived the lives they were supposed to live, kept the secrets of their gendered, raced, and classed lives, preserved the "moral order" at home and on the streets, and paid dearly and, typically, alone.

Rebecca, my grandmother, bore eighteen children in Poland. The last of them was my mother. Rebecca was a woman who smiled often, loved much, expected (and got) little, and would, I can only imagine, be shocked to hear that marital rape, sexual harassment, or safe abortions have been legally encoded (and eroded) during the past twenty years. Her photos, when she smiled, blossomed with the power of women, of humor, of relationships, of love. At the same time, my grandmother's spirit seems shriveled inside the body of a woman kept, fundamentally, out of control of her own economic, reproductive, and relational lives.

In the next generation, my mother, Rose, was born, when Rebecca had reached fifty-two (or fifty-six, depending on which relative you choose to believe). She lived under the rule of her oldest brother, who fiercely controlled family resources, movements, and family talk. In her early twenties, my mother found a man to free, protect, and love her. She married my father, Jack, onetime Lower East Side horse and buggy junk salesman. Now over seventy, she confides in me, her youngest. She just recently asked me to teach her to write a check. She has never learned to drive. Never used a credit card. Has never made a collect call. She smiles oddly when I speak of women's sexual pleasures.

It was probably ten years ago that my sister Sherry, my mother, and I attended a therapy session together. At one point in the hour, the therapist asked my mother for her thoughts about our conversation. It was probably then that this book was first conceived. My mother responded to the question: "My own mother, I'll never forget, she used to say . . ."

The therapist politely interrupted, "What do *you* think, Rose?" to which my mother continued, "If my husband, Jackie, were here, he would say . . ."

The therapist tried again, "Rose, what about *you?*"

With a knowing smile, she looked at us, grown women, her daughters, and said, "The girls always tell me . . ."

I remember having a tear stream down my face, hearing the therapist's voice, now muffled. Trying to clarify, "Rose, your mother is gone, Jack is not in the room, and your daughters can speak for themselves. What do *you* think, Rose?" My mother struggled to formulate an answer.

But with all those relationships evacuated, she said she couldn't. Her silence echoed the countless, contradictory voices sedimented shut, nestled between the layers of Rose. Daughter to Rebecca, wife to Jack, mother to Richard, Sherry, and Michelle, and grandmother to so many.

Each of the essays in this book is an attempt to wedge between women's layers, to hear what has been hidden, swallowed, suffocated, and treasured by, for, and despite women.

If all of our stories are indeed our own, if social research is largely autobiography, then the stories of this text are, of course, mine. What I have done across these essays is to chronicle my thinking with and because of friends, family, and strangers. Voices heard, muffled, suffocated, shouted in collective rage, and invented, as I have listened to women for what they say has been, could be, and what they long for.

This book is dedicated to Rebecca and Rose, Sherry and my niece Jackie. Four generations of women who have lived with secrets, told some, and have been haunted by many. Women with satin desires, rebellious passions, and feisty politics. But this book is also dedicated to those generations of women who simply choked on their secrets, took the blame and went slowly mad, in drink, drugs, violence, or joyful fantasies others would call delusions.

I thank—for love, friendship, and collaboration—co-authors Adrienne Asch, Linda Brodkey, Donnie Cook, Susan Gordon, and Pat Macpherson, as well as Donna Leitner, Elizabeth Sayre, and Jennifer Williams for manuscript assistance. Much appreciation to Abby Stewart from the University of Michigan and LeAnn Fields, from the University of Michigan Press, for encouragement. I invite us all, collectively and collaboratively, to disrupt, transgress, and invent possibilities for a deeply feminist psychology designed with and for women—displaying all our contradictions and differences.

Contents

Feminist Transformations of/despite Psychology

Michelle Fine and Susan Merle Gordon

The field of psychology has long enjoyed an internal debate about women (Crawford and Marecek 1988; Hare-Mustin and Marecek 1987). Traditionally, we have been the *objects* of these conversations, however, and not their subjects. With due respect to our foremothers, feminist psychologies have developed institutionally only over the past two decades. Now generating critique, reclaiming the topics of girls and women, and creating novel methods for exploring gender as noun and verb (Unger 1983; West and Zimmerman 1987), this work is rich and interdisciplinary, but not always recognizable as psychology.

Finding and representing a powerful, coherent, and sustained set of feminist voices within the discipline is no easy task (see Walsh 1987, on current controversies). Many interrogate gender differences. Some explore girls and women alone. Still others struggle over the dialectics of gender with race/ethnicity (Amaro and Russo 1987; Espin 1987; Ladner 1972; Lykes 1986; Rodgers-Rose 1980; Smith and Stewart 1983), social class (Rubin 1976), sexual orientation (Boston Lesbian Psychologies Collective 1987; Brown 1987), disability (Fine and Asch 1988), and/or age (Huddy and Goodchilds 1985). We exist at moments, at the margins and among ourselves. Whether or not we have transformed the discipline of psychology, and whether or not we would like to, remain empirical and political questions (see Grady 1981; Parlee 1979; Shields 1975; Unger 1982; Wallston 1981; Wittig 1985, for critiques).

At the level of theory, methods, politics, and activism, it is safe to say that feminist psychology has interrupted the discipline. And yet many of us have left our disciplinary homes. Some have literally exited the academy to work with activist organizations, conducting research, practice, and/or evaluations. Others remain academy bound but scattered throughout schools of education, social work, communications and law, in women's studies or African-American studies, working at the inter-disciplinary fringes, trying to articulate feminist epistemologies, theories, methods, and politics through the world of the university (Mayo 1982). Some survive inside traditional psychology departments, writing within the mainstream, while a few seek audience and collaboration among friends, students, and colleagues who have abandoned or been tossed out of the mainstream of psychology. If many of the critical daughters of psychology have left home and others remain "in the kitchen" doing the dirty work of critique, transformation, and creativity (e.g., Caplan and Hall-McCorquodale 1985), perhaps we need to reflect on where feminist psychologies and psychologists have gone, where we are going, and whether or not we want to reclaim the discipline.

In this chapter we explore the question: Is feminist psychology an inherent contradiction? Are psychology's obsessions compatible with notions of feminist epistemology (see Flax 1987; Harding 1987; Hartsock 1987)? These obsessions include notions of experimental control; explicit distance separating researcher from researched; conversion of subjects into objects; "universal laws" that render race/ethnicity, gender, and social class to be "noise"; a romance with sterile environments called laboratories in which human behavior can be perverted and then studied as if "natural" and "uncontaminated"; a commitment to generalizability that turns "real" social contexts into intrusions on science; and a fetish with imposed categories, comparisons, hierarchies, and stages. In the first half of this chapter, we consider how these contradictions (de)form the scholarship we call psychology of women/gender, and, in the second half, we imagine the contours of a project of political feminist psychology.

Feminist Transformations of Psychology

Women who have investigated the question of feminist influence on psychology have typically been quite generous to our forefathers, foremothers, and colleagues, measuring the "challenge" over the past twenty years in the broadest possible terms. Maxine Bernstein and Nancy Russo (1974), Brinton Lykes and Abby Stewart (1986), Mary Parlee (1979), Mary Roth Walsh (1987), and others document feminist influence in the increase of numbers of women published as authors, listed as editors, footnoted by authors, and included as "subjects"; the diminished proportions of male-only studies; the increased proportions of studies in which females are compared to males; and the use of methods and contexts broadened far beyond the laboratory into the realms of lived experience.

Building on this scholarship, we propose a more precisely defined set of criteria. If feminism has had a transformative impact on psychology, we would expect that psychologists who interrogate gender would do so with the following a priori understandings (Harding 1987):

1. *Power asymmetries* structure gender relations.
2. Gender always braids with social class, race/ethnicity, age, disability (or not), and sexual orientation, as well as social context to produce *socially and historically constituted subjectivities.*
3. The *meanings* of a social experience *as expressed by women* must be unraveled if that experience is to be fully analyzed.
4. *Contextualized research* is necessary to unearth women's psychologies as they reflect, reproduce, resist, and transform social contexts, hegemonic beliefs, and personal relationships.

With these criteria, dare we note that the transformation of psychology by feminism has been modest. Psychology, like other oppressive social institutions, has been relatively immune to the transformative power of feminism (and other civil rights movements).

Sociologists and psychologists today conclude that, while the feminism of the 1960s to 1980s has systematically affected women's consciousness, the traditional division of domestic labor, the organization of paid work, and the national distribution of wealth, income, and poverty have been relatively untouched. In the United States, women still do the housework (91 percent of married women), tend to children, make the dinners, care for the elderly, and live in disproportionate poverty—even while we may feel more "liberated" than twenty years ago. Girls and women across classes and racial and ethnic groups *have* changed, but the structures around us remain relatively intact. The discipline of psychology, like marriage, work, and parenting practices, has basically retained its shape, its boundaries, and its resistance to disruption in the eye of the feminist storm.

It is true that today more women are published, included as "subjects," and quantitatively compared to male subjects. These criteria, however, should be considered wholly inadequate to render psychological research feminist. While a vibrant strain of feminist psychology survives and flourishes, and while psychology of women courses are offered widely and enjoy extreme popularity, mainstream psychological research remains basically unchanged. For main/male stream psychology to display proudly its feminist heritage, gender, race/ethnicity, class, and other social dimensions of what feel like "personal experiences" would have to be placed squarely within the context of power. On this dimension, the transformative impact of feminism has been sorely lacking.

The Evidence on Transformation: Keeping Our Mouths Shut

A student recently informed me (MF) that a friend, new to both marriage and motherhood, now lectures her single women friends: "If you're married and want to stay that way, you learn to keep your mouth shut." Perhaps (academic) psychologists interested in gender have learned (or anticipated) this lesson in their "marriage" with the discipline of psychology. With significant exceptions, feminist psychologists basically keep our mouths shut within the discipline. We ask relatively nice questions (given the depth of oppression against women); we do not stray from gender into race/ethnicity, sexuality, disability, or class; and we ask our questions in a relatively tame manner. Below we examine how feminist psychologists conduct our public/published selves. By traveling inside the pages of *Psychology of Women Quarterly (PWQ)*, and then within more mainstream journals, we note a *disciplinary reluctance* to engage gender/women at all but also a *feminist reluctance* to represent gender as an issue of power.

In 1986, Brinton Lykes and Abby Stewart compared articles in *Psychology of Women Quarterly* to those in *Journal of Personality and Social Psychology (JPSP)*. They learned that *PWQ* more often analyzed data between males and females and included adults as "subjects." Moreover, only 15 percent of its studies were experiments, as compared with more than 50 percent in *JPSP*. They concluded that a feminist challenge to psychology has been felt, but not in the mainstream. We decided to expand the Lykes-Stewart analysis to study the feminist transformation of psychology through an assessment of what we decided to call the "penetration index," the "ovulation index," and the "transformative index."

The *penetration index* (PI) measures the extent to which mainstream journals in psychology cite articles from feminist journals. Drawing on three major psychological journals, *Developmental Psychology, Journal of Personality and Social Psychology,* and *Psychology of Women Quarterly,* we measured the frequency of citation of articles published in the seven feminist journals indexed in the *Social Science Citation Index (Feminist Studies, International Journal of Women's Studies, Psychology of Women Quarterly, Sex Roles, Signs, Women's Health,* and *Women's Studies International Forum* represented 0.005 of the 1,413 journals indexed in 1986).

Tracking the three psychological journals from 1981 through 1986, we found that *Developmental Psychology's* citations referred to a feminist journal article in a ratio of 0.03 (in 1981) and 0.02 (1986); *Journal of Personality and Social Psychology* referred to a feminist journal article in a ratio of 0.04 (in 1981) and 0.03 (1986); and *Psychology of Women Quarterly's* citations referred to a feminist journal article in a ratio of 0.32 (in 1981) and 0.37 (1986). Thus, on this first measure of penetration, we see a slow leak of feminist scholarship into the mainstream, little change over historic time, and a persistent community of co-citers among feminist scholars.

A second index of penetration measures the ratio by which studies from *PWQ* are cited in explicitly feminist versus other journals. That is, what share of the feminist citation pie is accounted for historically by feminist publications? Here we have more evidence of both the growing community of co-citers and the resistance to feminism within the mainstream. In 1981, 9 percent of the 1,035 *PWQ* cites were located in feminist journals, with 91 percent in other journals. By 1986, whereas the total number of citations had dropped by 10 percent to 932, we find that 23 percent are in feminist journals, and 77 percent are not. Feminists cite feminists more than we did five years ago, while others cite them less.

Since we developed a penetration index we were politically obligated to develop an *ovulation index* (OI). The OI measures the frequency of articles published in the mainstream and periodically released, which deal with gender and race. The data on the OI are disturbingly slim and disturbingly consistent from 1980 through 1986. Reviewing *American Psychologist, Developmental Psychology, Journal of Counseling Psychology,* and *Journal of Personality and Social Psychology,* we find that the percentage of studies (except in *American Psychologist,* where we relied on articles) dealing specifically with gender in 1980 ranged from 10 percent to 17 percent and in 1986 from 10 percent to 16 percent. Articles on race were even less frequent, ranging in 1980 from 2 percent to 5 percent, and in 1986 from 1.5 percent to 9 percent. Across these years and journals, only one article could be found that explicitly analyzed for social class differences, and that was in 1980; sexual preference emerged in 1986 *Developmental Psychology* and *JPSP* articles at a frequency of 1 percent each; and disability showed up as a researched topic in 1986 in 2–4 percent of the articles reviewed. The interactions of these variables were entirely absent from the volumes studied. In terms of ovulation, the flow is regular, slow, and relatively uneventful across studies of gender, race, social class, sexuality, and disability.

Finally, we come to the *transformative index* (TI), which turns our analyses away from the mainstream and onto feminist psychology itself. We examined *PWQ* volumes of 1985 and 1986 to establish a baseline of what feminist psychologists do methodologically, discursively, and politically that would/could/should transform the "malestream" (Hartsock 1987) of psychology. Our results were again disappointing. When feminism and psychology mate, feminism seems to bear only recessive genes.

Before launching into the transformative index for 1985–86, we digress for a moment to consider the findings of a similar review conducted by one of us (Fine 1985b) on *PWQ* articles published from 1978 through 1981. Of this earlier cohort of articles, it was found that 51 percent reported college women as their respondents with 9 percent mentioning nonwhite respondents. A full 71 percent examined only individual attributes, and 21 percent studied interpersonal relationships. Problematic themes wove through the conclusions: (1) authors ended their pieces on a note of progressive progress, with unchecked optimism about women in the future; (2) authors psychologized the structural forces that construct women's lives by offering internal explanations for social conditions; and (3) through the promotion of individualistic change strategies, authors invited women to alter some aspect of *self* in order to transform social arrangements. That analysis concluded with a caution about the creeping conservatism of the times and the discipline: "If we do not resist what I assume will be a concerted effort to undermine our advance, feminist psychology may assimilate to the powerful traditions of psychology" (1985b, 181).

Turning to *PWQ* for 1985–86, we note the persistence of individualism and conservatism, but a substantial diversification of samples studied. In 1985, of forty-two *PWQ* articles, thirty-seven reported studies of which eighteen (52 percent) included college student subjects and nine (24 percent) mentioned "diverse" populations (not only white, middle-class, heterosexual, and nondisabled). A full 86 percent (thirty-two) studied individuals rather than pairs, groups, collectives, relationships, or structures; and 24 percent of the studies' conclusions referred to some notion of *change.* In only 8 percent of these studies, however, was this change social, as opposed to individual. A year later, in 1986, there were thirty-four articles, and, of these, twenty-seven were studies. A third of the studies reported samples of college student subjects, with 41 percent describing samples selected for their diversity (by race / ethnicity and sexual orientation). One-third relied on women subjects only, and the remaining two-thirds compared females to males. Eighty-one percent (twenty-two) studied individuals, and an equal proportion concluded their essays with summarizing descriptions of the data. One-fifth attributed outcomes to gender differences, whereas 80 percent explained findings based on contextual or historic factors. Nineteen percent referred to change, and 7 percent offered thoughts on the relationship of the study to social change.

Feminist psychology published within *our* representative divisional journal does reform the samples, methods, and questions of psychology as well as broaden the scope of interpretation. But we also reproduce the individualism and conservatism of the larger discipline. Most feminist psychologists have yet to declare questions of power primary; to establish white, heterosexual, patriarchal control as central to relations and representations of gender; and to take seriously the spaces that women create as retreats, as celebrations, as moments of resistance, and as the closets for our social transformation. Even among ourselves, feminist psychologists, by necessity or desire, appear to be playing to a male psychological audience. In our attempts to bring feminism to psychology, we have perhaps undermined the politics and scholarship of feminism, refused questions of power asymmetry, and defaulted to the benign study of gender differences.

Refusing Power and Studying Differences: A Political Compromise on Gender

Rachel Hare-Mustin and Jeanne Marecek (1987) argue that to the extent that psychology (feminist and not) "does" gender at all, it does gender as difference. In this formulation, they describe two biases. The "alpha bias" occurs when gender differences are exaggerated, and the "beta bias" occurs when differences are minimized. Drawing on the Hare-Mustin-Marecek compelling metaview of gender inside psychology, we argue that this almost exclusive construction of gender-as-difference functions inside psychology as a political and scientific diversion away from questions of power, social context, meaning, and braided subjectivities.

Psychological researchers interested in gender typically rely on the simple and essential notion of differences. Within our culture and particularly our discipline, these empirical differences are then transformed into *either* hierarchy or a dualistic complementarity (as in the androgyny literature). To test male subjects only and then generalize to the human species is considered politically incorrect—even if still practiced regularly. To rely on female subjects only is to do a study on a "special interest group." But to incorporate both genders and divide by two is to conduct "good, nonsexist" psychology (see McHugh, Koeske, and Frieze 1986, for nonsexist guidelines).

We, as psychologists, do not typically study gender as power. We, as feminists, may "do" power between the genders but not within (with important exceptions see Collins 1988; Fine and Asch 1988; Golden 1984; Joseph and Lewis 1981; Smith and Stewart 1983) and remain ever reluctant to study that which interferes with feminist notions of sisterhood, communality, relational orientation, and cooperation (see Dill 1987; Fine and Asch 1988; Miner and Longino 1987; Rollins 1985). Perhaps, in the relatively unexciting space in which we compare women to men and call the results gender differences, we offer a political compromise satisfying minimally the Right and the Left.

The perversion of gender into the dominant study of gender differences may represent a safe, political compromise for feminist and nonfeminist scholars. But the consequences of that compromise are intellectually and politically serious. By drawing on a difference argument, not only do we deploy and legitimate essentialist understandings of gender (Chodorow 1978), but we also reproduce a series of dualistic beliefs about gender, sexuality, and race/ethnicity. Psychologists fetishize gender differences, as they do other differences, by flattening, normalizing, and making "scientific" those aspects of "personal" experience that are ideologically constructed and born of inequality. Teresa de Lauretis (1987) writes that a focus on sex differences keeps us in an "always already . . . political consciousness . . . of dominant cultural discourses." By posing universal oppositions, we are "imprisoned in the master's house" (2–3).

We want to make three points about the unexamined gender difference research frame. First, a focus on between-gender differences as the primary design for gender research creates, as it legitimates, a powerful and unarticulated commitment to heterosexuality as the frame for social research on gender. In Jungian terms, that which is masculine complements and completes that which is feminine. The androgyny literature is replete with this assumption (Bem 1974). To the extent that males and females bring distinct strengths and deficits to their lived experiences, their merger makes good sense and constitutes that which is *normal.*

Further obscured by the gender difference formulation is the political and/or psychoanalytic insight that to be male or masculine in our culture is to *not* be female or feminine. The former requires the eclipsing of the latter (Chodorow 1978; de Lauretis 1987; Harding 1987). And yet a gender difference frame implies the inherent compatibility of the two "roles." The frame fails to challenge the construction of social arrangements/relationships in which the processes and structures of gendering artificially biologize and then split off that which is conceived of as "male" and that which is conceived of as "female." A gender difference analysis simply reproduces the false splitting of the masculine from the feminine, camouflages oppressive structures that split and then "naturalize" gender differences and compulsory heterosexuality (Rich 1980; Rubin 1984), and renders invisible and unnatural a more full menu of human sexualities.

Third, and finally, the gender difference research frame renders the study of differences among and intimacy between women as either irrelevant to social theory or plainly bad science. We know from feminist scholarship and politics (Weitz 1984) that women alone—defined without men—always embody social danger. Whether lesbian, nun, prostitute, widow, single mother, or just a woman alone, she activates social anxieties, signals social dangers, and inherits social degradation. A threat automatically converted into an object of deprecation, she inherits disdain. Inside the discipline of psychology, we find that the study of women alone—without a comparison group of men—is typically disparaged as inadequate research. Whether it is a dissertation proposal of which colleagues may say, "You need to include men to compare these women to," or a review of the psychological literature in which females, if included at all, are typically compared to males, the assumption prevails that this comparison is necessary. When men are studied alone, they produce data on "human behavior." When women are studied alone, they produce barely credible data. The obsession with gender differences forces women's "subjugated knowledges" substantially underground (Belenky, Clinchy, Goldberger, and Tarule 1986; Foucault 1972).

By pitting that which is supposed to be male against that which is supposed to be female, psychologists mask all that we can learn about the construction and politics "in-between" (Poovey 1988) and within the genders. Indeed, we need new language, for we are not actually speaking here about the study of *sex* as biology or even *gender* as the social correlate of biological attributes. We are speaking of the study of the *politics* of *sex/gender* relations, which organize and reproduce, as they resist, and transform oppressive social arrangements (Flax 1987; Rubin 1984; Scott 1985). We are speaking of what may feel biological or psychological but is dialectically entwined with politics. In the absence of such research, we are saturated with studies of gender differences. And most psychologists maintain—implicitly if not explicitly—that, with respect to gender, our theories, methods, and politics are inherently neutral.

The Distortion of Gender in the Guise of Neutrality

If psychology has generated two primary positions in response to the "gender question," with the first arguing for gender differences, the second represents psychology as inherently gender (and power) neutral. The search for "truth" can be navigated through questions of gender, like all other questions. Gender presumably represents a dichotomous variable that can be examined within a laboratory, in a survey, through observations, or with an interview. Absent from the formulation is gender as a relational concept, knitted with power, context, and intimate meanings. We reflect now on these methodological scenes of ostensible neutrality.

What academic psychologists do well are experiments in laboratories. In 1980, this method accounted for 71 percent of studies reported in major social psychological journals. In 1985, it accounted for 78 percent. Psychologists typically generate theory and evidence from accessible populations—white, college-aged, privileged male undergraduates (Sears 1986) and write about that evidence as human behavior. In 1980, 75 percent of reviewed social psychological studies were conducted with students. In 1985, this profile accounted for 83 percent of studies. David Sears concludes his review of social psychological research with some distress, noting that the prestige of social psychological research seems to be linked to the inclusion of college students as subjects and to the location of a study inside experimental laboratories.

The experimental laboratory indeed distinguishes psychology from other social sciences. It is heralded as sterile, neutral, and fully appropriate for eliciting "objective" phenomena while holding the "noise" of social context and background variables silent. When I (MF) was an undergraduate, gender was still considered "noise" in social psychological studies. That is, women were considered noisy because our data did not conform to the male patterns (sometimes called universal laws), and so women were typically excluded from these studies. Today we are back in the lab. Removed from social relationships, interaction in the lab is typically limited to a subject and a white (often male) experimenter. There may be some strangers present, who are euphemistically called group members. Defining features of this context include a lack of trust, longevity, and connection. In caricature, this sounds like a scene designed for Clint Eastwood (a prototypic, if not real, male), and a scene that would drive women mad. Given the ambiguity of the circumstances, the absence of relationships and the anonymity, it is, for instance, a scene in which racist behaviors by white subjects may be most likely to be enacted (as long as they could be concealed) (Gaertner and Dovidio 1981). So much for the study of objective phenomena in "uncontaminated" spaces.

The ostensible sterility and neutrality of the lab mean only that hegemonic beliefs can be imported but not disrupted; that the social relationships and contexts in which women weave their lives are excluded as if irrelevant; that the ways in which women operate as community "glue" and as the institutionalized Other are rendered invisible. What we have in these scenes are female subjects who are actually turned into objects of the experimenter. Whereas feminist theorists have worked hard to distinguish the biological sex from the social gender (Unger 1982), the experimental laboratory removes women from their social contexts, so as not to reveal much about sex or gender. The subject is a product of the laboratory, gendered by what she imports into the lab and gender-perverted by the laboratory that extracts her from the context of her identity. This is no opportunity for the "untainted" display of sex or gender and certainly no test of the political aspects of the sex/gender system and its implications for individual or collective psychologies (Rubin 1984).

The laboratory is almost too easy a target for critique on gender studies. Surveys, observations, or even interviews—relatively more "radical" methods in standard psychology—can also distort gender if applied without attention to power asymmetries, context, and meaning. While they may claim dispassionate investigation by isolating and/or creating an individual woman, psychological observations, surveys, and interviews typically gather data from a woman alone, as if she were in her natural habitat. With power unexamined, context and background whited-out, women's meanings translated *for* her, and universal laws sought, such decontextualized psychology obfuscates the woman (Fine 1986a; Sherif 1987). We offer a negative example of gender-neutral research to illustrate the need for feminist *interruption* of traditional methods.

This example comes from feminist research that unearthed women's meanings—but that could as easily have obfuscated power, context, and meaning. Demie Kurz, sociologist at the University of Pennsylvania, collected divorced women's oral biographies of their lives with former husbands, focusing particularly on child support payments and experiences with domestic violence. Kurz relies on multiple methods, including standardized survey instruments and in-depth interviews, and she asks women to complete Strauss's Conflict Tactic Scale. Respondents circle the number of acts of violence they and their spouse enacted over the past year, and then Kurz invites the women to explain their ratings. One woman completed the Strauss Conflict Tactic Scale by circling almost identical numbers and frequencies of violent acts for herself and her spouse. Another proudly circled more for self than spouse. Trying to present a neutral face, Kurz asked, "So, you and he, you were violent together? You hit him and he hit you?" Both women—independently—laughed and said some version of, "What would you do if he hit you, sit there and smile?"

A third interviewee explained to Kurz that her former husband cleaned out their home one Sunday afternoon. "So he came when you weren't home and took everything?" "No, he used his car—he's too cheap to rent movers—and made ten trips, back and forth. And I stood there and watched." Typical passive woman, right? Wrong. "You didn't do anything?" asked Kurz. "Are you kidding, he was so violent with me I was terrified and glad only to get him out of the house."

Women can appear victimized, not coping, even "co-violent," help-less, or passive if researchers fail to probe for power asymmetries, to unearth the constraints and opportunities of context, and to interrogate local meanings (see Kurz 1988). In such circumstances, the presumption of gender neutrality—within a laboratory, survey, interview, observation, and archival analysis—will undermine all that can be understood about gender and power. By masking asymmetries, such research may discover differences and then ascribe them to biology or social roles, all the while obscuring power.

Reframing the Notion of Transformation: Toward Politics / despite Psychology

The discipline of psychology has appropriated and depoliticized feminism in two ways: through the search for gender differences and through the presumption of gender neutrality. The argument for neutrality suggests that no feminist effort need be asserted to unpack power, context, or meaning; and the search for gender differences flattens the asymmetries that organize gender relations while promoting heterosexuality as the exclusive frame for viewing social relations.

If feminist transformations of psychology per se have been disap-pointing in the mainstream and even within the pages of our own journal, *PWQ*, there nevertheless exists an explosion of feminist critique, epistemologies, theories, methods, and politics emerging from the corners of the academy and beyond, with psychologists cocreating, disrupting, advocating, listening, writing, screaming, and whispering (see Deaux 1984, for review). While we make no attempt to be comprehensive, we merely note *In a Different Voice* (Gilligan 1982), *Women's Ways of Knowing* (Belenky et al. 1986), *Lesbian Psychologies* (Boston Lesbian Psychologies Collective 1987), *The Psychology of Women: Ongoing Debates* (Walsh 1987), *The Black Woman* (Rodgers-Rose 1980), a recent volume of *PWQ* devoted to the study of Hispanic women (Amaro and Russo 1987), a current bibliography of psychological work on women of color (Mays n.d.), *Tomorrow's Tomorrow* (Ladner 1972), *Women with Disabilities: Essays on Psychology, Culture and Politics* (Fine and Asch

1988), and *Representations: Social Constructions of Gender* (Unger 1989a), which collectively enrich, finesse, critique, and create feminist psychologies. In each of these volumes, the tensions of our work are explored, the relationships between researcher and researched unpacked. Subjects get to be subjects, complexity and diversity are sought and welcomed, notions of objectivity are reformulated, and constructions of gender stretch broadly to encompass social and economic arrangements, ideologies, personal relationships, and inner selves. In the next section, we explore feminist psychologists' attempts to interrupt that which we have inherited from the fathers of psychology and reproduced in our own work. We look to the example of feminist therapy to help us imagine how we might evolve a truly political feminist project.

A Project of Political Feminist Psychology

The question of a political feminist psychology automatically raises the question of audience. For whom are we writing/researching? A few position themselves toward "ordinary" women. Some write for/with activists and practitioners, and an even smaller group write for lawyers and potential jurors, as in the case of expert witnesses working for the defense of battered women who kill (Blackman 1989) or adolescent women who seek confidential abortions (see Melton and Russo 1987). Our archival analyses, however, suggest that, for the most part, we are addressing psychologists, even between the relatively safe covers of *PWQ*. This may be due to concerns over tenure, professional acceptability, legitimacy, or the limits of our training. The consequences, however, are extreme.

While feminist psychology exists as a *potentially* expansive field of intellectual and political inquiry, it remains bound by a discipline designed to flatten, depoliticize, and individualize. These unacknowledged contradictions fill that which is called feminist psychology. They pervert our scholarship as they erode the politics of our work. Perhaps more than in other disciplines, feminists inside psychology, however, have choices. While broadening our audience beyond the discipline may be costly to those who remain in the academy, it is also compelling to imagine psychology deployed in ways that demystify ideology, that disrupt the seeming neutrality of relationships and structures, and that open ideological and material choices for all women. But a glance at the complexities confronted by feminist psychologists who do posit audiences outside the mainstream of psychology will help prevent romanticization of an idealized political feminist psychology. Whether we collaborate with activists, as in the work of Rhoda Linton and Michele Whitham on the Women's Peace Movement (1982); with legal advocates for battered women who kill, as in the work of Julie Blackman (1986, 1989) or Lenore Walker (1984); or with public educators (see Fine 1986b; Lather 1986; McIntosh 1983), the contradictions inside these relationships are by no means resolved.

If seeking social change rather than universal laws is our goal, we are still vulnerable to the possibilities of *gender essentialism* and *racial/ ethnic/class erasure.* How can woman be represented as a social and political category if not by camouflaging all the complexities and contradictions among us? We are still vulnerable to ignoring social context and contingencies—for how else can we develop courtroom strategies and public policies that can "generalize" across situations? And we are still vulnerable to hegemony, this time representing as true that which we believe, instead of that which men proclaim. It is sometimes hard to remember that *our* hegemony is little better than *theirs.*

In working with activists, we do not resolve these questions of power, context, and meaning simply by revealing the multiplicity of women's voices, the complexities of their contexts, and the contingencies of social arrangements. Nor can they be resolved by relying on the varied meanings women inscribe on their own lives or by representing individual psychologies within frames of inequitable power. By doing so, we merely relocate the contradictions and the discussions among "ourselves," but we still inherit dilemmas.

To illustrate: In rural Tennessee, Dr. Jacqui Wade, director of Afro-American Studies at the University of Pennsylvania and I (MF) were hired to evaluate a series of battered women's shelters (1986). It took little genius to notice the whiteness of staff and residents. It required little insight to hear that the women's needs were not always compatible with their children's needs (as in the desire to see paternal grandparents). Our work was conceived as collaborative with the shelters. Yet we ultimately generated what we considered to be important critical commentary—about race and racism and about children—which was not entirely shared by our collaborators. On these topics, we departed sharply from the women of the shelters. While they were the subjects of the research, the ones *for whom* the research was conducted, within the report which we wrote and narrated, they may have felt like objects. We discussed, negotiated, and traded insights. Yet there were moments of splitting and moments of critique. This is all to say that feminist psychologists writing within the academy do not have a monopoly on contradictions. Involvement in activist research does not relieve feminist psychologists of the hypocrisies with which we live daily. If we are compelled to social action, policy, legal advocacy, and/or practice, then we find ourselves faced with central dilemmas of praxis.

We turn now to imagining a project of political, feminist psychology, advanced through novel *ways of learning*, knitted to the conditions, complexities, asymmetries, pleasures, and dangers of women's lives. To excite feminist imaginations toward interruptive questions of epistemology, methodology, methods, and politics (Harding 1987), we offer a project that weaves four such ways of learning. Interrogating that which women do *traditionally* (sustain relationships and maintain social secrets) and that which women do *subversively* (generate feminist politics and imagine possibilities), we invite a project of psychology which empowers as it exposes, which offers critique as it reveals not only what is not but what could be. These four ways of learning are selective, not comprehensive. They challenge the authoritative position of the researcher; unsettle claims about objectivity, bias, and truth; and confuse intentionally the accepted segregation of social theory, method, and politics. All these posit political social change as the task of feminist psychology, and all these generate far more questions than answers.

To Unpack the Traditional Work of Women

Interrogating the Stuff of Relationships
If you really want to know either of us, do not put us in a laboratory or hand us a survey or even interview us separately alone in our homes. Watch me (MF) with women friends, my son, his father, my niece, or my mother, and you will see what feels most authentic to me. These very moments, which construct who I am when I am most me, remain remote from psychological studies of individuals or even groups. In the Psychology of Women class that I teach, students interview a woman "who is different from [them] in terms of race/ethnicity, social class, sexual orientation, or disability and write about her, [themselves], and what transpired between" or they "write a three-generation analysis of some issue that affected [their] grandmother, mother, and self." The

resulting essays are rich, filled with the stuff of relationships, the ways in which women blend together, and the ways in which women split off, positioned through and in opposition to other women:

What did ever happen to you and I? We were the best. I always knew I could count on you ... you were better than a sister. I was happy for and with you when you got married. I knew it was right for you. But I resented his intrusion into us. Our friendship had to be worked into his schedule. Somehow it didn't seem as bad when you were just dating him. You were always around. ... But when you got married, it was almost like I had to make dates with you ... and they always had to be at times that were convenient for him ... almost like I could have whatever was left of you after he had taken his fill. I didn't like that ... and then along came baby one ... you were into things that I had no interest in, and they seemed to swallow you whole. I guess it was easier to just find other things ... and other people than to try and compete. And I guess I envied you in some ways. I was working myself into exhaustion when you were on maternity leave picking out wallpaper for the nursery. You had someone to take care of you ... I only had myself to take care of me, and that scared me a lot. ... You scared me ... I didn't know who you were anymore, but I'm not sure who I am all the time either now ...

This is a small piece of Pam—in an attempt to capture the essence of this stranger who used to be my best friend. Pam was not what I expected. My rose-colored vision of a happy woman in complete control of her life didn't match the woman who opened the apartment door. Was the vision I had created of Pam for the past eighteen years naive? Probably, but at the same time perhaps it served a purpose in giving me an "ideal vision" when I felt things in my own life were less than ideal. It's interesting that Pam also has an ideal vision of my blissfully married life in suburbia—cat, dog, and children in tow—that served as a reference point for measuring her life. How sad that we were both measuring our lives by an imaginary ideal of the other's life. Our time together [they got together on Valentine's Day] showed us both that our unhappiness had just taken different forms. Pam focuses on what's missing from her life—the companionship, affection, and sex she would have were she not living alone. I focused on the burdensome aspects of the same companionship, affection, and sex that Pam craves. Two sides of the same coin . . .

I find myself growing tired of being patient and waiting for a "distant day." I feel a sense of urgency to no longer simply let my life lead me instead of leading my life. I must do something with this strong sense of connectedness I feel for this woman whose life is so different from mine. This woman who could be me. This woman who I could be. [This paper was situated inside a discussion of compulsory heterosexuality (Rich 1980).]

—Jill Tillman

As an adult, my interviewee remains active in social change. Fighting strong against laws which place a disproportionate amount of minorities behind bars, yet offer probation and light sentences to white men who commit the same crimes. This challenge of the system strikes me as brave, particularly since her family of origin distilled in her a fear of authority figures. I have never questioned the system in this way. I have advocated through personal experience the importance of changing some of these laws. However, I have never stood up against them. I black, and she white.

Recounting a piece of my childhood, I asked my interviewee whether the police had held such a strong arm in her community as they had done in mine. She said not. She could not imagine the cops chasing men down the streets and shooting at them, ill respective of others in the range of gunfire. She could not imagine radical, militant groups like the Black Panthers living a half a block away and watching fearfully as the police raided their home and dragged them all out one by one. She could not imagine seeing teenage men crippled for life from gang wars, drug wars, and the like. And yet she fights for causes which have not touched her life, but instead the lives of others, mostly black men and black women, Hispanic men and Hispanic women.

I am black, and she is Jewish. I cannot escape my skin color, and the texture of my hair can only be changed temporarily. She can waltz in and out of invisibility, utilizing her white skinned privileged for protection or gain. I do not have this option. I am not shielded from racism as she can sometimes be from anti-Semitism. Gomez recounts, "1980, my lover, white and Jewish, did not understand my outrage when she told me her friend, a white woman, had decided to cut off the nappy hair of her black, adopted daughter, rather than learn to deal with it. My lover understood oppression and discrimination, but, as a white-skinned woman with the approved hair texture, she'd never thought about the years of insidious assault black women face daily."

We emerge with our differences: Jewish, black, middle-class, working-class, straight, lesbian, motherless, and mother. Yet there are also common differences which have brought us closer together in reaching toward the same goals and fighting against the same obstacles: abolishment of racism and anti-Semitism, equal opportunity in jobs, housing, and education. We have experienced the wrath of dysfunctional families and emerge as strong and capable women, perhaps not so different after all.

—Allener Rogers

We have no easy way to analyze these essays, and yet, inside them, we find both the "stuff" of relationships and the "stuff" of women's identities. The subject is constructed as she constructs herself, in reflection, relation, and in resistance to the Other (see Fisher and Galler 1988). Psychological analyses of individuals, alone or in isolation, render invisible these relational aspects of self (Bhaba 1983; hooks 1981; Mead 1934). To begin research inside women's relationships and to work through these data are to seek women in a fundamentally radical and nonindividualistic way.

On Social Secrets: Desilencing the Social Underground
We know from feminist investigations that women are nestled not only inside relationships but precisely inside the most contradictory moments of social arrangements. Indeed, it is often women's work to be stuffed inside such spots and to testify that no contradiction exists (Smith 1987). No seams or wrinkles. Nothing shatters our coherent social existences. Wives are not supposed to give away the secret of male dependence, although they have plenty of evidence; secretaries are not supposed to tell about male incompetence or the incoherence they make presentable; lesbian women are not supposed to "flaunt" their sexualities (Nestle 1983); mistresses are not supposed to tell about the contradictions inside heterosexuality, monogamy, and the promises of marriage; women with

disabilities are not supposed to expose social obsessions with attractiveness and illusions of lifelong independence and health; prostitutes are not supposed to tell about the contradictions of intimacy and sexuality; daughters are not to speak of incest; and maids or domestics are not supposed to talk about the contradictions of the world of paid work and family life under advanced capitalism.

Women of all colors and classes are nestled inside these contradictory spots in which the pressures and structures of the economy rub against the pressures and structures of racism, sexism, and heterosexism. Women are sworn to both invisibility and secrecy (see Delacoste and Alexander 1988). Whether we turn to Judith Rollins's (1985) or Shellee Colen's (1986) stories of the relationships between domestics and the women who employ them or the *Village Voice* article on the relationships between black child care workers and the white children they tend to (Dobie 1988), we hear the screams and the silences that fill the contradictory spots (Caplan 1989). Whether we turn to Susan Schechter's (1982) account of African-American and Latina women residing in battered women's shelters under the rules and notions of "appropriate behavior" generated typically by white and affluent feminist women or we turn to my own work on rape survivors asked to cope in ways that privileged women and psychologists might (Fine 1984; and see also "Coping with Rape" in this volume), we see the contradictions that women are forced to swallow. Whether we ask disabled women about the value of feminism as currently practiced (Blackwell-Stratton, Breslin, Mayerson, and Bailey 1988) or ask lesbian women who have just come out to their now distant (straight) best friends whether or not they believe that heterosexual women are really more rational and connected than are men (Golden 1984), we understand that women daily collect data on social contradictions *between*, but also *within*, the genders.

We share Jean Baker Miller's (1976) insight that women are responsible not only for the maintenance of these relations and the repair of fractures but also for keeping silent about the extent to which men depend on women at home, at work, and on the street (see also Caplan 1989 and Flax 1987). Across social contexts, women's unpaid work includes collecting, retaining, and never revealing social secrets about men's and women's lives; about oppressive social and economic arrangements and the ideologies that make it "go down easier." This second way of learning—desilencing—calls for a moratorium on secret keeping. It tells—through letters, diaries, and groups—in contexts of relative safety and risks. Because women need to tell and because women, and girls, need to know.

To unearth the secrets is also to tap the costs of the silencing. Given that women are the repositories of social secrets and made to feel responsible for social problems, the hegemonic system works perfectly. Women traditionally have not needed to be coerced into secrecy. To speak has been to betray self. So many have preserved systems for which they have been held accountable—systems that betray, as they sustain them.

If they told, secrets of privilege, sexuality, danger, terror, violence, oppression, dependence, and fears would be exposed/transformed. We invite feminist scholars of psychology to engage in precisely these tasks to unearth the psychologies of women and men by identifying and invading those moments of social silencing and secrecy. Sitting at the margins, forced to the margins, or appropriated once at the margins, women collect social controversy and are sworn—typically through the "privilege" of heterosexuality—to secrecy. The "data" would expose a system that survives on the backs of women—disproportionately low-income women of color.

On Subversion: Women's Other Work

On Politics: Untying the Knots of Political Contradictions

If we move the project of feminist psychology from what women have traditionally done to the arena of subversion, our investigations would detour from what has been to what could be. The unearthing of secrets— now "inside" feminist politics and practice—is a significant task for activist researchers. When battered women's shelters are disproportionately white in staff and residents and defend this position because "black communities seem to take care of themselves better"; when feminist health collectives take on an AIDS testing program but refuse populations of intravenous (IV) drug-using women because "we're not ready to take this on"—then researchers can be helpful in unfreezing moments of problematic political decision making. We can learn the histories of such decisions and the care with which they are made and help unpack the dilemmas made in the name of politics and practice. (What may *appear* to feminist researchers to be an abdication of feminist principles needs to be explored through conversations with participants and decision makers.)

This way of learning unfreezes and unties political contradictions. It involves inviting staff, residents/clients, advocates, and professionals

from within and outside the organization to come together for group sessions to unravel the contradictions, dilemmas, and choices: to unpack the
politics, consequences, and costs. Freezing these moments to unfreeze the
conversations enables this mode of feminist research (Gordon 1988).
Researchers may pose questions that practitioners/activists seek to avoid
and may engage probes that threaten the impression of institutional coherence. Questions and ethical dilemmas will emerge, of course, about who
owns the data, whose voice/analysis/critique should be privileged, what
happens to organizational health once disrupted, and who gets to publish
what. This project is potentially both problematic and liberatory. Collaborative study and writing, in common and separate voices, can enable a
multiplicity of positions to be stated, critiqued, unraveled, and repacked
(Lewis and Simon 1986). Theory, practice, politics, and methods fuse
inside this moment and these contradictions of feminist scholarship.

On Possibilities: Studies of What Is Not
Teresa de Lauretis (1987) argues that the subject of feminism involves
"the movement back and forth between the representation of gender (in
its male-centered frame of reference) and what that representation leaves
out or, more pointedly, makes unrepresentable. It is the movement
between the (represented) discursive space of the positions made available by hegemonic discourses and the space-off . . . those other spaces,
both discursive and social, that exist since feminist practices have
(re)constructed them, in the margins . . . of hegemonic discourses, and in
the interstices of institutions, in counter practices and new forms of
community" (26).

In order to understand gender as a relational concept and one with
elastic boundaries, we need to investigate not only what is represented
and experienced as gender but also what is not represented, what is not
known, and what is not imaginable about gender and about women.
We need to disrupt prevailing notions of what is inevitable and "natural"
(see Tiefer 1987), as we invent images of what could be.

To illustrate what is not measured: In the battered women's shelter
research, the Conrad Hilton Foundation asked Michelle Fine and Jacqui
Wade to itemize a cost-benefit analysis of providing services per woman/
child. We agreed but insisted that we would also calculate the cost of *not*
providing services per woman/child. We asked each respondent—mothers
and children—to help us think about what would have happened to them
had *no* service been available. They itemized easily: broken bones, missed

days at school, foster care, employee absenteeism, welfare, moving children and/or mother to another state, fires, destroyed furniture, perhaps murder. The calculations embodied human as well as material costs.

To illustrate what is not illustrated: Feminist psychologists typically study a slice of the individual woman, as she pops up in her multiple roles—student, mother, friend, sexual object/subject, worker, daughter, and/or all of these. Less often studied are women inside collectives, women in their relationships (Simon 1988), the transformation of women over time (Baruch, Biener, and Barnett 1987), women in collaboration with women (Brodkey 1988), and women inside categories and communities we cannot yet imagine.

To illustrate what is not grieved: When injustice persists with no evidence of unhappiness, rebellion, or official grievance, we need to study the reasons why. An effective system of social injustice requires no coercive agents—only the strength of hegemony and/or punishment for dissent (Gramsci 1973). The most comprehensive system of injustice is one in which victims are victimized, nonvictims benefit, and "consensus" prevails that victims either "enjoy it" or at least they "don't mind." As Faye Crosby and her colleagues demonstrate (1989), the absence of grievance cannot be read as an indication of consent.

Feminists need to interrogate the absence of grievances, appeals, and rebellions by problematizing those factors that contribute to the social construction of quiescence (Gaventa 1980; Kaminstein 1988). At the University of Pennsylvania, as elsewhere, for example, conservative faculty and administration have taken the position that the very few incidents of formally filed sexual and racial harassment grievances signify the absence of harassment. Faculty, staff, and students in the feminist and African-American communities have argued, in contrast, that the *absence* of grievance substantiates the very depth of and terror imposed by harassment. Feminist research must get behind "evidence" that suggests all is well. We must demonstrate that which misrepresents justice, consensus, and "brotherhood" while silencing women. Feminist psychology can reframe what is as it activates images of what could be.

Feminist Psychology: An Inherent Contradiction?

Feminists inside research psychology suffer from extreme ambivalence. Trained and immersed in a highly positivist tradition, a discipline suffering from what Evelyn Fox Keller (1982) calls "physics envy" and yet rich with data about women (and men) which expose the superficiality of notions of objectivity, truth, stages, and even gender, it is not surprising that we are ambivalent.

To answer the most simple question—have we transformed psychology?—we would have to say, barely. When Michelle was up for tenure, a colleague, in an effort to be supportive, explained: "It's a pleasure to have someone doing feminine psychology around here."

Have we decentered the white, male, heterosexual, affluent, nondisabled standard? Probably not. Do we care? We're not so sure. Within psychology, we have achieved a small space for the intellectual and political nurturance of each other, our students, activists, practitioners, and policymakers. Our work—in quite explicitly feminist and in quite deformed ways—pops up in the public media. We are on television defending battered women who kill (Blackman 1986; Walker 1984); in print denouncing sexual harassment (Gutek, personal communication); in courtrooms defending the rights of young women to attend the finest all-male public high school in the city of Philadelphia (Fine 1983a; Unger 1983); and arguing that anti–abortion clinic protestors constitute a violation of the free speech of women seeking confidential abortions (LaFrance, personal communication). Feminist works are cited by some mainstream journals, and feminist scholars are being published inside the mainstream, particularly when we abide by the rules of traditional psychology.

But our impact on the discipline has ultimately been limited. Unlike sociology and anthropology departments, which seem to at least *know* that they need "a gender person," psychologists in psychology departments do not scramble to fill "the gender spot." In part, feminist psychologists have selected audiences elsewhere. But we have also basically asked nice questions, used "their" methods uncritically, and not been hysterical. We have typically failed to address systematically the notions of power; the dialectics of social inequity and individual psychologies; the braiding of gender, class, and race/ethnicity with age, disability, and sexual orientation. We have yet to develop a language for articulating that which is negotiated in between structures of oppression and individual/group psychologies (Bourdieu 1977). We have found no way inside the discipline to discuss "resistance" without it appearing childlike or overemotional. And we have been reluctant to introduce politics explicitly into our work and timid about exposing the inherently conservative politics that organize the field of psychology (Apfelbaum 1979; Buss 1979; Furby 1979; Wexler 1983).

Feminists can fit into psychology all too easily. We can do it by pretending that psychology is an apolitical discipline; by representing ourselves uncritically as objective researchers; by misrepresenting gender, within frames of sex roles, sex differences, or gender-neutral analyses without discussing power, social context, and meanings; and by constructing the rich and contradictory consciousness of girls and women into narrow factors and scales. But, by so doing, we reproduce and legitimate the individualism, conservatism, and dangers of psychology. We collude in the sexist and racist stances built into gender and race research that claims to be "power neutral" but is actually power justifying. Then we—like the women we study—sit inside moments of social contradiction, and we keep our mouths shut. We may build a humble critique from within the field which will undoubtedly be tamed and appropriated. Perhaps all psychologists will eventually include girls and women in their studies. Psychology, however, will then even more resiliently mask the power asymmetries that define gender, race/ethnicity, sexuality, disability, and class relations.

Feminist psychologists can enrich feminism inside psychology. But more important, in the 1990s, we can transform politics through feminist psychology. Psychology can be reconstituted as the stuff that fills women's (and men's) minds, bodies, and relationships; that feels so personal, rings so political, and has yet to be articulated between the two. Feminist psychologists must enter that space—to interrogate how women (and men) position and are positioned in ways that relay, inscribe, experience, and critique the social as a personal moment. And then we must learn how those personal moments can be strung together like beads into collective and disruptive feminist movements of politics and scholarship.

PART 1

On the Bodies of Women

The essays in this section examine the social politics of gender, race, class, sexuality, and disability as they are negotiated on and by women's bodies. Within this section, women's bodies serve as the space for looking at intimacy, pleasure, and violence.

> Female sexuality has historically proven to be the most problematic locus of representational issues for women. It has simultaneously promised the most intimate access any historical woman has to her femaleness, and consistently eluded anything like a woman-centered definition because female sexuality has occupied a critical place in men's contest for power and therefore in women's social oppression. (Poovey 1990, 30)

As Mary Poovey has written and these essays will explore, women's bodies serve as a telling platform upon which social politics are choreographed, resisted, and negotiated. Together these essays problematize how women's bodies and sexualities have been represented in official and feminist texts, how women narrate their/our own bodies, and how women make sense of violence done to them/us on local streets and in faculty offices.

Each of these essays, on its own, was written to probe the space between representations and experiences of women's bodies. "Sexuality, Schooling, and Adolescent Females: The Missing Discourse of Desire" lifts for analysis the discourses of morality, victimization, and danger located within sex education curricula, through which women's sexualities have officially been represented. The essay examines these frames on sexuality and explores why a discourse of women's desire has been so systematically absented such that female sexual agents have been rendered oxymoronic. She who desires is patently deviant. As powerfully

27

as patriarchy and heterosexism are reproduced by these texts, however, you will hear serious resistance voiced by adolescent women in these classrooms, struggling to make sense of the pleasures and dangers braided in their bodies and in their narratives.

The second essay, "Coping with Rape: Critical Perspectives on Consciousness," continues this analysis of women's embodiment of dangers through a conversation between Altamese, a young woman who had just been gang raped, and me, one evening she spent in the emergency room of a hospital where I was working as rape advocate. To listen to the conversation, a "detached" psychologist might conclude that Altamese was too resigned to the inevitability of her rape; perhaps, empathically, she would be described as having "learned to be helpless." A closer, critical listen to her story, however, forces us to hear how deeply and politically Altamese has contextualized her assault within her complex relations with social workers, the state, neighbors, and kin. Such a listen surfaces the individualism and universalism of traditional psychological theory and traditional feminist interventions, which result when social contexts narrated by women are neglected and when the political knowledge that women carry in their/our bodies is denied. Altamese refused to do what "good psychological coping" or "feminist advice" would prescribe, and her refusal is reread in this text as a moment of class and race resistance, reflecting what Leslie Roman calls an "asymmetry in subjectivity" which:

> best accounts for the process of the young women becoming social subjects. It acknowledges that the young women's contradictory intentions by gender and class favored their defense of one particular set of power and control relations over their challenge to them. Yet the concept allows researchers . . . to understand how the sporadically critical moments underlying young women's intentions—those which might be seen as "resistant" to one set of power and control relations—did not necessarily have socially transformative effects for either their class or gender relations. (1988, 178)

The story of Altamese raises up a critical issue for feminist psychologists: how to narrate women's resistances, particularly when their resistance is embodied in individual and privatized ways that enable women to survive and male violence to persist—unnamed.

The privatized politics of women's bodies surface again in the third text, "Presence of Mind in the Absence of Body." In this essay, Linda Brodkey and I offer a textual analysis of narratives produced by a sample of women graduate students who reported sexual harassment by faculty at the University of Pennsylvania. Throughout their essays, we detect a profound discursive flight by these women from their experiences of harassment, a powerful distancing from their embodied experiences, and a serious severing of their minds from their bodies. This essay explores the challenges of theorizing women's resistance, when women's bodies are situated within contradictions of gendered power asymmetries and the women are thoroughly committed to "getting through" as minds.

These essays, in concert, enable us to examine the politics danced upon, resisted through, embodied in, and transformed by women's bodies.

Sexuality, Schooling, and Adolescent Females: The Missing Discourse of Desire

Michelle Fine

Since late 1986, popular magazines and newspapers have printed steamy stories about education and sexuality. Whether the controversy surrounds sex education or school-based health clinics (SBHCs), public discourses of adolescent sexuality are represented forcefully by government officials, New Right spokespersons, educators, "the public," feminists, and health care professionals. These stories offer the authority of "facts," insights into the political controversies, and access to unacknowledged fears about sexuality (Foucault 1980). Although the facts usually involve the adolescent female body, little has been heard from young women themselves.

This essay examines these diverse perspectives on adolescent sexuality and, in addition, presents the views of a group of adolescent females. The essay is informed by a study of numerous current sex education curricula, a year of negotiating for inclusion of lesbian and gay sexuality in a citywide sex education curriculum, and interviews and observations gathered in New York City sex education classrooms.[1] The analysis examines the desires, fears, and fantasies that give structure and shape to silences and voices concerning sex education and school-based health clinics in the 1980s.

Despite the attention devoted to teen sexuality, pregnancy, and parenting in this country, and despite the evidence of effective interventions and the widespread public support expressed for these interventions (Harris and Associates 1985), the systematic implementation of sex education and SBHCs continues to be obstructed by the controversies surrounding them (Kantrowitz et al. 1987; Leo 1986). Those who resist sex education or SBHCs often present their views as based on rationality and a concern for protecting the young. For such opponents, sex education raises questions of promoting promiscuity and immorality and of undermining family values. Yet the language of the challenges suggests an effect substantially more profound and primitive. Gary Bauer, undersecretary of education in the U.S. Department of Education, for example, constructs an image of immorality littered by adolescent sexuality and drug abuse:

> There is ample impressionistic evidence to indicate that drug abuse and promiscuity are not independent behaviors. When inhibitions fall, they collapse across the board. When people of any age lose a sense of right and wrong, the loss is not selective. . . . They are all expressions of the same ethical vacuum among many teens. (1986, 2)

Even Surgeon General C. Everett Koop, a strong supporter of sex education, recently explained: "We have to be as explicit as necessary. . . . You can't talk of the dangers of snake poisoning and not mention snakes" (quoted in Leo 1986, 54). Such commonly used and often repeated metaphors associate adolescent sexuality with victimization and danger.

Yet public schools have rejected the task of sexual dialogue and critique, or what has been called "sexuality education." Within today's standard sex education curricula and many public school classrooms, we find: (1) the authorized suppression of a discourse of female sexual desire; (2) the promotion of a discourse of female sexual victimization; and (3) the explicit privileging of married heterosexuality over other practices of sexuality. One finds an unacknowledged social ambivalence about female sexuality which ideologically separates the female sexual agent, or subject, from her counterpart, the female sexual victim. The adolescent woman of the 1980s is constructed as the latter. Educated primarily as the potential victim of male sexuality, she represents no subject in her own right. Young women continue to be taught to fear and defend against desire, and in this context there is little possibility of their developing a critique of gender or sexual arrangements.

Prevailing Discourses of Female Sexuality Inside Public Schools

> If the body is seen as endangered by uncontrollable forces, then presumably this is a society or social group which fears change—

change which it perceived simultaneously as powerful and beyond its control. (Smith-Rosenberg 1978, 229)

Public schools have historically been the site for identifying, civilizing, and containing that which is considered uncontrollable. While evidence of sexuality is everywhere within public high schools—in the halls, classrooms, bathrooms, lunchrooms, and the library—official sexuality education occurs sparsely: in social studies, biology, sex education, or inside the nurse's office. To understand how sexuality is managed inside schools, I examined the major discourses of sexuality which characterize the national debates over sex education and SBHCs. These discourses are then tracked as they weave through the curricula, classrooms, and halls of public high schools.

The first discourse, *sexuality as violence*, is clearly the most conservative and equates adolescent heterosexuality with violence. At the 1986 American Dreams Symposium on education, Phyllis Schlafly (1986) commented: "Those courses on sex, abuse, incest, AIDS, they are all designed to terrorize our children. We should fight their existence, and stop putting terror in the hearts and minds of our youngsters." One aspect of this position, shared by women as politically distinct as Schlafly and the radical feminist lawyer Catherine MacKinnon (1983), views heterosexuality as essentially violent and coercive. In its full conservative form, proponents call for the elimination of sex education and clinics and urge complete reliance on the family to dictate appropriate values, mores, and behaviors.

Sexuality as violence presumes that there is a causal relationship between official silence about sexuality and a decrease in sexual activity— therefore, by not teaching about sexuality, adolescent sexual behavior will not occur. The irony, of course, lies in the empirical evidence. Fisher, Byrne, and White (1983) have documented sex-negative attitudes and contraceptive use to be negatively correlated. In their study, sexnegative attitudes do not discourage sexual activity, but they do discourage responsible use of contraception. Teens who believe sexual involvement is wrong deny responsibility for contraception. To accept responsibility would legitimate "bad" behavior. By contrast, Fisher et al. found that adolescents with sex-positive attitudes tend to be both more consistent and more positive about contraceptive use. By not teaching about sexuality, or by teaching sex-negative attitudes, schools apparently will not forestall sexual activity but may well discourage responsible contraception.

The second discourse, *sexuality as victimization*, gathers a much greater following. Female adolescent sexuality is represented as a moment of victimization in which the dangers of heterosexuality for adolescent women (and, more recently, of homosexuality for adolescent men) are prominent. While sex may not be depicted as inherently violent, young women (and today, men) learn of their vulnerability to potential male predators.

To avoid being victimized, females learn to defend themselves against disease, pregnancy, and "being used." The discourse of victimization supports sex education, including AIDS education, with parental consent. Suggested classroom activities emphasize "saying no," practicing abstinence, enumerating the social and emotional risks of sexual intimacy, and listing the possible diseases associated with sexual intimacy. The language, as well as the questions asked and not asked, represents females as the actual and potential victims of male desire. In exercises, role plays, and class discussions, girls practice resistance to trite lines, unwanted hands, opened buttons, and the surrender of other "bases" they are not prepared to yield. The discourses of violence and victimization both portray males as potential predators and females as victims. Three problematic assumptions underlie these two views:

—First, female subjectivity, including the desire to engage in sexual activity, is placed outside the prevailing conversation (Vance 1984).

—Second, both arguments present female victimization as contingent upon unmarried heterosexual involvement—rather than inherent in existing gender, class, and racial arrangements (Rubin 1984). While feminists have long fought for the legal and social acknowledgment of sexual violence against women, most have resisted the claim that female victimization hinges primarily upon sexual involvement with men. The full range of victimization of women—at work, at home, on the streets—has instead been uncovered. The language and emotion invested in these two discourses divert attention away from structures, arrangements, and relationships which oppress women in general, and low-income women and women of color in particular (Lorde 1980b).

—Third, the messages, while narrowly antisexual, nevertheless buttress traditional heterosexual arrangements. These views assume that, as long as females avoid premarital sexual relations with men, victimization can be avoided. Ironically, however, protection from male victimization is available primarily through marriage— by coupling with a man. The paradoxical message teaches females to fear the very men who will ultimately protect them.

The third discourse, *sexuality as individual morality*, introduces explicit notions of sexual subjectivity for women. Although quite judgmental and moralistic, this discourse values women's sexual decision making as long as the decisions made are for premarital abstinence. Secretary of Education William Bennett, for example, urges schools to teach "morality literacy" and to educate toward "modesty," "chastity," and "abstinence" until marriage. The language of self-control and self-respect reminds students that sexual immorality breeds not only personal problems but also community tax burdens.

The debate over morality in sex education curricula marks a clear contradiction among educational conservatives over whether and how the state may intervene in the "privacy of families." Noninterventionists, including Phyllis Schlafly, argue that educators should not teach about sexuality at all. To do so is to take a particular moral position which subverts the family. Interventionists, including Koop, Bennett, and Bauer, argue that schools should teach about sexuality by focusing on "good values" but disagree about how. Koop proposes open discussion of sexuality and the use of condoms, while Bennett advocates "sexual restraint" ("Koop's AIDS Stand Assailed" 1987). Sexuality in this discourse is posed as a test of self-control; individual restraint triumphs over social temptation. Pleasure and desire for women as sexual subjects remain largely in the shadows, obscured from adolescent eyes.

The fourth discourse, a *discourse of desire*, remains a whisper inside the official work of U.S. public schools. If introduced at all, it is as an interruption of the ongoing conversation (Snitow, Stansell, and Thompson 1983). The naming of desire, pleasure, or sexual entitlement, particularly for females, barely exists in the formal agenda of public schooling on sexuality. When spoken, it is tagged with reminders of "consequences"—emotional, physical, moral, reproductive, and/or financial (Freudenberg 1987). A genuine discourse of desire would invite adolescents to explore what feels good and bad, desirable and undesirable, grounded in experiences, needs, and limits. Such a discourse would release females from a position of receptivity, enable an analysis of the dialectics of victimization and pleasure, and would pose female adolescents as subjects of sexuality, initiators as well as negotiators (Golden 1984; Petchesky 1984; Thompson 1983).

In Sweden, where sex education has been offered in schools since the turn of the century, the State Commission on Sex Education recommends teaching students to "acquire a knowledge . . . [which] will equip them to experience sexual life as a source of happiness and joy in fellowship with other [people]" (Brown 1983, 88). The teachers' handbook goes on: "The many young people who wish to wait [before initiating sexual activity] and those who have had early sexual relations should experience, in class, [the feeling] that they are understood and accepted" (93). Compare this to an exercise suggested in a major U.S. metropolitan sex education curriculum: "Discuss and evaluate: things which may cause teenagers to engage in sexual relations before they are ready to assume the responsibility of marriage" (see Philadelphia School District 1986; and New York City Board of Education 1984).

A discourse of desire, though seldom explored in U.S. classrooms, does occur in less structured school situations. The following excerpts, taken from group and individual student interviews, demonstrate female adolescents' subjective experiences of body and desire as they begin to articulate notions of sexuality.

In some cases, young women pose a critique of marriage:

I'm still in love with Simon, but I'm seeing Jose. He's OK but he said, "Will you be my girl?" I hate that. It feels like they own you. Like I say to a girlfriend, "What's wrong? You look terrible!" and she says, "I'm married!" (Millie, a sixteen-year-old student from the Dominican Republic)

In other cases, they offer stories of their own victimization:

It's not like last year. Then I came to school regular. Now my old boyfriend, he waits for me in front of my building every morning, and he fights with me. Threatens me, gettin' all bad. . . . I want to move out of my house and live 'cause he ain't gonna stop no way. (Sylvia, age seventeen, about to drop out of twelfth grade)

Some even speak of desire:

I'm sorry I couldn't call you last night about the interview, but my boyfriend came back from [the] navy, and I wanted to spend the night with him; we don't get to see each other much. (Shandra, age seventeen, after a no-show for an interview)

In a context in which desire is not silenced, but acknowledged and discussed, conversations with adolescent women can, as seen here, educate through a dialectic of victimization and pleasure. Despite formal silencing, it would be misleading to suggest that talk of desire never emerges within public schools. Notwithstanding a political climate organized around the suppression of this conversation, some teachers and community advocates continue to struggle for an empowering sex education curriculum both in and out of the high school classroom.

Family life curricula and/or plans for a school-based health clinic have been carefully generated in many communities. Yet they continue to face loud and sometimes violent resistance by religious and community groups, often from outside the district lines (Boffey 1987; "Chicago School Clinic" 1986; Dowd 1986; Perlez 1986a, 1986b; Rohter 1985). In other communities, when curricula or clinics have been approved with little overt confrontation, monies for training are withheld. In New York City in 1987, for example, $1.7 million was initially requested to implement training on the Family Life education curriculum. As sex educators confronted community and religious groups, the inclusion of some topics as well as the language of others were continually negotiated. Ultimately, the chancellor requested only $600,000 for training, a sum substantially inadequate to the task.[2]

In this political context, many public school educators nevertheless continue to take personal and professional risks to create materials and foster classroom environments that speak fully to the sexual subjectivities of young women and men. Some operate within the privacy of their classrooms, subverting the official curriculum and engaging students in critical discussion. Others advocate publicly for enriched curricula and training. A few have even requested that community-based advocates *not* agitate for official curricular change, so "we [teachers] can continue to do what we do in the classroom, with nobody looking over our shoulders. You make a big public deal of this, and it will blow open."[3] Within public school classrooms, it seems that female desire may indeed be addressed when educators act subversively. But in the typical sex education classroom, silence, and therefore distortion, surrounds female desire.

The blanketing of female sexual subjectivity in public school class-rooms, in public discourse, and in bed will sound familiar to those who have read Luce Irigaray (1980) and Hélène Cixous (1981). These French feminists have argued that expressions of female voice, body, and sex-uality are essentially inaudible when the dominant language and ways of viewing are male. Inside the hegemony of what they call The Law of the Father, female desire and pleasure can gain expression only in the terrain already charted by men (see also Burke 1980). In the public school arena, this constriction of what is called sexuality allows girls one pri-mary decision—to say yes or no—to a question not necessarily their own. A discourse of desire in which young women have a voice would be informed and generated out of their own socially constructed sexual meanings. It is to these expressions that we now turn.

The Bodies of Female Adolescents: Voices and Structured Silences

If four discourses can be distinguished among the many positions artic-ulated by various "authorities," the sexual meanings voiced by female adolescents defy such classification. A discourse of desire, though absent in the "official" curriculum, is by no means missing from the lived experiences or commentaries of young women. This section introduces their sexual thoughts, concerns, and meanings, as represented by a group of African-American and Latina female adolescents—students and drop-outs from a public high school in New York City serving predominantly low-income youths. In my year at this comprehensive high school, I had frequent opportunity to speak with adolescents and listen to them talk about sex. The comments reported derive from conversations between the young women and their teachers, among themselves, and with me, as researcher. During conversations, the young women talked freely about fears and, in the same breath, asked about passions. Their struggle to untangle issues of gender, power, and sexuality underscores the fact that, for them, notions of sexual negotiation cannot be separated from sacrifice and nurturance.

The adolescent female rarely reflects simply on sexuality. Her sense of sexuality is informed by peers, culture, religion, violence, history, passion, authority, rebellion, body, past and future, and gender and racial relations of power (Espin 1984; Omolade 1983). The adolescent woman herself assumes a dual consciousness—at once taken with the excitement of actual/anticipated sexuality and consumed with anxiety and worry. While too few safe spaces exist for adolescent women's exploration of sexual subjectivities, there are all too many dangerous spots for their exploitation.

Whether in a classroom, on the street, at work, or at home, the adolescent female's sexuality is negotiated by, for, and despite the young woman herself. Patricia, a young Puerto Rican woman who worried about her younger sister, relates: "You see, I'm the love child and she's the one born because my mother was raped in Puerto Rico. Her father's in jail now, and she feels so bad about the whole thing, so she acts bad." For Patricia, as for the many young women who have experienced and/ or witnessed sexual violence, discussions of sexuality merge representations of passion with violence. Often the initiator of conversation among peers about virginity, orgasm, "getting off," and pleasure, Patricia mixed sexual talk freely with references to force and violence. She is a poignant narrator who illustrates, from the female adolescent's perspective, that sexual victimization and desire coexist (Benjamin 1983).

Sharlene and Betty echo this braiding of danger and desire. Sharlene explained: "Boys always be trying to get into my panties," and Betty added: "I don't be needin' a man who won't give me no pleasure but take my money and expect me to take care of him." This powerful commentary on gender relations, voiced by African-American adolescent females, was inseparable from their views of sexuality. To be a woman was to be strong, independent, and reliable—but not too independent for fear of scaring off a man.

Deidre continued this conversation, explicitly pitting male fragility against female strength: "Boys in my neighborhood ain't wrapped so tight. Got to be careful how you treat them." She reluctantly admitted that perhaps it is more important for African-American males than females to attend college, "Girls and women, we're stronger, we take care of ourselves. But boys and men, if they don't get away from the neighborhood, they end up in jail, on drugs or dead . . . or wack [crazy]."

These young women spoke often of anger at males, while concurrently expressing a strong desire for male attention: "I dropped out 'cause I fell in love and couldn't stop thinking of him." An equally compelling desire was to protect young males—particularly African-American males—from a system that "makes them wack." Ever aware of the ways that institutional racism and the economy have affected African-American males, these young women seek pleasure but also offer comfort. They often view self-protection as taking something away from young men. Lavanda offered a telling example: "If I ask him to use a condom, he won't feel like a man."

In order to understand the sexual subjectivities of young women more completely, educators need to reconstruct schooling as an empowering context in which we listen to and work with the meanings and experiences of gender and sexuality revealed by the adolescents themselves. When we refuse that responsibility, we prohibit an education that adolescents wholly need and deserve. My classroom observations suggest that such education is rare.

Ms. Rosen, a teacher of a sex education class, opened one session with a request: "You should talk to your mother or father about sex before you get involved." Nilda initiated what became an informal protest by a number of Latino students: "Not our parents! We tell them one little thing, and they get crazy. My cousin got sent to Puerto Rico to live with her religious aunt, and my sister got beat 'cause my father thought she was with a boy." For these adolescents, a safe space for discussion, critique, and construction of sexualities was not something they found in their homes. Instead, they relied on school, the spot they chose for the safe exploration of sexualities.

The absence of safe spaces for exploring sexuality affects all adolescents. It was paradoxical to realize that perhaps the only students who had an in-school opportunity for critical sexual discussion in the comfort of peers were the few students who had organized the Gay and Lesbian Association (GALA) at the high school. While most lesbian, gay, or bisexual students were undoubtedly closeted, those few who were "out" claimed this public space for their display and for their sanctuary. Exchanging support when families and peers would offer little, GALA members worried that so few students were willing to come out and that so many suffered the assaults of homophobia individually. The gay and lesbian rights movement had powerfully affected these youngsters, who were comfortable enough to support each other in a place not considered very safe—a public high school in which echoes of "faggot!" fill the halls.

In the absence of an education that explores and unearths danger and desire, sexuality education classes typically provide little opportunity for discussions beyond those constructed around superficial notions of male heterosexuality (see Kelly 1986, for a counterexample). Male pleasure is taught, albeit as biology. Teens learn about "wet dreams" (as the onset of puberty for males), "erection" (as the preface to intercourse), and "ejaculation" (as the act of inseminating). Female pleasures and questions are far less often the topic of discussion. Few voices of female sexual agency can be heard. The language of victimization and its underlying concerns—"Say No," put a brake on his sexuality, don't encourage—ultimately deny young women the right to control their own sexuality by providing no access to a legitimate position of sexual subjectivity. Often conflicted about self-representation, adolescent females spend enormous amounts of time trying to "save it," "lose it," convince others that they have lost or saved it, or trying to be "discreet" instead of focusing their energies in ways that are sexually autonomous, responsible, and pleasurable. In classroom observations, girls who were heterosexually active rarely spoke for fear of being ostracized (Fine 1986b). Those who were heterosexual virgins had the same worry. And most students who were gay, bisexual, or lesbian remained closeted, aware of the very real dangers of homophobia.

Occasionally, the difficult and pleasurable aspects of sexuality were discussed together, coming either as an interruption or because an educational context was constructed. During a social studies class, for example, Catherine, the proud mother of two-year-old Tiffany, challenged an assumption underlying the class discussion—that teen motherhood devastates mother and child; "If I didn't get pregnant, I would have continued on a downward path, going nowhere. They say teenage pregnancy is bad for you, but it was good for me. I know I can't mess around now. I got to worry about what's good for Tiffany and for me."

Another interruption came from Opal, a young African-American student. Excerpts from her hygiene class follow:

Teacher: Let's talk about teenage pregnancy.

Opal: How come girls in the locker room say, "You a virgin?" and if you say "Yeah" they laugh and say "Ohh, you're a virgin." And some black teenagers, I don't mean to be racial, when they get ready to tell their mothers they had sex, some break on them, and some look funny. My friend told her mother, and she broke all the dishes. She told her mother so she could get protection so she don't get pregnant.

Teacher: When my thirteen-year-old [relative] asked for birth control, I was shocked and angry.

Portia: Mothers should help so she can get protection and not get pregnant or diseases. So you was wrong.

Teacher: Why not say "I'm thinking about having sex?"

Portia: You tell them after, not before, having sex but before pregnancy.

Teacher (now angry): Then it's a fait accompli, and you expect my compassion? You have to take more responsibility.

Portia: I am! If you get pregnant after you told your mother and you got all the stuff and still get pregnant, you the fool. Take up hygiene and learn. Then it's my responsibility if I end up pregnant.

Field Note, October 23, Hygiene Class

Two days later, the discussion continued.

Teacher: What topics should we talk about in sex education?

Portia: Organs, how they work.

Opal: What's an orgasm?

[laughter]

Teacher: Sexual response, sensation all over the body. What's analogous to the male penis on the female?

Theo: Clitoris.

Teacher: Right, go home and look in the mirror.

Portia: She is too much!

Teacher: Why look in the mirror?

Elaine: It's yours.

Teacher: Why is it important to know what your body looks like?

Opal: You should like your body.

Teacher: You should know what it looks like when it's healthy, so you can recognize problems like vaginal warts.

Field Note, October 25, Hygiene Class

The discourse of desire, initiated by Opal but evident only as an interruption, faded rapidly into the discourse of disease—warning about the dangers of sexuality.

It was in the spring of that year that Opal showed up pregnant. Her hygiene teacher, who was extremely concerned and involved with her students, was also quite angry with Opal: "Who is going to take care of that baby, you or your mother? You know what it costs to buy diapers and milk and afford child care?"

Opal, in conversation with me, related, "I got to leave [school] 'cause, even if they don't say it, them teachers got hate in their eyes when they look at my belly." In the absence of a way to talk about passion, pleasure, danger, and responsibility, this teacher fetishized the latter two, holding the former two hostage. Because adolescent females combine these experiences in their daily lives, the separation is false, judgmental, and ultimately not very educational.

Over the year in this high school, and in other public schools since, I have observed a systematic refusal to name issues, particularly issues that caused adults discomfort. Educators often projected their discomfort onto students in the guise of "protecting" them (Fine 1987a). An example of such silencing can be seen in a (now altered) policy of the school district of Philadelphia. In 1985, a student informed me, "We're not allowed to talk about abortion in our school." Assuming this was an overstatement, I asked an administrator at the district about this practice. She explained, "That's not quite right. If a student asks a question about abortion, the teacher can define abortion; she just can't discuss it." How can definition occur without discussion, exchange, conversation, or critique, unless a subtext of silencing prevails (Greene 1986; Noddings 1986)?

Explicit silencing of abortion has since been lifted in Philadelphia. The revised curriculum now reads:

Options for unintended pregnancy:
(a) adoption
(b) foster care
(c) single parenthood
(d) teen marriage
(e) abortion

A footnote is supposed to be added, however, to elaborate the negative consequences of abortion. In the social politics that surround public schools, such compromises are apparent across cities.

The New York City Family Life Education curriculum reads similarly (New York City Board of Education 1984, 172):

List: The possible options for an unintended pregnancy. What considerations should be given in the decision on the alternatives?
—adoption
—foster care
—mother keeps baby
—elective abortion

Discuss:
—religious viewpoints on abortion
—present laws concerning abortion
—current developments in prenatal diagnosis and their implication for abortion issues
—why abortion should not be considered a contraceptive device
List: The people or community services that could provide assistance in the event of an unintended pregnancy
Invite: A speaker to discuss alternatives to abortion; for example, a social worker from the Department of Social Services to discuss foster care.

One must be suspicious when diverse views are sought only for abortion, and not for adoption, teen motherhood, or foster care. The call to silence is easily identified in current political and educational contexts (Fine 1987a; Foucault 1980). The silence surrounding contraception and abortion options and diversity in sexual orientations denies adolescents information and sends the message that such conversations are taboo—at home, at church, and even at school.

In contrast to these "official curricula," which allow discussion and admission of desire only as an interruption, let us examine other situations in which young women were invited to analyze sexuality across categories of the body, the mind, the heart, and, of course, gender politics.

Teen Choice, a voluntary counseling program in New York City held on-site by non–board of education social workers, offered an instance in which the complexities of pleasure and danger were invited, analyzed, and braided into discussions of sexuality. In a small group discussion, the counselor asked of the seven ninth-graders, "What are the two functions of a penis?" One student responded, "To pee!" Another student offered the second function: "To eat!" which was followed by laughter and serious discussion. The conversation proceeded as the teacher asked, "Do all penises look alike?" The students explained, "No, they are all different colors!"

The freedom to express, beyond simple right and wrong answers, enabled these young women to offer what they knew with humor and delight. This discussion ended as one student insisted that, if you "jump up and down a lot, the stuff will fall out of you, and you won't get pregnant," to which the social worker answered with slight exasperation that millions of sperm would have to be released for such "expulsion" to work and that, of course, it wouldn't work. In this conversation, one could hear what seemed like too much experience, too little information, and too few questions asked by the students. But the discussion, which was sex-segregated and guided by the experiences and questions of the students themselves (and the skills of the social worker), enabled easy movement between pleasure and danger, safety and desire, naïveté and knowledge, and victimization and entitlement.

What is evident, then, is that, even in the absence of a discourse of desire, young women express their notions of sexuality and relate their experiences. Yet official discourses of sexuality leave little room for such exploration. The authorized sexual discourses define what is safe, what is taboo, and what will be silenced. This discourse of sexuality miseducates adolescent women. What results is a discourse of sexuality based on the male in search of desire and the female in search of protection. The open, coed sexuality discussions so many fought for in the 1970s have been appropriated as a forum for the primacy of male heterosexuality and the preservation of female victimization.

The Politics of Female Sexual Subjectivities

In 1912, an education committee explicitly argued that "scientific" sex education "should . . . keep sex consciousness and sex emotions at the minimum" (Leo 1986). In the same era, G. Stanley Hall proposed diversionary pursuits for adolescents, including hunting, music, and sports, "to reduce sex stress and tension . . . to short-circuit, transmute it and turn it on to develop the higher powers of the men [*sic*]" (1914, 29, 30). In 1915, Orison Marden, author of *The Crime of Silence*, chastised educators, reformers, and public health specialists for their unwillingness to speak publicly about sexuality and for relying inappropriately on parents and peers, who were deemed too ignorant to provide sex instruction (Imber 1984; Strong 1972). And, in 1921, radical sex educator Maurice Bigelow wrote:

> Now, most scientifically-trained women seem to agree that there are no corresponding phenomena in the early pubertal life of the normal young woman who has good health (corresponding to male masturbation). A limited number of mature women, some of them physicians, report having experienced in the pubertal years localized

tumescence and other disturbances which made them definitely conscious of sexual instincts. However, it should be noted that most of these are known to have had a personal history including one or more such abnormalities such as dysmenorrhea, uterine displacement, pathological ovaries, leucorrhea, tuberculosis, masturbation, neurasthenia, nymphomania, or other disturbances which are sufficient to account for local sexual stimulation. In short such women are not normal. (179)

In the 1950s, public school health classes separated girls from boys. Girls "learned about sex" by watching films of the accelerated development of breasts and hips, the flow of menstrual blood, and then the progression of venereal disease as a result of participation in out-of-wedlock heterosexual activity.

Thirty years and a much-debated sexual revolution later (Ehrenreich, Hess, and Jacobs 1986), much has changed. Feminism, the civil rights movement, the disability and gay rights movements, birth control, legal abortion with federal funding (won and then lost), and reproductive technologies are part of these changes (Weeks 1985). Due both to the consequences of and the backlashes against these movements, students today do learn about sexuality—if typically through the representations of female sexuality as inadequacy or victimization, male homosexuality as a story of predator and prey, and male heterosexuality as desire.

Young women today know that female sexual subjectivity is at least not an inherent contradiction. Perhaps they even feel it is an entitlement. Yet, when public schools resist acknowledging the fullness of female sexual subjectivities, they reproduce a profound social ambivalence that dichotomizes female heterosexuality (Espin 1984; Golden 1984; Omolade 1983). This ambivalence surrounds a fragile cultural distinction between two forms of female sexuality: *consensual* sexuality, representing consent or choice in sexuality, and *coercive* sexuality, which represents force, victimization, and/or crime (Weeks 1985).

During the 1980s, however, this distinction began to be challenged. It was acknowledged that gender-based power inequities shape, define, and construct experiences of sexuality. Notions of sexual consent and force, except in extreme circumstances, became complicated, no longer in simple opposition. The first problem concerned how to conceptualize power asymmetries and consensual sexuality. Could consensual female heterosexuality be said to exist within a context replete with structures, relationships, acts, and threats of female victimization (sexual, social, and economic) (MacKinnon 1983)? How could we speak of "sexual preference" when sexual involvement outside of heterosexuality may seriously jeopardize one's social and/or economic well-being (Petchesky 1984)? Diverse female sexual subjectivities emerge through, despite, and because of gender-based power asymmetries. To imagine a female sexual self, free of and uncontaminated by power, was rendered naive (Foucault 1980; Irigaray 1980; Rubin 1984).

The second problem involved the internal incoherence of the categories. Once assumed fully independent, the two began to blur as the varied practices of sexuality went public. At the intersection of these presumably parallel forms—coercive and consensual sexualities—lay "sexual" acts of violence and "violent" acts of sex. Sexual acts of violence, including marital rape, acquaintance rape, and sexual harassment, were historically considered consensual. A woman involved in a marriage, on a date, or working outside her home "naturally" risked receiving sexual attention; her consent was inferred from her presence. But today, in many states, this woman can sue her husband for such sexual acts of violence; in all states, she can prosecute a boss. What was once part of "domestic life" or "work" may today be criminal. On the other hand, violent acts of sex, including consensual sadomasochism and the use of violence-portraying pornography, were once considered inherently coercive for women (Benjamin 1983; Rubin 1984; Weeks 1985). Female involvement in such sexual practices historically had been dismissed as nonconsensual. Today such romanticizing of a naive and moral "feminine sexuality" has been challenged as essentialist, and the assumption that such a feminine sexuality is "natural" to women has been shown to be false (Rubin 1984).

Over the past decade, understandings of female sexual choice, consent, and coercion have grown richer and more complex. While questions about female subjectivities have become more interesting, the answers (for some) remain deceptively simple. Inside public schools, for example, female adolescents continue to be educated as though they were the potential *victims* of sexual (male) desire. By contrast, the ideological opposition represents only adult married women as fully consensual partners. The distinction of coercion and consent has been organized simply and respectively around age and marital status—which effectively resolves any complexity and/or ambivalence.

The ambivalence surrounding female heterosexuality places the victim and subject in opposition and derogates all women who represent female sexual subjectivities outside of marriage—prostitutes, lesbians, single mothers, women involved with multiple partners, and, particularly, black single mothers (Weitz 1984). "Protected" from this derogation, the typical adolescent woman, as represented in sex education curricula, is without any sexual subjectivity. The discourse of victimization not only obscures the derogation, it also transforms socially distributed anxieties about female sexuality into acceptable, and even protective, talk.

The fact that schools implicitly organize sex education around a concern for female victimization is suspect, however, for two reasons. First, if female victims of male violence were truly a social concern, wouldn't the victims of rape, incest, and sexual harassment encounter social compassion and not suspicion and blame? And, second, if sex education were designed primarily to prevent victimization but not to prevent exploration of desire, wouldn't there be more discussions of both the pleasures and relatively fewer risks of disease or pregnancy associated with lesbian relationships and protected sexual intercourse or of the risk-free pleasures of masturbation and fantasy? Public education's concern for the female victim is revealed as deceptively thin when real victims are discredited and when nonvictimizing pleasures are silenced.

This unacknowledged social ambivalence about heterosexuality polarizes the debates over sex education and school-based health clinics. The anxiety effectively treats the female sexual victim as though she were a completely separate species from the female sexual subject. Yet the adolescent women quoted earlier in this text remind us that the female victim and subject coexist in every woman's body.

Toward a Discourse of Sexual Desire and Social Entitlement: In the Student Bodies of Public Schools

I have argued that silencing a discourse of desire buttresses the icon of woman-as-victim. In so doing, public schooling may actually disable young women in their negotiations as sexual subjects. Trained through and into positions of passivity and victimization, young women are currently educated away from positions of sexual self-interest.

If we resituate the adolescent woman in a rich and empowering educational context, she develops a sense of self that is sexual as well as intellectual, social, and economic. In this section, I invite readers to imagine such a context. The dialectic of desire and victimization—across spheres of labor, social relations, and sexuality—would then frame schooling. While many of the curricula and interventions discussed in this essay are imperfect, data on the effectiveness of what *is* available are nevertheless compelling. Studies of sex education curricula, SBHCs, classroom discussions, and ethnographies of life inside public high schools demonstrate that a sense of sexual and social entitlement for young women *can* be fostered within public schools.

Sex Education as Intellectual Empowerment

Harris and Yankelovich polls confirm that over 80 percent of American adults believe that students should be educated about sexuality within their public schools. Seventy-five percent believe that homosexuality and abortion should be included in the curriculum, with 40 percent of those surveyed by Yankelovich et al. ($N=1015$) agreeing that twelve-year-olds should be taught about oral and anal sex (see Harris and Associates 1985; Leo 1986).

While the public continues to debate the precise content of sex education, most parents approve and support sex education for their children. An Illinois program monitored parental requests to "opt out" and found that only six or seven of eight hundred fifty children were actually excused from sex education courses (Leo 1986). In a California assessment, fewer than 2 percent of parents disallowed their children's participation. And, in a longitudinal five-year program in Connecticut, seven of two thousand five hundred students requested exemption from these classes (Scales 1981). Resistance to sex education, while loud at the level of public rhetoric and conservative organizing, is both less vocal and less active within schools and parents' groups (Hottois and Milner 1975; Scales 1981).

Sex education courses are offered broadly, if not comprehensively, across the United States. In 1981, only seven of fifty states actually had laws against such instruction, and only one state enforced a prohibition (Kirby and Scales 1981). Surveying 179 urban school districts, Sonnenstein and Pittman (1984) found that 75 percent offered some sex education within senior and junior high schools, while 66 percent of the elementary schools offered sex education units. Most instruction was, however, limited to ten hours or less, with content focused on anatomy. In his extensive review of sex education programs, Kirby (1985) concludes that less than 10 percent of all public school students are exposed to what might be considered comprehensive sex education courses.

The progress on AIDS education is more encouraging, and more complex (see Freudenberg 1987) but cannot be adequately reviewed in this article. It is important to note, however, that a December, 1986, report released by the U.S. Conference of Mayors documents that 54 percent of the seventy-three largest school districts and twenty-five state school agencies offer some form of AIDS education (Benedetto 1987). Today debates among federal officials—including Secretary of Education Bennett and Surgeon General Koop—and among educators question *when* and *what* to offer in AIDS education. The question is no longer *whether* such education should be promoted.

Not only has sex education been accepted as a function of public schooling, but it has survived empirical tests of effectiveness. Evaluation data demonstrate that sex education can increase contraceptive knowledge and use (Kirby 1985; Public/Private Ventures 1987). In terms of sexual activity (measured narrowly in terms of the onset or frequency of heterosexual intercourse), the evidence suggests that sex education does not instigate an earlier onset or increase of such sexual activity (Zelnik and Kim 1982) and may, in fact, postpone the onset of heterosexual intercourse (Zabin, Hirsch, Smith, Streett, and Hardy 1986). The data for pregnancy rates appear to demonstrate no effect for exposure to sex education alone (see Dawson 1986; Kirby 1985; Marsiglio and Mott 1986).

Sex education as constituted in these studies is not sufficient to diminish teen pregnancy rates. In all likelihood, it would be naive to expect that sex education (especially if only ten hours in duration) would carry such a "long arm" of effectiveness. While the widespread problem of teen pregnancy must be attributed broadly to economic and social inequities (Jones et al. 1985), sex education remains necessary and sufficient to educate, demystify, and improve contraceptive knowledge and use. In conjunction with material opportunities for enhanced life options, it is believed that sex education and access to contraceptives and abortion can help to reduce the rate of unintended pregnancy among teens (Dryfoos 1985a, 1985b; National Research Council 1987).

School-Based Health Clinics: Sexual Empowerment

The public opinion and effectiveness data for school-based health clinics are even more compelling than those for sex education. Thirty SBHCs provide on-site health care services to senior, and sometimes junior, high school students in more than eighteen U.S. communities, with an additional twenty-five communities developing similar programs (Kirby 1985). These clinics offer, at a minimum, health counseling, referrals, and follow-up examinations. Over 70 percent conduct pelvic examinations (Kirby 1985), approximately 52 percent prescribe contraceptives, and 28 percent dispense contraceptives (Leo 1986). None performs abortions, and few refer for abortions.

All SBHCs require some form of general parental notification and/or consent, and some charge a nominal fee for generic health services. Relative to private physicians, school-based health clinics and other family planning agencies are substantially more willing to provide contraceptive services to unmarried minors without specific parental consent (consent in this case referring explicitly to contraception). Only 1 percent of national Planned Parenthood affiliates require consent or notification, compared to 10 percent of public health department programs and 19 percent of hospitals (Torres and Forrest 1985).

The consequences of consent provisions for abortion are substantial. Data from two states, Massachusetts and Minnesota, demonstrate that parental consent laws result in increased teenage pregnancies or increased numbers of out-of-state abortions. The Reproductive Freedom Project of the American Civil Liberties Union, in a report that examines the consequences of such consent provisions, details the impact of these statutes on teens, on their familial relationships, and, ultimately, on their unwanted children (Reproductive Freedom Project 1986). In an analysis of the impact of Minnesota's mandatory parental notification law from 1981 to 1985, this report documents over seven thousand pregnancies in teens aged thirteen to seventeen, three thousand five hundred of whom "went to state court to seek the right to confidential abortions, all at considerable personal cost." The report also notes that many of the pregnant teens did not petition the court, "although their entitlement and need for confidential abortions was as strong or more so than the teenagers who made it to court. . . . Only those minors who are old enough and wealthy enough or resourceful enough are actually able to use the court bypass option" (Reproductive Freedom Project 1986, 4).

These consent provisions, with allowance for court bypass, not only increase the number of unwanted teenage pregnancies carried to term but also extend the length of time required to secure an abortion, potentially endangering the life of the teenage woman and increasing the costs of the abortion. The provisions may also jeopardize the physical and emotional well-being of some young women and their mothers, particularly when paternal consent is required and the pregnant teenager resides with a single mother. Finally, the consent provisions create a class-based health care system. Adolescents able to afford travel to a nearby state or able to pay a private physician for a confidential abortion have access to an abortion. Those unable to afford the travel or those who are unable to contact a private physician are likely to become teenage mothers (Reproductive Freedom Project 1986).

In Minneapolis, during the time from 1980 to 1984 when the law was implemented, the birthrate for fifteen- to seventeen-year-olds increased 38.4 percent, while the birthrate for eighteen- and nineteen-year-olds—not affected by the law—rose only 0.3 percent (Reproductive Freedom Project 1986). The State of Massachusetts passed a parental consent law that took effect in 1981. An analysis of the impact of that law concludes that "the major impact of the Massachusetts parental consent law has been to send a monthly average of between ninety and ninety-five of the state's minors across state lines in search of an abortion. This number represents about one in every three minor abortion patients living in Massachusetts" (Cartoof and Klerman 1986). These researchers, among others, write that parental consent laws could have more devastating effects in larger states, from which access to neighboring states would be more difficult.

The inequalities inherent in consent provisions and the dramatic consequences that result for young women are well recognized. Twenty-nine states and the District of Columbia, for example, now explicitly authorize minors to grant their own consent for receipt of contraceptive information and/or services, independent of parental knowledge or consent (see Melton and Russo 1987, for full discussion; National Research Council 1987; for a full analysis of the legal, emotional, and physical health problems attendant upon parental consent laws for abortion, see Reproductive Freedom Project). More recently, consent laws for abortion in Pennsylvania and California have been challenged as unconstitutional.

Public approval of SBHCs has been slow but consistent. In the 1986 Yankelovich survey, 84 percent of surveyed adults agree that these clinics should provide birth control information; 36 percent endorse dispensing of contraceptives to students (Leo 1986). In 1985, Harris found that 67 percent of all respondents, including 76 percent of blacks and 76 percent of Latinas, agree that public schools should establish formal ties with family planning clinics for teens to learn about and obtain contraception (Harris and Associates 1985). Mirroring the views of the general public, a national sample of school administrators polled by the Education Research Group indicated that more than 50 percent believe birth control should be offered in school-based clinics; 30 percent agree that parental permission should be sought; and 27 percent agree that contraceptives should be dispensed, even if parental consent is not forthcoming. The discouraging news is that 96 percent of these respondents indicate that their districts do not presently offer such services (Benedetto 1987; Werner 1987).

Research on the effectiveness of SBHCs is consistently persuasive. The three-year Johns Hopkins University study of school-based health clinics (Zabin et al. 1986) found that schools in which SBHCs made referrals and dispensed contraceptives noted an increase in the percentage of "virgin" females visiting the program as well as an increase in contraceptive use. They also found a significant reduction in pregnancy rates: There was a 13 percent increase at experimental schools after ten months versus a 50 percent increase at control schools; after twenty-eight months, pregnancy rates decreased 30 percent at experimental schools versus a 53 percent increase at control schools. Furthermore, by the second year, a substantial percentage of males visited the clinic (48 percent of males in experimental schools indicated that they "have ever been to a birth control clinic or to a physician about birth control," compared to 12 percent of males in control schools). Contrary to common belief, the schools in which clinics dispensed contraceptives showed a substantial postponement of first experience of heterosexual intercourse among high school students and an increase in the proportion of young women visiting the clinic prior to "first coitus."

Paralleling the Hopkins findings, the St. Paul Maternity and Infant Care Project (1985) found that pregnancy rates dropped substantially in schools with clinics, from seventy-nine births/thousand (1973) to twenty-six births/thousand (1984). Teens who delivered and kept their infants had an 80 percent graduation rate, relative to approximately 50 percent of young mothers nationally. Those who stayed in school reported a 1.3 percent repeat birthrate, compared to 17 percent nationally. Over three years, pregnancy rates dropped by 40 percent. Twenty-five percent of young women in the school received some form of family planning and 87 percent of clients were continuing to use contraception at a three-year follow-up. There were fewer obstetric complications; fewer babies were born at low birth weights; and prenatal visits to physicians increased relative to students in the control schools.

Predictions that school-based health clinics would advance the onset of sexual intimacy, heighten the degree of "promiscuity" and incidence of pregnancy, and hold females primarily responsible for sexuality were countered by the evidence. The onset of sexual intimacy was postponed, while contraception was used more reliably. Pregnancy rates substantially diminished, and, over time, a large group of males began to view contraception as a shared responsibility.

It is worth restating here that females who received family planning counseling and/or contraception actually postponed the onset of heterosexual intercourse. I would argue that the availability of such services may enable females to feel they are sexual agents, entitled and therefore responsible, rather than at the constant and terrifying mercy of a young man's pressure to "give in" or of a parent's demands to "save yourself." With a sense of sexual agency and not necessarily urgency, teen girls may be less likely to use or be used by pregnancy (Petchesky 1984).

Nontraditional Vocational Training: Social and Economic Entitlement

The literature reviewed suggests that sex education, access to contraception, and opportunities for enhanced life options, in combination (Dryfoos 1985a, 1985b; Kirby 1985) can significantly diminish the likelihood that a teenager will become pregnant, carry to term, and/or have a repeat pregnancy and can increase the likelihood that she will stay in high school through graduation (National Research Council 1987). Education toward entitlement—including a sense of sexual, economic, and social entitlement—may be sufficient to affect adolescent girls' views on sexuality, contraception, and abortion. By framing female subjectivity within the context of social entitlement, sex education would be organized around dialogue and critique, SBHCs would offer health services, options counseling, contraception, and abortion referrals, and the provision of real "life options" would include nontraditional vocational training programs and employment opportunities for adolescent females (Dryfoos 1985a, 1985b).

In a nontraditional vocational training program in New York City designed for young women, many of whom are mothers, participants' attitudes toward contraception and abortion shifted once they acquired a set of vocational skills, a sense of social entitlement, and a sense of personal competence (S. Weinbaum, pers. com., 1987). The young women often began the program without strong academic skills or a sense of competence. At the start, they were more likely to express more negative sentiments about contraception and abortion than when they completed the program. One young woman, who initially held strong antiabortion attitudes, learned that she was pregnant midway through her carpentry apprenticeship. She decided to abort, reasoning that, now that she has a future, she can't risk losing it for another baby (S. Weinbaum, pers. com., 1987). A developing sense of social entitlement may have transformed this young woman's view of reproduction, sexuality, and self.

The Manpower Development Research Corporation (MDRC), in its evaluation of Project Redirection (Polit, Kahn, and Stevens 1985), offers similar conclusions about a comprehensive vocational training and community-based mentor project for teen mothers and mothers-to-be. Low-income teens were enrolled in Project Redirection, a network of services designed to instill self-sufficiency, in which community women served as mentors. The program included training for what is called "employability," Individual Participation Plans, and peer group sessions. Data on education, employment, and pregnancy outcomes were collected at twelve and twenty-four months after enrollment. Two years after the program began, many newspapers headlined the program as a failure. The data actually indicated that at twelve months, the end of program involvement, Project Redirection women were significantly *less likely* to experience a repeat pregnancy than comparison women; *more likely* to be using contraception; *more likely* to be in school, to have completed school, or to be in the labor force; and twice as likely (20 percent versus 11 percent, respectively) to have earned a graduate equivalency diploma. At twenty-four months, however, approximately one year out of the program, project and comparison women were virtually indistinguishable. MDRC reported equivalent rates of repeat pregnancies, dropout, and unemployment.

The Project Redirection data demonstrate that sustained outcomes cannot be expected once programs have been withdrawn and participants confront the realities of a dismal economy and inadequate child care and social services. The data confirm, however, the effectiveness of comprehensive programs to reduce teen pregnancy rates and encourage study or work as long as the young women are actively engaged. Supply-side interventions—changing people but not structures or opportunities—that leave unchallenged an inhospitable and discriminating economy and a thoroughly impoverished child care / social welfare system are inherently doomed to long-term failure. When such programs fail, the social reading is that "these young women can't be helped." Blaming the victim obscures the fact that the current economy and social welfare arrangements need overhauling if the sustained educational, social, and psychological gains accrued by the Project Redirection participants are to be maintained.

In the absence of enhanced life options, low-income young women are likely to default to early and repeat motherhood as a source of perceived competence, significance, and pleasure. When life options are available, however, a sense of competence and "entitlement to better" may help to prevent second pregnancies, may help to encourage education and, when available, the pursuit of meaningful work (Burt, Kimmich, Goldmuntz, and Sonnenstein 1984).

Femininity May Be Hazardous to Her Health: The Absence of Entitlement

Growing evidence suggests that women who lack a sense of social or sexual entitlement, who hold traditional notions of what it means to be female—self-sacrificing and relatively passive—and who undervalue themselves are disproportionately likely to find themselves with an unwanted pregnancy and to maintain it through to motherhood. While many young women who drop out, pregnant or not, are not at all traditional in these ways, but are quite feisty and are fueled with a sense of entitlement (Fine 1986a; S. Weinbaum, pers. com., 1987), it may also be the case that young women who do internalize such notions of "femininity" are disproportionately at risk for pregnancy and dropping out.

The Hispanic Policy Development Project reports that low-income female sophomores who, in 1980, expected to be married and/or to have a child by age nineteen were disproportionately represented among nongraduates in 1984. Expectations of early marriage and childbearing correspond to dramatic increases (200 to 400 percent) in nongraduation rates for low-income adolescent women across racial and ethnic groups (Hispanic Policy Development Project 1987). These indicators of traditional notions of womanhood bode poorly for female academic achievement.

The Children's Defense Fund (1986) recently published additional data that demonstrate that young women with poor basic skills are three times more likely to become teen parents than women with average or above-average basic skills. Those with poor or fair basic skills are four times more likely to have more than one child while a teen; 29 percent of women in the bottom skills quintile became mothers by age eighteen versus 5 percent of young women in the top quintile. While academic skill problems must be placed in the context of alienating and problematic schools and not viewed as inherent in these young women, those who fall in the bottom quintile may nevertheless be the least likely to feel entitled or in control of their lives. They may feel more vulnerable to male pressure or more willing to have a child as a means of feeling competent.

My own observations, derived from a year-long ethnographic study of a comprehensive public high school in New York City, further confirm some of these conclusions. Six months into the ethnography, new pregnancies began showing. I noticed that many of the girls who got pregnant and carried to term were not those whose bodies, dress, and manner evoked sensuality and experience. Rather, a number of the pregnant women were those who were quite passive and relatively quiet in their classes. One young woman—who granted me an interview anytime, washed the blackboard for her teacher, rarely spoke in class, and never disobeyed her mother—was pregnant by the spring of the school year (Fine 1986b).

Simple stereotypes, of course, betray the complexity of circumstances under which young women become pregnant and maintain their pregnancies. While U.S. rates of teenage sexual activity and age of "sexual initiation" approximate those of comparable developed countries, the teenage pregnancy, abortion, and childbearing rates in the United States are substantially higher. In the United States, teenagers under age fifteen are at least five times more likely to give birth than similarly aged teens in other industrialized nations (Jones et al. 1985; National Research Council 1987). The national factors that correlate with low teenage birthrates include adolescent access to sex education and contraception and relative equality in the distribution of wealth. Economic and structural conditions that support a class-stratified society and limit adolescent access to sexual information and contraception contribute to inflated teenage pregnancy rates and birthrates.

This broad national context acknowledged, it might still be argued that, within our country, traditional notions of what it means to be a woman—to remain subordinate, dependent, self-sacrificing, compliant, and ready to marry and/or bear children early—do little to empower women or enhance a sense of entitlement. This is not to say that teenage dropouts or mothers tend to be of any one type. Yet it may well be that the traditions and practices of "femininity," as commonly understood, may be hazardous to the economic, social, educational, and sexual development of young women.

In summary, the historic silencing within public schools of conversations about sexuality, contraception, and abortion, as well as the absence of a discourse of desire—in the form of comprehensive sex education, school-based health clinics, and viable life options via vocational training and placement—all combine to exacerbate the vulnerability of young women whom schools, and the critics of sex education and SBHCs, claim to protect.

Conclusion

Adolescents are entitled to a discussion of desire instead of the anti-sex rhetoric that controls the controversies around sex education, SBHCs, and AIDS education. The absence of a discourse of desire, combined with the lack of analysis of the language of victimization, may actually retard the development of sexual subjectivity and responsibility in students. Those most "at risk" of victimization through pregnancy, disease, violence, or harassment—all female students, low-income females in particular, and nonheterosexual males—are those most likely to be victimized by the absence of critical conversation in public schools. Public schools can no longer afford to maintain silence around a discourse of desire. This is not to say that the silencing of a discourse of desire is the primary root of sexual victimization, teen motherhood, and the concomitant poverty experienced by young and low-income females. Nor could it be responsibly argued that interventions initiated by public schools could ever be successful if separate from economic and social development. But it is important to understand that, by providing education, counseling, contraception, and abortion referrals, as well as meaningful educational and vocational opportunities, public schools could play an essential role in the construction of the female subject— social and sexual.

And, by not providing such an educational context, public schools contribute to the rendering of substantially different outcomes for male and female students and for male and female dropouts (Fine 1986a, 1986b). The absence of a thorough sex education curriculum, of school-based health clinics, of access to free and confidential contraceptive and abortion services, of exposure to information about the varieties of sexual pleasures and partners, and of involvement in sustained employment training programs may so jeopardize the educational and economic outcomes for female adolescents as to constitute sex discrimination. How can we ethically continue to withhold educational treatments we know to be effective for adolescent women?

Public schools constitute a sphere in which young women could be offered access to a language and experience of empowerment. In such contexts, "well-educated" young women could breathe life into positions of social critique and experience entitlement rather than victimization, autonomy rather than terror.

NOTES

1. The research reported in this essay represents one component of a year-long ethnographic investigation of students and dropouts at a comprehensive public high school in New York City. Funded by the W. T. Grant Foundation, the research was designed to investigate how public urban high schools produce dropout rates in excess of 50 percent. The methods employed over the year included: in-school observations four days/week during the fall, and one to two days/week during the spring: regular (daily) attendance in a hygiene course for twelfth-graders; an archival analysis of more than one thousand two hundred students who compose the 1978–79 cohort of incoming ninth-graders; interviews with approximately fifty-five recent and long-term dropouts; analysis of fictional and autobiographical writings by students; a survey distributed to a subsample of the cohort population; and visits to proprietary schools, programs for graduate equivalency diplomas, naval recruitment sites, and a public high school for pregnant and parenting teens. The methods and preliminary results of the ethnography are detailed in Fine (1986a).

2. This information is derived from personal communication with former and present employees of major urban school districts who have chosen to remain anonymous.

3. Personal communication.

Coping with Rape: Critical Perspectives on Consciousness

Michelle Fine

Prosecute? No, I just want to get home. While I'm pickin' some guy out
of some line, who knows who's messin' around with my momma and
my baby.
—Altamese Thomas, 24-year-old rape survivor
October, 1981, hospital emergency room

At 2:00 A.M. one October morning, Altamese Thomas was led out of
a police car, entered the hospital in pain, smelling of alcohol. Altamese
had been drinking with some women friends in a poor, high crime,
largely black neighborhood in Philadelphia. She found herself in an alley,
intoxicated, with pants down. She reports being gang-raped. The story
unfolds, from intake nurse, the police, and from Altamese herself.

I was awakened, in the small office for volunteer rape counselors,
when the emergency room nurse telephoned me: "A Code-R just arrived."
"Code-R" is the euphemism used to describe a woman who has been
raped. I spent the remainder of the evening and some of the morning
with Altamese. A twenty-four-year-old black mother of three, two of
her children have been placed by the state in foster care. From 2:00 A.M.
until 7:00 A.M., we held hands as she smarted through two painful
injections to ward off infection; traveled through the hospital in search
of X-rays for a leg that felt (but wasn't) broken; waited for the sex
offender officers to arrive; watched Altamese refuse to speak with them;
and returned to the X-ray room for a repeat performance—and we talked.

I introduced myself and explained my role. Interested primarily
and impatiently in washing "the dirt off" and receiving necessary medical
care, Altamese was unambivalent about her priorities. She did not

want to prosecute nor talk with social workers or counselors. She couldn't call upon her social supports. She just wanted to get home. For five hours we talked. Our conversation systematically disrupted my belief that I understood anything much about the psychology of taking control in the face of injustice. This article which stems from my dialogue with Altamese, provides a critical analysis of the class, race, and gender biases woven into the social psychological literature on coping with injustice.

The Psychology of Taking Control

When confronting life crises, injustices, or tragedies, psychologists argue, people fare best by assuming control over their circumstances. Accepting responsibility for one's problems and/or solutions correlates with psychological and physical well-being, across populations as diverse as rape survivors, disabled adults, the institutionalized elderly, unemployed men and women, school children with academic problems, even high school dropouts. This article examines the assumptions that underlie present formulations of Taking-Control-Yields-Coping. Weaving relevant theory and research with excerpts from the dialogue between this rape survivor and the author, it will be argued that the prevailing coping-through-control ideologies are often limited by class, race, and gender biases. Further, these models are disproportionately effective for only a small and privileged sector of society.

Psychologists have demonstrated that individuals cope most effectively with unjust or difficult circumstances by controlling their environments. This may involve attributing behavioral blame for the onset of bad events or personal responsibility for initiating change. Taking control may require participating in social programs for "getting help" and relying upon one's social supports.

The current Taking-Control arguments often assume that people *can* control the forces that victimize them, *should* utilize available social programs, and *will* benefit if they rely on social supports. What is not explicit is that these prescribed means of coping are likely to be ineffectual for most people. Persons of relatively low ascribed social power—by virtue of social class position, ethnicity, race, gender, disability, or sexual preference—cannot control those forces that limit their opportunities. But, while it has been proposed that many then learn to be helpless

(Seligman 1975), I maintain instead that they do assert control in ways ignored by psychologists. For many, taking control involves ignoring advice to solve one's problems individually and recognizing instead the need for collective, structural change. Taking control may mean rejecting available social programs as inappropriate to one's needs or recognizing that one's social supports are too vulnerable to be relied upon. Such acts of taking control have long been misclassified by psychologists as acts of relinquishing control.

Access to Means of Taking Control: A Function of Social Power

The control-yields-well-being proposition is empirically robust and admittedly compelling. As a psychologist interested in the social psychology of injustice, I study and support efforts that encourage people to take control of their lives. A review of this literature reveals, however, *individualistic* coping strategies, effective for persons of relatively high social power, promoted *as if* they were optimal and universal ways to cope. By establishing a hierarchy of appropriate ways to take control, this literature often (1) denies the complex circumstances many people confront, (2) de facto delegitimates those strategies for taking control employed by persons of relatively low social power, (3) encourages psychological and individualistic responses to injustice, which often reinforce existing power inequities, and (4) justifies prevailing social structures.

Advancing the position that people need to exert individual control over their lives presumes that all people are able to do so, that all people want to do so, and that, to improve their life circumstances, people need to change themselves rather than social structures. Three fundamental problems with this formulation emerge.

First, if asserting individual control promotes psychological health, it may be because individualism is socially reinforced in our society. Positive reinforcement follows individualistic acts (e.g., "pulling oneself up by the boot-straps") with social disapproval displayed for collective acts (e.g., in school, these collective acts may be considered cheating; at work, trouble making). The health that is associated with acts of individualistic control may therefore derive from social and ideological supports in our culture, not because individual control is inherently healthy.

Given that psychological well-being stems in part from social rewards for individualism and internality, a second problem emerges with this model of coping. If unfair treatment occurs and control of that treatment is unlikely, a presumption of internality may be delusional. Externality may benefit persons whose life conditions are indeed beyond their control. To nurture the much encouraged illusion of internality in many circumstances would be unreasonable. In situations of low probability of success for redressing an injustice, attempts to redress injustice personally can breed helplessness.

It may be true that, when persons of relatively high social power assert a single act of "taking control" (e.g., voice a grievance or file a complaint), they are likely to succeed. In contrast, the undocumented worker who is sexually harassed by her factory foreman might be foolish to file a grievance. "Bearing it" does not mean she has given up but, rather, that she determined a solution by which she can be in control and employed. Establishing strategies to survive, when change is unlikely, needs to be recognized as an act of control.

A third problem with current control formulations is that they often decontextualize coping. The presumption that psychologists can extract optimal ways to assume control over failure or adversity *across situations* reduces the complexities of the situations ad absurdum.

The strategies popular in the literature and undoubtedly effective in many cases may benefit persons of relatively high social power (e.g., by attributing successes to stable internal factors and failures to unstable factors; taking responsibility for solutions; relying on social supports or utilizing available social programs). As psychologists, however, we lack an understanding of how people who are systematically discriminated against and restricted to low power positions take control. We fail to understand how they determine what is controllable and what is not. We dismiss control strategies that look like "giving up" but are in fact ways to survive. Even more serious, we avoid the study of those ways of taking control which systematically disrupt traditional power relations. Our literature legitimates existing power asymmetries.

There are two major consequences to these theoretical problems. First, control efforts enacted by low power persons are often misdiagnosed as giving up. Such attempts to take control tend to be misread as counterproductive ("Why don't they do something about their work conditions if they are dissatisfied rather than slowing down on productivity?"); distorted as self-effacing ("Even she blames herself for the rape."); diagnosed as masochistic ("She must enjoy the abuse; why else would she stay?"); classified as learned helplessness (Seligman 1975) ("She always says, 'I can't do anything about it.'"); or denigrated as psychological resistance ("I tried to offer help, but he won't listen!") by laypersons and psychologists alike. These behaviors may indeed function as strategies of asserting control, if not resistance.

Second, the existing body of research on allegedly healthy ways of coping reproduces existing power inequities by prescribing *as optimal* those ways of coping which are effective for high power persons. Social programs designed for low power persons are often organized toward coping strategies (such as individualism and reliance on social institutions) effective for high power persons. The models are deceptive for persons of low social power who depend on higher power persons, economically, socially, and/or psychologically, and have other low power persons (e.g., kin) highly dependent upon them. This precarious web of interdependencies creates conditions in which social institutions are likely to be unresponsive and individualism to be inappropriate. Many low power persons will not improve their own circumstances at expense to others, and most are unlikely to have access to standard tools of control (e.g., grievance procedures, money, or leverage with Congressional representatives). If they do, these tools are unlikely to promote the kinds of changes they need. Consequently, when low power persons decide *not* to use the resources or programs offered them (e.g., "Because my mother is sick, and I have to take care of my children."), their disadvantaged circumstances may come to be viewed as deserved. The perception that they are *unwilling* to act on their own behalf provides evidence of helplessness, if not laziness. Their need to rely on high power persons is then confirmed. The power asymmetries built into these relationships are systematically justified.

Below, through a dialogue between the author and a woman who survived a rape—a dialogue situated in a hospital emergency room the evening of the rape—we analyze how persons of relatively low social power do assert control, and how easily a psychologist can misread these as efforts to give up.

| *Altamese Thomas* | *Michelle Fine* |
| | 3:00 A.M.   Altamese, the police will be here to speak with you. Are you interested in prosecuting? Do you want to take these guys to court? |

No, I don't want to do nothin'
but get over this. . . . When I'm
pickin' the guy out of some line,
who knows who's messin' around
with my momma or my baby.
Anyway, nobody would believe
me. [Can I wash now?]

3:30 A.M.   [Once the exam is
over you can wash and brush
your teeth. First we need to wait
for the doctor for your exam.]
Wouldn't your friends testify as
witnesses?

Where I live, nobody's gonna testify. Not to the police. Anyway,
I'm a Baptist, and I know God is
punishing him right now. He
done bad enough, and he's
suffering.

4:00 A.M.   Maybe if we talked
about the rape, you would feel
better.

You know, I don't remember
things. When I was little, lots of
bad things happened to me, and
I forget them. My memory's bad;
I don't like to remember bad
stuff. I just forget. When I was a
young child, my momma told me
about rape and robberies. I told
her she was wrong. Those things
happen in the movies, not here.
When I saw such things on the
streets I thought they was making a movie. Then one day a
lady started bleeding, and I knew
it was no movie.

4:30 A.M.   . . . Do you think
maybe you would like to talk

with a counselor in a few days
about some of your feelings?

I've been to one of them. It just
made it worse. I just kept thinking about my problems too
much. You feel better when
you're talking, but then you got
to go back home, and they're still
there. No good just talking when
things ain't no better.

Is there anyone you can talk to
about this?

Not really. I can't tell my mother,
not my brothers either. They
would go out and kill the guys.
My mother's boyfriend too. I
don't want them going to jail
'cause of me.

You said you sometimes meet
with a social worker. Can you
talk with your social worker?

She's the one who took away my
kids. If they take my baby, I
would kill myself. I ain't gonna
get myself in trouble; all I got is
my baby, and she already thinks
I'm a bad mother. But I love my
babies, and I try hard to take
care of them. [I just don't understand why men have to rape.
Why do they have to take when
they could just ask?]

How about one of your teachers
at —— college? Can you talk to
them?

Those teachers think I'm stupid.
Sometimes they call on me, and I
don't answer. When you got
problems, your mind is on the

moon. He calls on you, and you
don't know what he's saying.
They treat you like a dog, and
you act like a dog.

5:30 A.M.   Soon you will get to
leave here and go home, where
you'll feel safe.

It ain't safe there. I live in the
projects with my baby. I can't go
back there now. It feels safer
here. . . . I hurt so much.

7:00 A.M.   Can I call you next
week just to see how you're
doing?

Sure . . .

Asserting Relational Control

At first glance, one might say that Altamese abdicated control: She gave
up. Unwilling to prosecute, uninterested in utilizing her social supports,
she relied on God for justice. Resistant to mental health, social service,
and educational and criminal justice assistance, she rejected available
options. Her coping mechanisms might be said to include denial, repression, and paranoia. She doesn't trust her friends to testify, her family
to listen, her social worker to be supportive, her teachers to understand,
or the police to assist. She has refused available mechanisms of control.

And yet, through our dialogue, it was obvious that each of her
decisions embodies a significant assertion of control. Likely to be misclassified as helpless or paranoid, she asserted strategies for taking control
which ensure both her well-being and that of her kin. Altamese organized
coping around relational concerns. Worried about her mother, child, and
siblings, she rejected options offered to help her cope. She viewed my
trust in the justice system as somewhat absurd; my commitment to
talking about the rape to friends, social workers, teachers, or family as
somewhat impulsive; my expectations of witnessess coming forth as
almost naive; and even my role as volunteer counselor as somewhat
unusual.

Altamese Thomas	*Michelle Fine*
So, you're a nurse?	
	7:00 A.M. Actually, I volunteer here, talking with women who have been raped.
You mean you do this for fun?	
	I do it because I think it's important. Do you?
. . . I don't know how you can do it all the time.	

Most people are denied the means to assume control over fundamentally changing their lives. Although prevailing ideology argues otherwise, Altamese and the millions of women who are unemployed, poor, minority and/or disabled, and responsible for a network of kin have limited options. Although pursuing college, she may perhaps qualify for a low-pay job someday. Given unemployment statistics, her personal style, life circumstances, and lack of qualifications, her chances are slim.

The standard means of taking control promoted by counselors, policymakers, and researchers tend to be individualistic and most effective for a privileged slice of society. Trusting social institutions, maximizing interpersonal supports, and engaging in self-disclosure are strategies most appropriate for middle-class and affluent individuals whose interests are served by those institutions, whose social supports can multiply available resources and contacts, and for whom self-disclosure may in fact lead not only to personal change but also to structural change.

For Altamese, who is unable to trust existing institutions, self-disclosure would have exposed wounds unlikely to be healed. Responsible for a network of kin, Altamese could not rely on but had to protect her social supports. Resisting social institutions, withholding information, and preserving emotional invulnerability emerged as her strategies for maintaining control. Expecting God to prosecute, loss of memory to ensure coping, and fantasy to anesthetize reality, Altamese is by no means helpless.

While her social and economic circumstances are such that Altamese cannot change the basic oppressive structures that affect her, the social and psychological strategies she employs are mechanisms of control—protection for self and others. An abstract pursuit of justice was not possible given her social context, commitments, and concerns. She organized the realities of her life so as to manage effectively the multiple forces that *are* out to get her and her kin. Like Carol Gilligan's concept of women's relational morality (1982), Altamese exhibited what may be considered relational coping.

With little attention paid to relational concerns and a systematic neglect of power relations, psychologists have prescribed ways to cope as if a consensus about their utility had been established; as if there were no alternatives; as if universals could be applied across contexts; and as if these strategies were uninfluenced by our position in social and economic hierarchies. As the creators of what Foucault (1972) calls "power-knowledge," psychologists have an obligation to expose the dialectics of psychological control and structural control as experienced by women and men across lines of social class, ethnicity, and race, levels of physical ability and disability, and sexual preferences. In the absence of such knowledge, psychologists impose, as healthy and universal, what may be narrow and elitist strategies for taking control.

One particular strategy, examined below, involves the prescription that persons treated unjustly or confronted by tragedy utilize available social programs. If Altamese is any indication, such social programs are likely to be severely underutilized so long as they are designed top-down *for* (and not by) the persons supposedly served.

Coping with Options

One way to take control over adversity, supported by much psychological research (including my own), is to do something to improve one's own life circumstances—to use available options. To battered women, it may be suggested that they leave their abusive homes; to the unemployed, that they enroll for skills retraining; to the underpaid, that they learn to be assertive; to rape victims, that they "ventilate" and prosecute. Social programs have proliferated to offer individuals these services. These programs are generally designed by relatively high power individuals for persons who have what are considered personal problems. Offered as *opportunities* to improve the quality of life experienced by low power persons, these programs generally aim to correct presumed deficits. Some disabled persons have the opportunity to work in sheltered workshops, often earning less than minimum wages, trained for nonmarketable skills. Some battered women have the opportunity to be sheltered in facilities that exclude women with drug or alcohol addictions, are located in unsafe neighborhoods, and limit a maximum stay to two weeks, promising an alternative to violent homes. Some African-American high school dropouts have the opportunity to earn their graduate equivalency diplomas (GEDs), promising greater vocational mobility, despite the fact that black adolescent unemployment figures range from 39 percent to 44 percent for high school graduates and dropouts, respectively.

As efforts to fix people and not to change structures, many of these options reinforce the recipient's low power position. It is therefore most interesting that, when such persons dismiss these options as inappropriate, ineffective, or as decoys for the "real issues," these persons are often derogated. Individuals who reject available options, such as disabled adults who picket the Jerry Lewis Telethon [which raises money to help "fight" disabilities], claiming it to be condescending and reinforcing of the worst stereotypes, are viewed as ungrateful, unappreciative, and sometimes even deserving of their circumstances. The same option that appears valuable to a high power person may be critiqued as a charade by low power persons.

To demonstrate: There exists substantial evidence that high power persons do see social options (e.g., an appeal, grievance procedure, opportunity to flee) as more potentially effective than low power persons do. Experimental and survey data document that, in social contexts in which an option to injustice is available, victims are more likely than nonvictims to consider their circumstances unjust, but nonvictims are more likely to rate the option as powerful to promote change. Victims see injustice; nonvictims see the potential for change. But victims are *not* more likely than nonvictims to use an option to change their circumstances. Why would victims reject an opportunity to avenge injustice?

To investigate this question, victim and nonvictim responses to open-ended questions about injustice and appeals were reviewed (Fine 1980). Victims claim to be reluctant to appeal an injustice not because they do not recognize injustice, they do; not because they feel they deserved to be treated unfairly, they do not; not because they respect victimizers who commit injustice, they do not. Victims appear to be reluctant because they are in fact less likely to win an appeal and usually have more to lose than nonvictims who would appeal. The appeal procedure in this study was designed as an opportunity for the victim to redress inequity but actually offered her only a remote chance of success.

To appeal successfully, the victim or nonvictim had to convince at least one other member of a three-person group that an inequity had occurred. If she appealed, a victim (1) would appear self-serving, (2) could not be sure she would be supported in her appeal, (3) could, if she lost the appeal, get double confirmation that her treatment was justified, and (4) could indeed have much to lose by initiating an appeal.

In marked contrast, a nonvictim who appeals on behalf of the victim (1) would appear benevolent, (2) could be relatively sure of support from the victim, (3) could enjoy public praise for her benevolence, and (4) could gain psychologically and socially from the appeal. It is little wonder, then, that observers view options as more viable for victims than victims do themselves. It is perhaps in this role as observers that psychologists have encouraged victims' utilization of available programs and services. By not understanding how disempowering it may be to be offered an inappropriate option, while reminded that "this is your last chance," even the most benevolent observer/helper can create secondary injury.

Conclusions

> At fifteen life had taught me undeniably that surrender, in its place, was as honorable as resistance, especially if one had no choice.
> —Maya Angelou, *I Know Why the Caged Bird Sings*

As social scientists generate master strategies for taking control and promote them as universally applicable, the paradox of "therapeutic hegemony" emerges. Those individuals with the least control over the causes of their problems, much less the means for structural resolution, are prescribed psychological models for individual efficacy. As long as individual victims (or survivors) act alone to improve their circumstances, oppressive economic and social arrangements will persist. The effects of such acts of psychological control may ultimately be indistinguishable from the effects of surrender. Even acts of resistance, if initiated individualistically, ultimately buttress power differentials. Altamese's unwillingness to use the justice system, her nonreliance on kin, and her trust that God will provide or punish do nothing for the women that these rapist(s) will attack next. Nor do they stem the wave of violence against women. What these behaviors accomplish is that they give Altamese a control strategy by which she can survive, with her remaining child, her mother, and her brothers, in a community where she can get some support. Unfortunately, these behaviors also allow psychologists to continue to weave the fantasy that Altamese needs to be educated about options available to her and taught to be assertive about her needs. Psychologists can remain ever convinced that, if *only* Altamese would learn to use it, the system would work to her advantage. . . .

Epilogue

And so, as psychologists, we are faced with a conceptual dilemma. Should we expand the definition of taking control to incorporate the lived experiences of women and men across class, race, and ethnic lines? Or do we dispense with the concept of taking control totally, rejected as too narrow to be salvaged? I would argue the former. Taking control is undoubtedly a significant psychological experience; knowing that one can effect change in one's environment makes a difference. How individuals accomplish this, however, does vary by economic and social circumstance, gender, and perhaps personal style. The lived experiences of individuals like Altamese need to be integrated into our conceptions of taking control in order for the concept to have meaning for those persons most likely to confront injustice. A feminist psychology needs to value relational coping and to contextualize, through the eyes of those women affected, the meanings of victimization and taking control. The continued assessment of "women's coping" as helplessness needs to be reframed.

Author's Note

I include this note to describe methodological and ethical dilemmas faced in writing this article as a social psychologist. I also hope to persuade others, particularly clinicians interested in using this "method," to consider its inherent ethical dilemmas.

This article, which reflects critical thinking about social psychological theory, was provoked by a discussion with a woman I have chosen to call Altamese. This conversation was between me, as a volunteer rape counselor (not as clinician—which I am not—nor as researcher) in an urban hospital and Altamese, an emergency room patient. The conversation took place because I work at the hospital in this capacity, not because I intended to do research on the topic of rape. The information reported does not, therefore, conform to the traditional standards of ethical practices of data collection.

The ethical dilemmas, as I see them, arise in a way not addressed by the 1983 ethical principles (enumerated by the American Psychological Association [APA]): Altamese was not "informed" because, at the time, there was no research to be informed of; she was not "debriefed" because our only conversation took place in the course of my offering her support, not through the use of a predefined research instrument. Because of these factors, I remain somewhat ambivalent about the presentation of this material.

The problem is, simply, what to do with information gathered in a context in which research was not being conducted, in which the assumption is one of privacy, from which a publishable article evolves two years later? Three issues need to be examined: anonymity, informed consent, and assumptions about privacy.

Anonymity concerns appear to be the easiest to satisfy in both the present work and any other that utilizes a similar methodology. In the present work, names, demographics, and life circumstances have been changed radically so that anonymity is well guarded. The details of the rape and reactions to it have been omitted so that no one could identify this woman—perhaps not even she herself. When information provided in any private setting is subsequently introduced in a manuscript, revealing data should be deleted, changed, and/or "checked back" (if possible) for use.

Informed consent is more complicated. In this case, there was no presumption of "doing research." There would have been no reason, therefore, to request such consent. And two years later, with neither telephone nor forwarding address available, it is impossible to ascertain consent today. Of course, as someone suggested, it is possible that Altamese did sign a statement upon entering the emergency room which "OKed" the research use of relevant information, but one cannot assume this to be informed consent.

In thinking about informed consent, it must be clear that (1) if a researcher is explicitly interested in gathering clinical information for research purposes, all clients need to complete informed consent forms noncoercively (so that they have the option to receive services even if they do not agree to be involved in research); and (2) even if informed consent is provided, clients have the right to delete certain quotes or information from a manuscript if they feel revealed or betrayed by that section of the manuscript.

The third issue is, for me, the most complicated: what to do when information is provided in a context presumed to be private and confidential. Do researchers have a right to use this information for research/ theoretical ends? I want to say a blanket no, but again my own work leaves me wanting a more qualified response. A central consideration here is the issue of risk. In the present case, I can see no risk. Clearly, if Altamese were prosecuting these rapists, the potential risk would be enormous and publication out of the question.

This legal aspect of risk acknowledged, however, we still need to consider how we would feel if information we provided confidentially showed up in a journal article. The more explicit we can be with clients about the potential research purposes and the more we can involve clients in the importance of writing about this material (e.g., to make "public" what are experienced as "private" and "personal" problems), the less damage we will do to the trust levels between ourselves and our clients/ informants; the better we will understand how clients/informants view violations of confidentiality and breaches of contracts; and, presumably, the better the information we will gather (perhaps too optimistic).

This article is about an encounter between two women and incorporates my impressions of that encounter. I have elected to use the material, while trying to describe my ambivalent feelings about the encounter and about this article based on the encounter. In this note, I have tried to reflect on the ethical dilemmas I have confronted and offer suggestions to individuals who may be interested in utilizing such a methodology systematically and intentionally:

1. Develop informed consent procedures so that all clients/potential informants are aware that information could be used for research purposes, providing services even if research consent is denied, and recognizing that introducing the topic of informed consent may systematically alter the nature of the relationship. The question needs to be asked: Are there some counseling relationships in which counselors cannot simultaneously be collecting research-relevant information?

2. Beyond this safeguard, the potential risks to clients of using their

information for research purposes need to be weighed and discussed with clients.

3. Our responsibilities to people who provide us with information need to be respected. Researchers need to be particularly careful about abusing information provided when people assume the exchange to be private, confidential, and safe.

NOTES

Many people deserve thanks for the production of this article. David Surrey was helpful in reviewing, and listening about this material. His theoretical contributions and support are most appreciated. Dell Hymes provided invaluable outside analytic insight. Rhoda Unger and two anonymous reviewers have been supportive and conceptually most helpful. Theresa Singleton typed through numerous versions, until we got it "right." Her patience and goodwill are appreciated. Altamese Thomas, a pseudonym, and the millions of women who have survived rape, have taught me a lot about being a psychologist and being a woman.

Presence of Mind in the Absence of Body

Linda Brodkey and Michelle Fine

We commonly tell stories about what happens to us and what we make of our experience. In a sense, then, the stories documenting our lives tell what we find worth remembering and contemplating and sharing with others. It is, of course, the "others" who complicate the telling of stories, for stories are not usually told to ourselves alone but to those we hope will understand our construction of events. The stories included in this essay concern the sexual harassment of students by professors. We have tried to reconstruct the historical and institutional circumstances of telling along with the stories told because the transformative potential of the narratives cannot be understood apart from the context in which they were written and read.[1]

The sexual harassment narratives were written by undergraduate and graduate women at the University of Pennsylvania in response to an open-ended question on the Penn Harassment Survey (PHS).[2] These students are of the generation of women for many of whom, as Annette Kolodny (1988) recently put it, "feminism is either outdated—because of the naive belief that 'there aren't any problems any more'—or a distorted melange of media images and Reagan-era backlash." For some of them, Kolodny adds, "feminism is both personal and problematic" because their mothers "tried to reject traditional family roles in a society that offered their offspring no compensating structures and amid a movement too new to prepare us all for the consequences of such radical change" (461). Yet the women who wrote these narratives know what sexual harassment is. Their narratives confirm the findings of survey research on college and university campuses: Women students are routinely harassed; postsecondary institutions have been egregiously hesitant to address harassment (much less write, publish, and enforce sexual harassment policies); and remedies for reporting and grieving sexual harassment favor if not harassers, then their institutions (Robertson, Dyer, and Campbell 1988). After reading and reflecting on these narratives, we have come to believe that the future of academic feminism is activism and that activism begins in pedagogy.

The narratives clarify the findings of the Penn survey, namely, that women are reluctant to report sexual harassment and reticent when they do tell because they suspect that institutional indifference will lead to reprisals of one sort or another. We think their fears are justified and, in turn, warrant feminist curriculum intervention. What we have learned from women's narratives of their experiences of harassment, however, suggests that we will need to encourage all students, and women in particular, to explore not so much the fact but the complexities of harassment. After all, harassment sits at the nexus of gender, power, and sexuality in the academy—as it does in all institutions. Exploring it will take the students and us far outside the boundaries of legal definitions and institutional remedies. It will even take us outside of current feminist analyses of gender and sexuality, for most women students judge sexual harassment to be beyond the reach of law and feminism.

To teach this new generation is to try to understand that its members encounter sexual harassment as women whose civil rights have been guaranteed since birth and hence as women who have believed themselves to be protected by those laws—and have only recently found that they are not. And to work with them is also to realize that, even as their narratives reveal the partiality of their visions of gender and sexuality, they critique the partiality of our more seasoned feminist analyses of gender inequity and sexual violence. We are arguing for feminist pedagogies to accompany what Donna Haraway calls "situated and embodied knowledges," the partiality and plurality of which contest "various forms of unlocatable, and so irresponsible, knowledge claims" (1988, 583). Partial perspectives exert a sobering influence on feminist pedagogies, privileging self-conscious acts of critical vision and imagination which are openly hostile to the already established vantage points of either relativism or totalization, which Haraway sees as "promising vision from everywhere and nowhere" (584). Yet she is also suspicious of all "innocent" positions, including what can be seen from the vantage points of subjugation, and offers positioning as a responsible political and epistemological feminist practice for continuing the conversation on gender already in progress in the academy. The pedagogical and political project, then, is to interrogate the ways in which the sexual harassment narratives undermine the transformative potential of narration by effectively withdrawing their narrators from the conversation we had hoped they would enter.

Telling It Like It Is/Was and Like It Isn't/Wasn't

Given that the Penn Harassment Survey focused primarily on sexual harassment and given the demographics of students at Penn, the narratives written by undergraduate and graduate women raise almost exclusively the concerns of white women from the middle and upper social classes. Yet their narratives confirm the findings of other campus surveys and hence frustrate any hopes we may have had that knowledge of civil rights defends women against their harassers. Of particular concern here are the narratives written in response to question 21:

> It would be helpful to us if you would describe this experience in detail. Please do so omitting any incriminating information (e.g., names, courses, etc.). You may include a separate piece of paper if necessary.

Ignoring for the moment the likelihood that the proviso to omit incriminating information may have also discouraged many women students from including details of any kind and the fact that the quarter inch allotted for response was inadequate, we offer the narrative below as typical, inasmuch as the woman provides a markedly attenuated description of the event itself relative to the elaborate explanation of both her professor's behavior and her decision not to report him.

> When the incident happened, his attention lasted about one month. It did not occur to me that it was "sexual harassment" per se because I don't tend to think in terms of deviant behavior.
>   I perceived a troubled man experiencing a mid-life crisis—and more important—a colleague with whom I genuinely shared intellectual commitments and interests. Unfortunately, he saw a young, bright cutsie who could help him with his work and who could potentially serve as an escape route from his unsatisfactory marriage. Basically, all I had to do was make my "No" repetitive and

very clear, but the situation was so muddled and, in many ways, not so cut and dried as "sexual harassment." Things occurred on a very subtle level and are not reported for this reason. All professors have to say is "She's unstable, paranoid, imagining things or lying, etc." Graduate women don't have a leg to stand on. (PHS, file 403-31)

Many statements in this account warrant commentary. She refers to "the incident" but never describes what her professor actually did. We're not then certain if she considers the "attentions that lasted about one month" sexual harassment and hence "deviant behavior" or if, as she later asserts, "the situation was so muddled and, in many ways, not so cut and dried as 'sexual harassment.'" She contrasts her complex view of him ("I perceived a troubled man experiencing a mid-life crisis—and more important—a colleague with whom I genuinely shared intellectual commitments and interests") with his simple view of her ("Unfortunately, he saw a young, bright cutsie who could help him with his work"). Here lies her conflict. And it matters because she has located the danger in his gendering of her, that is, in being turned into a woman. For she goes on to explain that his professional abuse is but a preface to an attempt to transform her into a woman whose body "could potentially serve as an escape route from his unsatisfactory marriage." She tells us that she dealt with her harasser as one might a perverse child—"Basically, all I had to do was make my 'No' repetitive and very clear"—and then explains that she and all the others have no other recourse, since "all professors have to say is 'She's unstable, paranoid, imagining things or lying, etc.'" And her last words, "Graduate women don't have a leg to stand on," summarizes both her own situation and her position on the gendering of women by their male professors.

Leaving Your Body to Science

We have a good deal of sympathy for this graduate woman's rendering of the academic world she inhabits, where her experience of gender has been reduced to slut and madwoman. While we delight in her refusal to take her professor's extracurricular forced-choice exam, we are, nonetheless, troubled by the argument that she and other women students use to represent their strategies for resisting harassers, for it certainly looks as if their practice is to transcend their bodies and deny that women students are women. We say this because of the stunning regularity with which women students position themselves in their narratives as disinterested bystanders who have witnessed rather than experienced sexual harassment and who have been asked not to describe what happened to them but to explain why professors harass their women students.

This behavior increases when his wife leaves town, if we are in a situation involving liquor or if we are in the presence of other individuals who find this behavior entertaining. (PHS, file 947-31)

Male faculty in a department in which I conduct research make suggestive comments, joke and tease most of the time. There are no female faculty members of the department and my assumption has always been that they were simply ignorant of how their behavior was affecting the females who are associated in this department. (PHS, file 431-61)

He was drunk which I'm sure contributed to the problem. (PHS, file 344-51)

What troubles us about the women's explanations of the extenuating circumstances surrounding acts of harassment is the extent to which each has positioned herself as a narrator who, because she has personally transcended the experience, is "free" to evaluate her harasser's behavior from the vantage point of an expert witness. She does this by assuming a clinical posture with respect to sexual harassment, treating the event as a mere symptom of a disease she must diagnose. Instead of a personal narrative recounting her own anger, sorrow, pain, or even pleasure, she impersonally catalogs his motives: He drinks; his wife is out of town; his colleagues egg him on; he's socially maladroit; he's old; he doesn't know any better. She's taking good care of him. That wouldn't concern us all that much except that the narrative positions women assign themselves suggest that they understand their own survival to depend on the ability to cleave their minds from their bodies. This mind/body split reproduces in each of them the very cultural ideology that has historically been used to distinguish men from women and justify gender oppression. By severing mind from body and then privileging the mind's dispassionate, even clinical, explanation of events, each woman materially reproduces in her narrative the very discursive dichotomies that have historically been used to define a seemingly endless string of culturally positive terms (male/mind/reason/culture) in contrast to a negative string (female/body/intuition/nature) (see, e.g., Caplan 1986).

We take such representations of self-as-mind by women students as pleas to be seen by professors as *not* women. In poststructural terms, the women attempt to achieve unity and coherence as writers in an academic discourse, often called science, that has in recent history offered a few privileged white males the comforting belief that they and they alone legislate reality. These men reside in a world in which "mind over matter" means that what counts is what each individual man can know, understand, and represent as empirical. While poststructural theories argue convincingly that the unity afforded our divided sense of ourselves as discursive subjects is an illusion (e.g., Belsey 1980; Brodkey 1989), we are presumably most attracted to discourses that promise to represent us to ourselves and others as empowered subjects—as the agents who speak the discourse rather than the objectified subjects of which it speaks. For many faculty and students, scientific discourse regulates academic speech and writing. And we think the women students are trying to reproduce a version of scientific discourse by positioning themselves as narrators who, having transcended their bodies, are then entitled to use their dispassionate observations as the bases of their clinical explanations of men's motives and cynical speculations on institutional reprisals. What happened to their bodies (sexual harassment) is not problematic and hence plays little part in the narratives; why it happened (his motives) and what would happen (reprisals), however, remain problematic long after the event and hence the narratives tell the story of a torturous struggle to represent themselves as genderless.

We see each woman student as offering to pay an exorbitant, not to mention impossible, price for the coherent self represented in her narrative. In exchange for her mind, she leaves her body to science. Such a strategy for resisting harassment, however, uncritically accepts the illusory coherence of scientific discourse and presumes that human subjectivity is essentially rather than multiply determined (overdetermined) in democratic societies. Yet there is overwhelming evidence in theory, research, and practice that mind, body, gender, and sexuality are not facts we must live with but social constructions we have learned to live by.

Learning to Stand Together

Our goal in this essay is to discern the potential for a liberatory pedagogy of political analysis in the sexual harassment narratives. We understand such inquiry to be transformative, that is, intellectual work in which students and teachers think in terms of both epistemology (ways of knowing the world) and activism (ways of acting in the world). To this end, we have found it useful to review the narratives first in light of feminist standpoint theory (e.g., Hartsock 1985) and then in light of critical pedagogy (e.g., Giroux 1988) calling for educational projects of possibility which pose teachers and students as intellectual and political agents.

In *Money, Sex, and Power*, Nancy Hartsock (1985) argues that, because women experience themselves as continuous with the world and men experience themselves as discontinuous with the world, they stand in materially different relationships with themselves, other people, and the world of objects. Thus, women and men view the world from entirely different and indeed opposing standpoints. Hartsock traces the construction of these opposing and gendered epistemologies to early childhood experiences of body and boundary as described in the work of Nancy Chodorow (1978), reasoning that girls, "because of female parenting, are less differentiated from others than boys, more continuous with and related to the external object world." Such a division of labor in parenting, argues Hartsock, means that "girls can identify with a concrete example present in daily life" while "boys must identify with an abstract set of maxims only occasionally present in the form of the father" (238). Relationality is particularly useful in explaining how women reason from experience. And it is plausible to conclude, as Hartsock has, that designating women as the primary caretakers of children results in gender-differentiated epistemologies, in which even harassed women would tend to see, create, and value relationality.

While Hartsock's notions inform us about what women might have been trying to do in their narratives, the idea that a single feminist standpoint could account for all women is not plausible. It obscures the complexity and diminishes the importance of differences, such as race and class, in women's lives. Further, the theory does not address the extent to which personal development through "object relations" is confounded by the cultural hegemony that affects the way women think about, talk about, and organize against harassment in the academy. In other words, the struggle toward standpoint cannot be abstracted from the struggle against the distractions and attractions of dominant ideology (Gramsci 1971). It is, after all, inside an academic hierarchy of asymmetrical relations between students and teachers that women students answered question 21 like "good" students, thereby representing their personal experience of sexual harassment in the same disinterested terminology used in the survey.

Saturating standpoint theory with the understanding that cultural hegemony is also determining, we are better able to understand how women students might have independently arrived at similar political stances in their narratives of sexual harassment. Instead of *describing* what happened, their narratives try to *explain* what happened by imagining what might have motivated their harassers and what might have happened had they reported the harassment. A standpoint of relationality may account for the formal structure of the narratives, but the contents spell hegemony. The transcendent narrator is a standpoint from which a writer can relate the concerns of harasser and harassed alike. But the motives and reprisals women name come out of that dreary stockpile of conclusions/premises/arguments which individualism and proceduralism commonly use to explain why "you can't fight city hall" and why men can't be held accountable for harassment.

The political potential of the standpoint of relationality as an activist epistemology is severely tested by the content of the sexual harassment narratives, inasmuch as it becomes clear that, when women link the incident to men's motives and institutional reprisals, they are left standing alone and wishing they were not women. Their analysis of motives and reprisals leads them to believe that, since men harass women for untold reasons, women who report harassment will be subjected to more of the same arbitrary treatment from the institution. The dispassionate language in which graduate women speculate on institutional reprisals is academic, and this strikes us as all the more eerie not only because it reproduces the mind/body split but also because their fears are far from academic. Consider, for instance, the way in which this student juxtaposes form and content in the following passage:

> *I think* female graduate students *probably* bear the brunt of sexual harassment at the University. *Most* of the guys who harass you or *just make life difficult* are your teachers and dissertation committee members. Graduate students here have no power. We're dependent

on our departments for financial aid, and are afraid that these professors *could* black-ball us in our future careers. (PHS, file 344–51; emphasis added)

Because sexual harassment is woven into the very fabric of faculty-student relations, women do not, as a matter of course, appeal to legal remedies; institutional procedures only further jeopardize their professional lives. Student complaints about sexual harassment are not likely to be taken as seriously by the institutions as allegations of capricious grading or irregular office hours. While the modulated phrasing may mean that women students are confronting irrational behavior from their professors by responding rationally, and relationally, this very act of using their heads effectively preempts these women's taking an activist stance.

Hartsock understands the epistemology of standpoint as liberatory:

Because of its achieved character and its liberatory potential, I use the term "feminist" rather than "women's standpoint." Like the experiences of the proletariat, women's experience and activity as a dominated group contains both negative and positive aspects. A feminist standpoint picks out and amplifies the liberatory possibilities contained in that experience. (1985, 232)

We do not see relationality in the sexual harassment narratives as liberatory, or even potentially so, and think it could only become so if feminist educators were willing to work with students to imagine liberatory possibilities not raised when analysis fetishizes individual men's motives and institutional reprisals. In other words, we see relationality as an epistemology that helps to explain the reasoning of women students who experience inequity, bypass their outrage, and rationalize that the way it is, is all there is.

A subjugated standpoint does not necessarily facilitate collective activism on behalf of women who, in the absence of support, have individually devised ad hoc strategies for deflecting harassment. With such strategies, a particular woman may be able to prevent or protect herself against individual acts of harassment. Such strategies, however, neither interrupt nor disrupt the material and ideological gender asymmetries organizing the academy. Such strategies do not call public attention to sexual harassment as simply the most overt and explicit of those practices reminding women that we are not card-carrying members (pun intended) of the academic club (and again).

What we've learned from reading these narratives is that, if the women appear not to have said "what really happened," that was because we were only listening for the legal categories that "count" as sexual harassment: that is, evidence of social transgressions that are specified by the Equal Employment Opportunity Commission (EEOC) guidelines and that can be documented empirically in terms that the court understands. The voices of women students in the sexual harassment narratives speak of a pervasive, routinized, and institutionalized sexual intimidation calling for a far more radical institutional project than heretofore suggested by either adversarial law or positioned feminism.

The violent behaviors that feminism and law bracket as sexual harassment and that institutions then treat as exceptional practices do not begin to capture the sense of danger lurking in the women's narratives. The unspoken oppression strikes us as all the more brutal when, as in the example below, difficulties with language suggest she may also be a foreign student:

> I went to private office to visit this person. He greeted me at the door, closed the door and locked it. He leaned over me, standing very close and started unbuttoning my overcoat. I fumbled with coat buttons trying to make light of/ignore his behavior, and trying to dissipate his sexual attention. He helped me remove my hat, coat, scarf and hang them up. He took my hand and led me over to couch in office. We had often sat in that part of the office before to chat, with him on couch (often lounging) and me on chair facing him. He sat down on couch and pulled me by my hand to sit next to him. I pulled to try to sit in chair as per usual; he would not let go. He lay down on couch and pulled me down to sit next to him on edge of couch, near his hip level. He released my hand and I moved back to far end of couch. There were no chairs nearby. I could not move to sit elsewhere without drawing tremendous attention to my action: (1) I would be overtly rejecting him if he was seriously pursuing me sexually; (2) I would be quite rude if he then decided to pretend he had no sexual intentions. My first thought was not to provoke him since the door was locked and the office quite soundproof. He kept urging me to sit closer to him and I declined. He finally took my hand and pulled me, I resisted but

moved closer as a last resort before an outright struggle and possible scream. He kept holding my hand. He then tried to pull me down on top of him, coaxing me verbally. I refused. I stayed upright and using as much strength as necessary and shook my head no, looking him straight in the eye. Luckily, he wanted to seduce me, not assault me violently. (PHS, file 1974–31)

Her narrative reminds us that, even though legal categories account for his behavior, she appeals not to law but popular psychology to explain her professor's motives: "I felt that this incident was due more to an ego-attack of older man (mid-60s) rather than the machinations of a sexual psychopath." If a stranger had attacked her on the street, no doubt she could have seen it as an assault. But she casts her professor's "strange" behavior in the most benign light possible—by comparing him to a psychopath—presumably so that she can imagine completing her studies:

We have resumed our usual interactions. In this case, there was enough of a personal friendship to use as a basis to deal with the incident on a person-to-person way. Had that not been the case, however, I would have risked losing the support of an internationally renowned scholar with impressive professional contacts and influence. That's quite a bit of leverage to have over someone, isn't it? (PHS, file 1974–31)

This narrative is unusual because its extensive analysis is grounded in a description of the event itself. To be sure, she offers the usual explanations of motives, but she elaborates the harassing incident in tandem with her many modes of resistance before stating her ambivalence about the institutional vulnerability of graduate student women.

When oppression is normalized, privatized, and rooted in a powerful and pervasive institutional ambivalence toward the oppressed, a woman student is more likely to pose and resolve the conflict in her narrative by glossing the incident and concentrating on explanations:

A mutual sexual attraction grew between myself and a professor. It was in part physical—in many settings and to people at large, the professor projects his sexuality—but was also based upon the discovery of shared values. This bond struck a chord with me, as

> I felt very lonely and isolated, for the usual—and institutionalized—
> reasons that graduate students feel this way. (PHS, file 1851-31)

Her seeming calm is soon belied, however, by a catalog of fears iterated
in many of the narratives: "I shortly grew alarmed both at the power of
my own feelings and the increasing power of the professor's feelings";
"Although I did not feel physically threatened—that seemed unlikely—I
became afraid that he would begin to manipulate me by using the power
of my own feelings and my need for him"; "This fear arose as I learned
how he was irrationally competitive with us [graduate students]"; "I felt
that I had lost both his respect and his important professional support";
"I knew if needed he would not 'go to bat' for me in the personally influential ways that professors have to work for their students" (PHS, file
1851-31). In a later, more sustained passage, she explains why the fears
that simmer internally are not to be expressed formally:

> It seemed impossible to resolve the situation by talking it over with
> him—the relationship always had an unspoken nature about it, and
> he very likely would have stonewalled me, making me feel totally
> responsible for what had happened. I did not feel that it would be
> helpful to speak to any other faculty members given my own
> involvement and the provocative and controversial nature of a sexual
> and political relationship which is not even supposed to exist. I also
> feared discrediting myself and I felt that the faculty's personal loy-
> alties rested with this professor. (PHS, file 1851-31)

The women who wrote the narratives know they've been treated
unfairly by their professors. And, while they do not blame themselves,
their reluctance to insist that professors are responsible leaves women
students recognizing harassment but transfixed rather than transformed
by their knowledge of oppression (see Fine 1986a). The fact that personal
knowledge does not necessarily become grounds for political action is
clear not only from the narratives but also from the survey. Even though
45 percent of graduate and professional women students reported some
sexual harassment over the past five years, over 80 percent handled it
"by ignoring or going along with it or by avoiding contact with the
offender." And, indeed, only between 0 and 6 percent of graduate students
(depending on the type of harassment) report filing a formal grievance

in response to an incident of harassment (deCani, Fine, Sagi, and Stern 1985, viii).

Feminist interpretation means reading these stories as true but partial accounts of sexual harassment. But feminist pedagogy strives to recover the intellectual and creative energy dispersed when women try to transcend their bodies and find themselves standing alone against their harassers. This is a pedagogy that would transform that wasted individual energy into a collective desire to identify and examine the institutional practices that succor sexual harassment and begin to institute counterpractices that do not. The possibilities for pedagogy in the next section arise out of our analysis of the narratives and pose a feminist project in terms of transforming the scene of institutional harassment so that women in the academy are free to study and teach—with our bodies and minds intact.

Learning How to Speak in the Academy

In this section, we set out to amplify in pedagogy some political projects that we now think may have been attenuated in the sexual harassment narratives. We do this realizing that the survey itself may have encouraged harassed women to resolve prematurely the tensions and complexities their narratives posed. The designers of the survey had hoped that open-ended questions would offer women students an opportunity for both critique and empowerment. Instead, women respondents commonly took this opportunity to consolidate experiences about which they were seemingly quite ambivalent and effectively returned all responsibility for advocacy to the committee. At least, this is how we have come to understand the lengths some women went to in thanking the committee:

> Thanks for your concern over this issue. I realize that I was less than responsible to my fellow students for not pursuing a formal "complaint" but I'm glad to help with the survey. (PHS, file 1799-11)

> I do appreciate being able to tell someone about this who will take this information seriously. (PHS, file 1851-31)

> I thank you for conducting this questionnaire. I hope you publish

the results and information on the procedure for reporting situations. (PHS, file 1486-11)

Thanks for listening! (PHS, file 1418-31)

We take seriously Henry Giroux's reminder that "oppositional political projects . . . should be the object of constant debate and analysis" (1988, 69). We recommend basing the curriculum on a *negative critique* of these and/or other individualistic and futile attempts to interrogate or interrupt forms of institutional oppression organized around gender, race, and social class. Central to this project is the demystification of institutional policies and practices that cloak social inequities. We need to engage young women and men in exploring how our analyses of the causes and consequences of social inequities construct not only our understandings of the present but also our images of what is possible in the near or far future. Unable to imagine institutional change, the women who wrote the sexual harassment narratives default to reworking relationships with faculty or, even more consequentially, to reworking or denying their bodies.

Feminist pedagogy begins by animating the policies and procedures that contribute to harassment. The faceless image of authority sustains the illusion that institutions are immutable and hence oppression inevitable. This is the illusion feminists must first seek to dispel if we hope to enable young women and men to see oppression as mutable through critical and collective reflection and action. A pedagogy intentionally remote from political activism incidentally fosters the very alienation, individualism, and cynicism we confronted in these narratives. We were heartened to find young women who grew up in the wake of civil rights legislation and witnessed the victories and losses of feminists in the courts and state legislatures struggling against harassment. Their collective narrative, however, is a story of despair, for each woman encounters the lechery of professors alone, with little hope that law can, or that the institution will, intercede on her behalf. And so she tries to rise above the scene of harassment in narratives reminding us that the halls of academe are littered with the bodies women students leave hostage in their flight from professional treachery.

We could set an intellectual and political process in motion by asking students to imagine how a series of university representatives might respond to the narratives. What would the university counsel, the lawyer whose job it is to subvert grievances and suits against the institution, make of a narrative about the institutional threat of violence rather than an actual act of violence? How might the director of the Women's Center respond? Or a feminist professor? A nonfeminist professor? A faculty member who has been or thinks he may be named in a sexual harassment suit? The editor of the student newspaper or the alumni magazine? And what about the dean of the school? The man or woman chairing the department? The president of the university? The president of student government or the faculty senate? The counseling staff? What changes if we know that the narrator is white, black, straight, gay? The harasser white, black, straight, gay? While the list is far from complete, it points out that, since institutions speak not one but several "languages," students need to apprise themselves of the range of "dialects" representing their university.

At any given moment in its history, the representatives of a university will be unevenly committed to preserving the status quo, which means that the possibilities for political change are always contingent on revealing heterogeneity within what only appears to be a single voice to outsiders. While it is nearly always the case that the university lawyer will not hear such a narrative, the other representatives are not nearly so predictable in their responses. The related narrative task suggested by the first is, of course, revision. Having imagined what university representatives might do with the narrative as written, how might a particular narrative be rewritten to secure a hearing from each of the representatives? We are not suggesting an *exercise* in writing for audiences but recommending that students do this kind of imaginative work before they meet and interview representatives concerning their jobs and their positions on harassment of women and minority constituencies on campus. This collaborative work requires students to take careful notes, report back to peers and faculty, and compare findings and impressions; they should do this before making any decisions about who and what to write and before making plans for more sustained collective action. We see what can be learned from representatives of the institution as a first lesson in understanding how power is or is not dispersed locally and as a first step toward interrupting the illusion that institutional authority is literally anonymous.

What happens next is, of course, contingent on what students and teachers are willing to deem appropriate under the circumstances. Students might go on to write a white paper on the status of women students on their campus, a series of articles for the student or a city newspaper, a pamphlet for entering students and their parents, a broadside for students, faculty, and staff. Or they might decide that their preliminary research warrants additional studies of the institution and its relations with students on a number of issues that include but are not bounded by sexual harassment. The point is that it would be pedagogically irresponsible to set up an intellectual exploration such as we are suggesting and assume that students will have succeeded only if they reproduce familiar feminist analyses, that is, execute what we have already conceptualized. There is no feminist standpoint they must find. There is, instead, a feminist project, struggling to find the crevices in the institutional facade that glosses over oppression of students, staff, and faculty across lines of race, class, and gender.

The unevenness of institutional commitment to the status quo does not mean that any particular strategy meant to engage university representatives in a conversation will result in desired/desirable political change. We have only to review the recent political successes of the New Right in the academy and elsewhere to realize that heterogeneity is itself no guarantee that discussions will move administrations to more progressive policies. While speaking is certainly a form of action, institutional representatives often understand talk as a way of appeasing and defusing student, faculty, and staff activists. Students as well as educators need to bear in mind that talking and writing to representatives may not be enough unless they are also willing to enlist support from institutions that are (or have representatives who are) interested in their university. Included among the possibilities are: the press, professional organizations, legislators, community activists committed to gender and race equity, alumni, well-known political "radicals" willing to visit campus and speak out for students, and parents who thought that education would support, not undermine, their children. While political networking is as difficult to learn as to maintain, such a network is critical both as a lever for starting conversation inside the institution and as an alternative if or once a conversation breaks down. Outside the boundaries arbitrarily set by the academy, moreover, young women and men are sometimes better positioned to notice and interrupt the institution's version of reality and protectionism and, so, better positioned to represent themselves as informed and critical agents of change.

Learning What to Do When Talk Is Just Talk

Women have been known to contemplate and even commit outrageous acts when conversation fails. The most dramatic example we know of happened at the University of Pennsylvania in the early 1980s. Once a week, with great regularity, the campus was secretly decorated with photographs of prominent male faculty, whose pictures were captioned WANTED FOR CRIMES AGAINST WOMEN and signed by the "Women's Army." Along with others, we presumed this to be the work of a small group of undergraduate women who, distressed that conversation with the provost, university government, and individual faculty failed to draw sufficient attention to problems of sexual harassment, resorted to extraordinary methods for naming the problem.

University officials and many faculty were alarmed that the Women's Army was irresponsibly accusing men. Which it was. Yet we also read these actions as evidence of the women's despair over adamant institutional refusal to listen and act. At the time, Penn had an elaborate set of mechanisms for voicing student dissent, but "listening" was revealed as a way to appropriate such dissent, that is, to appease "angry young women." We have heard that, at some other institutions, young women on campus welcome parents on Parents' Day with the gruesome statistics of the likelihood that their daughter will be harassed and/or raped during her four years at college.

We are not recommending these strategies. They are not attempts to alter the conditions of women's lives. They are the voices of despair that institutional indifference provokes. People have been known, however, to throw caution to the wind when institutions refuse to talk or when they intentionally set out to confound by offering talk in lieu of policy. Women are particularly vulnerable once engaged in conversation, since the willingness to talk is considered the most important evidence of growing trust and cooperation. And most of us, needless to say, find it excruciatingly difficult to break frame and "go public," even when it becomes evident that the official conversation is fruitless.

While the work of the Women's Army and its sisters elsewhere does not provide models of political projects aimed toward transformation, the outrageous is nonetheless of untold pedagogical value. Worst-case scenarios stretch the sense of possibility even as they terrorize the imagination. Images of the "irrational strategies" we may want to avoid help us to imagine how to insist that institutions take seriously their conversations with women.

Feminist Archives for Intellectual Activism

The analysis suggests the need for an archive of feminist intellectual activism to chronicle the varied ways of identifying, analyzing, interrupting, and, under exceptionally perverse circumstances, disrupting gender-based power asymmetries in the academy. Feminist activism must reposition itself inside a larger politics of solidarity with "other self-conscious political projects" (Harding 1986, 163), which, at the very least, would also include struggles around race/ethnicity, class, disability, and sexual orientation. Such an archive could already be stocked with: reports of the reemergence of women's consciousness-raising groups on campus; core curricula that mainstream feminist, African-Americanist, and Third World scholarship (and organized efforts to marginalize or eliminate them); charters for establishing women's centers; arguments for developing gay men's and lesbian women's studies programs; policies of professional organizations which monitor the use of sexist language in presentations and publications (Conference on College Composition and Communication) or the presence of African-American studies and women's studies courses within accredited programs.

As impressive as we find this list, the narratives caution us that far more is needed. This new generation of women is equipped with a striking sense of entitlement and yet beset by fears that its members' female bodies are liabilities, their minds male, their professors likely to corrupt their intellectual relationships, and their legal rights hollow. We can't anticipate what they will contribute to either the archive or the struggle, but social history assures us that it will not be precisely what we added. After all, they inherited rather than advocated for the gains of the 1970s, yet they share the threat of stunning disappointments in the 1980s and 1990s.

Perhaps the lesson we most need to learn is that it is as important for students as it is for teachers to become researchers—students as well as teachers are intellectuals and need to see themselves as informed political agents. We have learned that teachers and students need to collaborate critically across generations, histories, life circumstances, and politics to create curricula and pedagogies that seek to transform institutions not by reproducing or resisting the practices of oppression but by confronting the institution on intellectual grounds. Only thus can we imagine a context in which every woman's story could realize its full liberatory potential, and no woman would decline to tell her story because "any information would be incriminating" (PHS, file 2174-C31).

NOTES

1. We take this opportunity to thank the Quad Women's Group, the undergraduate women at Penn who, in the four years we met with them weekly, surprised and delighted us with stories of their lives as students, daughters, lovers, and friends. This article is infused with dreams, desires, and fears that materialized in those sessions and emerge here in our own academic dream of a story in which women stand together in their struggle to reclaim the bodies that accompany their minds.

2. The Penn Harassment Survey was sent to students, faculty, and staff in March, 1985, and the *Report of the Committee to Survey Harassment* at the University of Pennsylvania was published the following fall in the *Almanac*, the weekly university publication for staff and faculty (deCani, Fine, Sagi, and Stern 1985). The committee reported that 1,065 of the 2,251 usable questionnaires included answers to open-ended questions. Concerning undergraduate and graduate women's responses to the open-ended question asking them to describe an experience of harassment, thirty-seven of the sixty-six undergraduate responses reported harassment by either professors or teaching assistants, and forty-four of the sixty-eight graduate responses concerned professors. While we did not include their narratives in this article, readers will be interested to learn that, of the thirty-six untenured women faculty at Penn who wrote about harassment, seventeen reported being harassed by faculty (thirteen of whom were senior) and one by her dean; that twelve of twenty responses from tenured women faculty definitely concerned another faculty member (including two department chairs); and that eighteen of the thirty-two women staff who responded reported being harassed by either their supervisors or faculty (ix–x). That any woman at Penn is potentially subject to harassment, regardless of status, reminds us that some men violate women's civil rights as a matter of course and that they do so with relative impunity inside the academy.

PART 2

Shadows and Silences,
Constructed and Resisted

If women's bodies display the individually embodied and negotiated politics of gender, a look at socially constructed shadows and silences reveals those collective spaces in which women's stories have been buried and repressed, and in which women's resistances have been fermenting. The three essays in this section examine critically the social partitions that separate public talk from structured silences, men from women, the lives of privilege from the lives of Others. These essays wander through and unravel these dualisms, pressing not only those who are served by these splits but also uncovering life on the Other side. Within this analytic work, the writings of Joan Scott have been influential. Scott invites feminist scholars not to engage in the sameness versus difference debate but, instead, to problematize the debate surrounding "difference." She writes:

> It seems to me that the critical feminist position must always involve two moves. The first is the systematic criticism of the *operations of categorical difference, the exposure of the kinds of exclusions and inclusions—the hierarchies*—it constructs and a refusal of their ultimate "truth." A refusal, however, not in the name of an equality that implies sameness or identity, but rather (and this is the second move) in the name of an equality that rests on differences—differences that confound, disrupt and render ambiguous the meaning of any fixed binary opposition. To do anything else is to buy into the political argument that sameness is a requirement for equality, an untenable position for feminists (and historians) who know that power is constructed on and so must be challenged from the ground of difference. (1991, 146; emphasis added)

The three articles in this section take as their project an examination of how differences are constructed as natural and how they are justified through ideological shadows and silences. The first essay, "'The Public' in Public Schools: The Social Construction/Constriction of Moral Communities," examines ethnographically the distinctions made within public high schools among student bodies. These distinctions ideologically center privileged groups (e.g., high achievers, elite, white students, and males) and profoundly decenter Others. Cloaked in a discourse of the "common good," the public integrity of the whole is accomplished, (de)legitimating the Other as less, and ultimately producing a community (of the entitled), ironically and fragilely secured by the exiling of Others. Life in the ideological shadows is examined, as are the frailties of the "common good."

The second essay, "Silencing in Public Schools," reflects on those daily practices of public education that split off not only the bodies but also the social consciousness voiced by low-income students in urban schools, particularly African-American and Latino students. This essay examines how fiercely bureaucracy seeks to repel critical talk but also reveals how fiercely students resist the compulsion to silence. This essay draws support from Valerie Smith, who writes in her text *Split Affinities*:

> Unacknowledged cultural narratives, such as those which link racial and gender oppression, structure our lives as social subjects; the ability of some people to maintain dominance over others depends upon these narratives remaining pervasive but unarticulated. In my teaching . . . I take seriously the responsibility to teach texts by and about black women. . . . However, it is to me equally important to work with my students toward the recognition of the kinds of *silences that structure the social hierarchy in which we live.* (1991, 278; emphasis added)

Any deep examination of structured shadows and silences bumps up against the insight that within spaces of oppression lies the fermenting of resistance—renaming lack, filling silence, and infusing outrage into spoken talk. In the final essay, "Beyond Pedestals: Revisiting the Lives of Women with Disabilities," Adrienne Asch and I slice open the representations and experiences of women with physical disabilities. These women have been portrayed as if they suffer because of biology rather than because of the social conditions of exclusion they confront daily.

Ideologies about "what is natural" loiter dangerously around their lives so that their disproportionate poverty, exclusion from education and career opportunities, rejection as lovers, spouses, and mothers, victimization by sexual abuse and denial of health services are presumed to be due to "defects" in their bodies rather than injustices in disability, class, and gender politics. In this essay, we pry open the partitions between able-bodied and disabled and problematize notions that then sit uncomfortably "in between"—that is, notions of femininity, heterosexuality, autonomy, attractiveness, and women's *in*dependence.

Together these three essays reframe conditions of exclusion and privilege, and they resituate scenes of silence and shadows as "homes" in which political resistances may be nurtured. As bell hooks writes:

> At times, home is nowhere. At times, one knows only extreme estrangement and alienation. Then home is no longer just one place. It is locations. Home is that place which enables and promotes varied and ever changing perspectives, a place where one discovers new ways of seeing reality, frontiers of difference. One confronts and accepts dispersal and fragmentation as part of the construction of a new world order that reveals more fully where we are, who we can become, an order that does not demand forgetting. "Our struggle is also a struggle of memory against forgetting." (1990, 148)

As you will hear from students inside and outside schools and from women with disabilities, social exiling, as hooks suggests, can become the grounds for percolating collective critique of culture and for dismantling the very categories used to exclude. Through the critical and sometimes collective insights gathered at the margins, these three articles speak to feminist research that can reframe those who have been cast as the Other, dismantle the partitions, and, more important, resuscitate buried images of strength, power, and critique from those deported to silence and shadows.

"The Public" in Public Schools: The Social Construction/ Constriction of Moral Communities

Michelle Fine

Public schools constitute moral communities. While this statement will appear self-evident to some, it surely requires elaboration for others. To the extent that any state offers public education, every child and adolescent in that state is assured legal access to it. Moreover, that access is deemed essential for social and economic participation in democratic society (Ryan 1982). But, because public schooling in our society is considered a social good available to all children, we sometimes forget that it *is* socially distributed and that decisions about how it *should be* distributed are ever reconsidered.

Public schooling further fits the criteria for moral communities in that political negotiations, although typically unacknowledged, determine who shall enter, remain in, and become excluded from these communities. Policies and practices in schools regularly monitor the following: Who gets what? How much should they get? In what contexts? For how long? Toward what ends? Who is entitled to receive special resources (mentally gifted? special education? tracking? Headstart?)? How can fair allocations of tax resources be determined and sustained (Goertz 1982)? How should student bodies be distributed by race, class, and gender to assure diversity, equity, and excellence (Bastian et al. 1986)?

In the introductory article of *Journal of Social Issues* (Spring 1990), Susan Opotow described three defining characteristics of a moral community: collective considerations of fairness, reallocations of community resources, and personal sacrifices for others. Public schools are organized around fair (equal) access. Community monies are explicitly redistributed for the "common good" (Raskin 1986). And citizens are required to pay taxes to meet the educational needs of other individuals. Therefore, it seems reasonable to conclude that public schools constitute moral communities.

Educational Exclusion for the "Common Good"

If we begin with the assumption that public schools comprise moral communities, we must recognize that, in the 1990s, the issue of exclusion from public schools no longer revolves around the simple matter of access. All children can receive public schooling by virtue of the compulsory education laws of the 1920s, the decision in *Brown v. Board of Education of Topeka, Kansas,* and then *Brown II,* the Bilingual Education acts, Public Law 94-142 (the Education for All Handicapped Children Act), and the development of the Harvey Milk School at the Institute for the Protection of Lesbian and Gay Youths in New York City. With *access* to this moral community established as legitimate and universal, the issue of social justice has shifted to the process of exclusion, that is, students' differential *experiences* and *outcomes* once inside these communities (Giroux 1988; Hilliard 1988; Meier 1987).

The present article offers a conceptual analysis of educational ideologies and practices that attempt to justify, in the name of the common good, what is actually exclusion from public education (Raskin 1986). Drawing on three cases involving public high schools, this analysis describes how the concepts of "merit," "choice," and "tradition" have been used to legitimate and gloss over the exclusion of some students from their public schools. The three cases are quite distinct in the nature of the exclusion and the ideologies that supported it. My involvement across the three, however, shared a common quality, for, in each case, my work began when students' exclusion was being negotiated.

Overview of Case Settings

At Comprehensive High School in New York City, I worked as a qualitative social researcher, engaged in a year-long ethnography seeking to understand how an urban comprehensive high school could have dropout rates that exceeded half of any ninth-grade cohort. The research was conducted within the school and in the neighboring community where these low-income African-American and Latino students resided. This research focused on the institutional production of high school dropouts, a form of exclusion that may be likened to a *slow leak* from this moral community.

Dwight Morrow High School in Englewood, New Jersey, is an integrated high school that serves as the public school for residents of Englewood and neighboring Englewood Cliffs. The Board of Education of Englewood Cliffs, representing a community of primarily white and Asian affluent parents, initiated litigation, seeking to send its students to Tenafly High, a neighboring public high school, whose student body is almost exclusively white or Asian and affluent. I was brought in to study and then testify about interracial and interclass relations within the two schools. The exclusion here involved class and race exclusivity at Tenafly High, the school that the Englewood Cliffs's board of education sought to join. The situation may be likened to a *spontaneous break* in this moral community, surfacing abruptly through the litigation.

The third case involved an elite public boys' school, Central High in Philadelphia. In the midst of gender-based litigation, I was invited to document the impact of young women's exclusion from and potential attendance at Central High. The situation here may be considered an *historically sustained* form of exclusion.

My inquiries originated at the exit doors of Comprehensive High and in the courtrooms where arguments over inclusion at Dwight Morrow, Tenafly, and Central High were being litigated. Through the details of these distinct cases, this article explores the justificatory ideologies and practices of several different kinds of moral exclusion from contemporary public high schools and the resultant construction of ironically exclusive "public communities."

The Cases: Methods and Analyses

Dropouts from Comprehensive High: A Slow Leak Due to "Academic Inability"

In September, 1984, I recorded in my field notes the statement of the principal of Comprehensive High (a pseudonym), who welcomed parents to the school with his opening remark:

Welcome to Comprehensive High. We are proud to say that 80 percent of our graduates go on to college.

The W. T. Grant Foundation had funded my year-long ethnography to study the question, "Why do urban students drop out of high school?" But, after three months in the field, an equally compelling question surfaced: "Why do they stay?" At Comprehensive High, a zoned high school in upper Manhattan, the student body was predominantly African-American and Latino, largely low-income and working-class. In the fall, I conducted observations four days per week throughout the school, in the dean's office, guidance office, attendance room, lunchroom, and the library. I attended some classes regularly, including English, English as a Second Language, Sociology, and Hygiene, and sporadically showed up in Bookkeeping, Remedial Reading, Typing, History, Chemistry, and Music (for a detailed analysis of methods, see Fine 1987b).

To complement the rich qualitative information being gathered, a cohort analysis of over fourteen hundred students who began ninth grade in 1978–79 estimated the percentage who had graduated, dropped out, or transferred over six years. Working closely with the parents' association, the union chapter chair, community advocates, and the principal, and interviewing well over fifty recent and long-term dropouts, I was able to develop an understanding of the dynamics that helped turn a majority of the entering high school students into dropouts (see Fine 1987b).

A glimpse of the quantitative data may give readers a sense of the scope of exclusion that powerfully affected this public urban high school. Of the 1,430 students who formed the 1978–79 ninth-grade cohort, only 20 percent ultimately graduated from this school by June of 1985 (their seventh year). The 66 percent dropout rate (some had transferred) stood in stark contrast to the principal's pronouncement. Those who graduated were almost all headed for college. Most, however, never made it to the graduation ceremony (U.S. Commission on Civil Rights 1982).

At Comprehensive High, as elsewhere, two ideologies prevailed to explain the high dropout rates: inadequate academic ability and student choice. But ethnographic work revealed that low-income adolescents leave high school for a myriad of reasons. Some left to care for families: "My momma has lupus, and I must care for her, my sisters, and brothers. Later for me."

Others doubted the taken-for-granted (middle-class) linear relation between a high school diploma and future economic security: "Reason I stay in school is 'cause every morning I see this bum sleeping by the subway and I think 'not me,' but then I think, 'Bet he has a high school diploma.'" Still others challenged the traditional curriculum, which severed what they knew historically, culturally, and personally from what was presented as truth (Delpit 1988; Fine 1987b). Here is an example:

> November 2, English class. White female teacher in discussion with students about a recent shooting that occurred outside the school:
> *Teacher:* Can you imagine any circumstances under which killing would be justified?
> *Opal:* If a guy tries to beat up my mother, I'd kill him.
> *Teacher:* Well, it's not likely that your mother would be beat up. She would have to be in a fight with someone she knew.
> *Alicia:* Shit, Missy, what city you live in?

Many students felt coerced to leave, told by administrators that they had been absent too often or that they could not return after having been suspended. A student's mother reported:

> When they discharged my son, I thought it was over, until the guidance counselor told me that the dean couldn't do it [i.e., legally keep her son out of school]. But she told me not to tell them that she told me. I knew it was a cover-up then.

Finally, there were students whom one might say willfully dropped out, that is, "by choice." Throughout September, these students entered the attendance office, perhaps six per morning, saying, "I'm seventeen, and I want to drop out." Appropriate papers were handed to them, which students were asked to sign and get a parent or guardian to cosign. Given a sheet of paper listing outreach centers and graduate equivalency diploma (GED) programs, these adolescents were discharged into a world devoid of the opportunities they imagined available. None was told that New York state has the lowest national GED pass rate at 48.5 percent; none was told that it is difficult to get into military service without a diploma (as many planned to do) and that those accepted have an extremely high rate of less-than-honorable discharge; and none was told that the private business schools, which many planned to enroll in, had reputations of unethical recruitment practices, dishonest promises, and 70 percent dropout rates. One dean explained to me,

> In a system like this you need boundaries. I can't worry about kids after they're gone. It's tough enough while they are here. My job is like the pilot on a hijacked plane; I have to throw off the hijackers.

Two-thirds of the students were considered as the alleged hijackers, while passengers constituted only 20 percent of the original students. (See analyses in Fine 1987b.)

The story from Comprehensive High represents an exclusion that may be considered as a slow leak from this moral community. While those with poor academic histories left predictably early, most low-income adolescents who were ever in attendance at Central High School eventually exited prior to graduation. They left in ways that were institutionalized, invisible, and accepted as if inevitable. This outcome, however, raises the question, Would the public accept "lack of ability" or students' "personal choice" as sound justifications if two-thirds of a white, middle-class student body disappeared prior to graduation? Or would we reject these rationalizations and be outraged by such an educational exclusion?

Dwight Morrow and Tenafly High Schools: A Spontaneous Break for "Parental Choice"

The case of *Board of Education of the Borough of Englewood Cliffs v. Board of Education of the City of Englewood v. Board of Education of the Borough of Tenafly* raises another set of questions about educational exclusion through litigation. The case was brought by the Board of Education of the Borough of Englewood Cliffs, representing primarily white and Asian affluent parents seeking to take their children *out* of an integrated public high school. This case pitted demands for parental choice squarely against demands for racial and class equity.

In 1987, three contiguous public school districts were involved in litigation over where students from Englewood Cliffs, New Jersey, should attend public high school. A community too small in population to warrant its own high school, Englewood Cliffs sent its adolescents to a neighboring public high school in Englewood City, a community integrated by race, ethnicity, and social class. The one public high school in Englewood City, Dwight Morrow High School, had a student body that was racially integrated and cross-class, including approximately 20 percent low-income, 66 percent African-American, 18 percent Latino, 12 percent white, and 4 percent Asian.

The Board of Education of Englewood Cliffs sued to sever its sending-receiving relationship with Englewood City, arguing that instead the Cliffs parents should be allowed to send their secondary students to Tenafly High School (THS), located in a neighboring, predominantly white, affluent community, rich in resources, and impressive in mean standardized test scores. The student body at THS was 80 percent white, 18 percent Asian, 1 percent African-American, and 1 percent Latino, with virtually no low-income students. Over the prior five years, Tenafly High School had already accepted large numbers of students from Englewood Cliffs on a private tuition basis. At the time of the litigation, a full 12 percent of Tenafly High School students were paying $5,480 per year to attend this public high school, and, over the prior five years, 82 percent of them had come from either Englewood or Englewood Cliffs.

The Board of Education of Englewood City sought to (1) retain the sending-receiving relationship between Englewood Cliffs and Englewood City, (2) impose an injunction against Tenafly High School's private tuition policy, and (3) regionalize the three districts. In the words of the attorneys for Englewood City:

> Without question, regionalization is necessary to root out racial segregation and to advance the objectives of integration in all three districts. . . . If all Cliffs and some Englewood students are welcome to cross the border to receive their education at THS (Tenafly High School)—not only welcome, but so desired that the Tenafly Board has fought to avoid injunction—why not others? Why not those who are not affluent and cannot afford tuition? Why not those who are not the brightest and the best, but are average kids who can be motivated to succeed? Why not special education children? Why not more blacks and more Hispanics? Why not regionalization? (Mytelka and Trachtenberg 1987, 7)

The Board of Education of Englewood Cliffs argued that the educational quality at Dwight Morrow High School was inferior and that the principle of parental choice should enable parents to opt out of Dwight Morrow High School. From the point of view of Englewood

City, however, these notions of "quality" and "choice" were thinly veiled strategies to facilitate racial prejudice and white flight. *Quality* was a euphemism for racial and class segregation; *choice* was being espoused for predominantly wealthy white and Asian parents. A decision to sever the sending-receiving relationship, Englewood argued, would provoke an *impression* in Englewood of poor educational quality, despite evidence to the contrary, and would facilitate a communitywide exodus of middle-class parents across race/ethnic groups from Dwight Morrow High School, thus eroding the race and class integration of the school and undermining state interests in educational equity and quality through diversity.

I served as an expert witness for Englewood City. I was invited by the Board of Education of Englewood City to study the social, academic, and psychological climate surrounding integration at Dwight Morrow High School, to investigate how African-American, white, Latino, and Asian-American students viewed their school and the litigation, and to ask how they would feel if the Englewood Cliffs students were permitted to leave. I also interviewed a small sample of young women and men at Tenafly High School to ascertain their views of race relations, the litigation, and the consequences should Englewood Cliffs's petition prevail. Over the course of the year, I conducted in-depth observations at Dwight Morrow, held extensive interviews with administrators, faculty, over twenty students, both individually and in groups, and interviewed eight students individually at Tenafly High School. The students interviewed ranged racially, ethnically, and by social class. Some were selected because of their active involvement in school activities, while others were chosen randomly.

The arguments posed by the lawyers were echoed by the interviewed students. Students at Dwight Morrow spoke generously, and proudly, of the virtues of racial and class integration. The interviews conducted with the students from Tenafly High School, in contrast, reflected what seemed to be the chilling effects of an elite, segregated public education.

Only one of the Tenafly students indicated any concern for the social and racial issues raised by the lawsuit. A young Asian boy stated simply, "It does seem like discrimination." The remaining seven assured me that

> You should do what the majority wants, and the majority from the Cliffs want to come here.

> I don't want to attend school with kids who wear torn clothes.

You get people from rich society here. I'd rather hang out with kids with money than kids who are totally poor.

They [the black students at Dwight Morrow] can pay to come here also. If blacks can't afford it, they should go to school with blacks. You are out for yourself.

My parents pay taxes, and so I deserve the best education possible.

Never thought about it.

Tenafly is like a private school; people dress nice and come from good homes.

The interviews from Tenafly were truly sobering. In the short duration of our time together, these students expressed positions that displayed a candid disregard for persons less fortunate, or merely different, than they. In my expert report, I discussed these interviews as follows:

> The extent to which these students, privileged by social class and race, take for granted their "entitlement" and perceive no social consequence in having a basically Black high school and basically White high school separated by only a few miles, suggests the dramatic extent to which segregation reinforces, in the minds of White students, a sense of inherent superiority and the justice of unjust outcomes. (Fine 1987a)

I concluded that these Tenafly students were taught in a segregated context, denied the thorough and efficient education that New Jersey law requires, socially miseducated, and deprived of the diverse social and academic experiences available to students at Dwight Morrow High.

The litigating Board of Education from Englewood Cliffs was asking for the creation of an educational community organized through class and racial exclusion and asking that this be sanctioned by the state. The board sought this form of education partially through the popular language of "parental choice." But like notions of "inadequate academic ability" and "student choice" at Comprehensive High, here parental choice to leave Dwight Morrow High School and attend Tenafly incorporated a social ideology that argued for, at the same time that it obscured, educational exclusion.

Both the New Jersey State Commissioner of Education and the presiding administrative law judge found the arguments of Englewood Cliffs uncompelling. They rejected the "poor quality" argument, determined that Dwight Morrow High School provided quality education, and found that a change to the homogeneous Tenafly High School would deprive Englewood Cliffs students of the enriching educational benefits of diversity. The commissioner determined that Englewood Cliffs's relationship with Dwight Morrow High School would not be severed and that Tenafly would be forbidden to accept students from Englewood and Englewood Cliffs as private tuition students. Regionalization, however, was denied. All parties are now appealing the decision.

While parental choice and constant parental search for educational quality need not be incompatible with educational equity (Bastian 1989), the rhetoric of choice typically enters educational discourse when a privileged group seeks refuge from one public context and entrance into another, more elite context. From the perspective of the Englewood Cliffs board and in the attitudes that seemed to permeate Tenafly High School, exclusion appeared to be the motivation behind erroneous assertions of poor quality and demands for parental choice.

Central High School: Historically Sustained Exclusion to Preserve "Tradition"

In late 1984, progressive men throughout Philadelphia called to beg me not to testify on behalf of gender integration of Central High School: "Oh no, not Central. It's a great school. A great tradition. Don't let it fall. It will be ruined." I grew suspicious rather quickly. The voice of Zero Mostel echoed repeatedly: "TRADITION!" I asked myself, "Whose tradition?"

In *Elizabeth Newberg, Pauline King and Jessica Bonn v. Board of Public Education, School District of Philadelphia*, three adolescent women sued for access to Central High School, the most prestigious public high school in Philadelphia. Central High had the highest mean test scores in the city, prided itself on the finest resources and private endowment, and still enjoys a national reputation as one of the top public schools in the country. Because Central and Girls High School comprised the only elite academic high schools in Philadelphia, students who attended them came from across the city.

The three young women who initiated the suit had been students at Girls High (two were still there at the time of the litigation). With budding feminist sensibilities, they felt entitled to "attend the best school in the city," they believed they deserved access to Central, and they argued that a public institution that stood for exclusion on the basis of gender was inherently discriminatory. The defense for preserving Central High as a single-sex school stood, in contrast, firmly on the foundation of tradition. Young women's exclusion was justified by a long and proud Philadelphia custom specifying that this institution should be one in which young men could socialize with other young men without the "distractions" of young women's presence.

The rhetoric of tradition was well managed. One-third of the judges in Philadelphia were alleged to be graduates of Central High School. Many graduates swore on the stand to Central's academic history of excellence and that this excellence was inseparably keyed to its being an all-male school. Adult men testified that they still carried Central High School cards in their wallets and displayed Central High School bachelor's degree diplomas on their office walls, and they reiterated with romance and misty eyes their days as young boys at Central.

My involvement with this school came in two waves. In 1984, I was invited to testify about the value of gender integration, and the social and academic impact of sustaining an exclusively male public high school. In preparation, I interviewed the three young women plaintiffs extensively, spoke with administrators at Central High, and read thoroughly the literatures on gender segregation and integration in secondary school. My second wave of involvement with Central High came four years later, through supervision of a dissertation by Arlene Holtz (1989) on the long-term inpact of the lawsuit on Central's school climate and gender relations.

In 1984, after intensive interviews with the young women, I concluded that the judicial sanctioning of an exclusively male public high school could reinforce in the minds of the general public, the young men at the school, and young women and men across the city that males were essentially superior. It could legitimate sex-based discrimination and seemingly substantiate popular beliefs about biological differences between male and female educational capabilities. The trial ended with the judge (who was, by the way, not a graduate of Central High) ruling in favor of the plaintiffs. The graduating class of 1985 was, therefore, the last to be all male. The president of the Alumni Association, in his address to this group, is quoted by Holtz as saying:

This brings to an end a tradition that has lasted almost 150 years. We of the Alumni Association think that this is just one of the traditions that has made Central High School absolutely the finest high school in America. (cited in Holtz 1989, 16)

And the class sponsor concluded his remarks in kind:

So in the future when we should meet,
Let us remember the last of the elite.

To this day, Central's nationally reputed archive, the official chronicle of the institution's history, remains silent on the litigation. There is no evidence of the young women's victory. According to Holtz (1989), many young women students have seemingly been accepted by the young men and some faculty at Central, but the acceptance is often shown by disparaging the young women attending school next door—at Girls High. And so a tradition of exclusion still prevails, although in a revised form.

How Ideologies Facilitate and Obscure Exclusion

In contexts of universal access such as public education, moral exclusion occurs routinely but is obscured by social ideologies of justice. Such ideologies rationalize exclusion practices and justify existing boundaries. More profoundly, they seem to comfort those individuals who are insiders.

Critical theorist Catherine Belsey describes social ideology as:

real in that it is the way in which people really live their relationship to the social relations which govern their conditions of existence, but *imaginary* in that it discourages a full understanding of these conditions of existence and the ways in which people are socially constituted within them. (1980, 46; emphasis added)

The ideologies surrounding school exclusion—academic inability at Comprehensive High, parental choice to attend Tenafly High, and tradition at Central High—provided coherence and meaning to the institutions and individuals that spawned them. But these ideologies also required the exclusion of some groups and made it seem as if their absence were simply for the collective best (Pratt 1985; Raskin 1986).

At Comprehensive High, students once included as community

members were ushered out with a rationale ostensibly based on *merit*. Over time, two-thirds of the students were viewed as inferior and perceptually transformed into a threat to the well-being of those who remained. Likewise, using the language of *choice*, the Englewood Cliffs Board of Education argued that parents should be able to choose their public schools, and their children should be offered what they saw as "the best"—in this case, a school segregated by race and class. Dwight Morrow High, and its students "with torn clothes," were viewed as a threat to their children's intellectual growth. According to this perspective, by receiving a class- and racially segregated education, elite children would presumably serve the common good most effectively.

Finally, the ideology of *tradition* at Central High also invoked a nostalgic image of a common good. Couched in the language of history, order, and "the way things have always been," tradition comforted its devotees. When the tradition of male bonding at Central High was brought under legal scrutiny, there were public pronouncements that the school would be damaged, male students would be distracted, and a long-standing tradition of excellence would be destroyed. The common good could presumably be salvaged only if the school remained all male.

When Exclusion Is Challenged

The image of a single common good unravels once the diverse needs and entitlements of those placed outside the "deserving" community are revealed. In these three cases, once notions of tradition, male bonding, natural academic abilities, and quality education were stripped of their seeming objective neutrality, they revealed a set of educational contexts that had survived largely through slow, spontaneous, or sustained exclusion. Upon close examination, each of these three schools seemed to have salvaged its internal meaning and identity by constructing partial and perverse images of discarded others. For Comprehensive High, the discarded group was dropouts; for Englewood Cliffs and Tenafly High School, low-income students and students of color; and, at Central High, young women. In contrast to these *discarded others*, the students, faculty, and parents who "belonged" enjoyed a righteous sense of their collective selves—they were smarter, classier, or more masculine.

But, once the Other emerged as a critical and deserving subject (through research and/or litigation), the rationalizations for maintaining an exclusive community grew fragile. At these points, the illicit use of moral exclusion to maintain a moral community was rendered visible: much of what held the insiders together was feelings of superiority to the excluded group outside.

Consequences of Moral Exclusion in Public Education

What is the moral of this story about moral communities? It is frightening to consider that public schools claim universal inclusion yet invent highly exclusive boundaries to control who is actually in and out and then represent these boundaries as protecting the common good. While the notions of merit, choice, and tradition may appear liberal, benign ideologies of public schooling, they actually provide a cover for moral exclusion, and they carry sweeping consequences for those excluded and even damage those who are ostensibly protected.

Consider these "protected" individuals. They include young women and men who graduated from Comprehensive High and witnessed 66 percent of their peers drop out or be pushed out while no one protested. Students at Tenafly High suffered socially deficient education and were trained to believe they deserved, simply by virtue of race and class privilege, an exclusionary school. And young men at Central High School long recognized that female students were being denied entrance into the finest school in the city of Philadelphia simply because they were young women. Across the three schools, students were being educated within publicly sanctioned communities of exclusion, sheltered from a rich education of diversity and critique. But, even worse, the schools taught these young women and men to see public exclusion as natural, justifiable, and perhaps even necessary for the common good.

The analysis in this article challenges scholars and practitioners interested in public education to probe beneath the surface of ostensibly neutral (even "progressive") ideologies and to expose the dynamics of moral exclusion which are often veiled by liberal arguments phrased in terms of the supposed common good.

Silencing and Nurturing Voice in an Improbable Context: Urban Adolescents in Public School

Michelle Fine

October, 1986, national conference on education: Phyllis Schlafly demands that elementary, junior, and senior high school courses on child abuse and incest be banned as "terrorizing tactics against children."

Later that same month: Judge Thomas Gray Hull of the Federal District Court in Greeneville, Tennessee, upholds Fundamentalist parents' right to remove their children from public school classes in which offending books, including *The Wizard of Oz* and *Diary of a Young Girl,* are taught.

One might wish to imagine that demands for silencing in public schools resonate exclusively from the conservative New Right. In this article, I will argue that Schlafly and these Fundamentalist parents merely caricature what is standard educational practice—the silencing of student and community voices.

Silencing signifies a terror of words, a fear of talk. This article examines such practices as they echoed throughout a comprehensive public high school in New York City, in words and in their absence; these practices emanated from the New York City Board of Education, textbook publishers, corporate "benefactors," religious institutions, administrators, teachers, parents, and even students themselves. The essay explores what doesn't get talked about in schools: how "undesirable talk" by students, teachers, parents, and community members is subverted, appropriated, and exported, and how educational policies and procedures

115

obscure the very social, economic, and therefore experiential conditions of students' daily lives while they expel critical "talk" about these conditions from written, oral, and nonverbal expression.

In the odd study of *what's not said* in school, it is crucial to analyze (1) whom silencing protects; (2) the practices by which silencing is institutionalized in contexts of asymmetric power relations; (3) how muting students and their communities systematically undermines a project of educational empowerment (Freire 1985; Giroux 1988; Shor 1980); and (4) how understanding the practices of silencing can make possible a public education that gives voice to students and their communities.

Why silencing in urban public schools? If we believe that city schools are public spheres that promise mobility, equal opportunity, and a forum for participatory democracy (Giroux and McLaren 1989), indeed one of few such sites instituted on the grounds of equal access (Carnoy and Levin 1985); if we recognize the extent to which these institutions nonetheless participate in the very reproduction of class, race, and gender inequities; and if we appreciate that educators working within these schools share a commitment to the former and suffer a disillusionment by the latter, then it can be assumed that the practices of silencing in public schools do the following:

1. Preserve the ideology of equal opportunity and access while obscuring the unequal distribution of resources and outcomes
2. Create within a system of severe asymmetric power relations the impression of democracy and collaboration among "peers" (e.g., between white, middle-income school administrators and low-income black and Hispanic parents or guardians)
3. Quiet student voices of difference and dissent so that such voices, when they burst forth, are rendered deviant and dangerous
4. Remove from public discourse the tensions between (a) *promises* of mobility and the material *realities* of students' lives; (b) explicit claims to democracy and implicit reinforcement of power asymmetries; (c) schools as an ostensibly *public* sphere and the pollution wrought on them by *private* interests; and (d) the dominant language of equal educational opportunity versus the undeniable evidence of failure as a majority experience for low-income adolescents

Silencing removes any documentation that all is not well with the workings of the U.S. economy, race and gender relations, and public schooling as the route to class mobility. Let us take a single piece of empirical data provided by the U.S. Department of Labor to understand why urban schools might be motivated to silence.

In 1983, the U.S. Department of Labor published evidence that a high school diploma brings with it quite discrepant opportunities based on one's social class, race, and gender, and, further, that the absence of such a diploma ensures quite disparate costs based on the same demographics. Although public rhetoric has assured that dropping out of high school promotes unemployment, poverty, and dependence on crime or welfare, the national data present a story far more complex. Indeed, only 15 percent of white male dropouts (age twenty-two to thirty-four) live below the poverty line, compared with 28 percent of white females, 37 percent of African-American males, and 62 percent of African-American females (U.S. Department of Labor 1983). Further, in a city like New York, dropouts from the wealthiest neighborhoods are more likely to be employed than high school graduates from the poorest neighborhoods (Tobier 1984). Although having a degree corresponds to employment and poverty levels, this relationship is severely mediated by race, class, and gender stratification.

In the face of these social realities, principals and teachers nevertheless continue to preach, without qualification, to African-American and Latino students and parents a rhetoric of equal opportunity and outcomes, the predictive guarantees of a high school diploma, and the invariant economic penalties of dropping out. Although I am no advocate of dropping out of high school, it is clear that silencing—which constitutes the practices by which contradictory evidence, ideologies, and experiences find themselves buried, camouflaged, and discredited—oppresses and insults adolescents and their kin who already "know better."

The press for silencing disproportionately characterizes low-income, minority urban schooling. In these schools, the centralization of the public school administration diminishes community involvement; texts are dated (often ten to fifteen years old) and alienating, in omission and commission; curricula and pedagogies are disempowering, often for students and teachers; strategies for discipline more often than not result in extensive suspension and expulsion rates; and calls for parental involvement often invite bake sale ladies and expel "troublemakers" or advocates. These practices constitute the very means by which schools silence. Self-proclaimed as fortresses against students' communities, city schools offer themselves as "the only way out of Harlem" rather than in partnership with the people, voices, and resources of that community.

Silencing more intimately shapes low-income public schools than relatively privileged ones. In such contexts, there is more to hide and control and, indeed, a greater discrepancy between pronounced ideologies and lived experiences. Further, the luxury of examining the contradictory evidence of social mobility may only be available to those who continue to benefit from existing social arrangements, not those who daily pay the price of social stratification. The dangers inherent in questioning from "above" are minor relative to the dangers presumed inherent in questioning from "below." In low-income schools, then, the process of inquiring into students' lived experience is assumed, a priori, unsafe territory for teachers and administrators. Silencing permeates classroom life so primitively as to render irrelevant the lived experiences, passions, concerns, communities, and biographies of low-income, minority students. In the process, the very voices of these students and their communities, which public education claims to enrich, shut down.

This essay focuses on silencing primarily at the level of classroom and school talk in a low-income, "low-skill" school. Surely there are corporate, governmental, military, and bureaucratic mandates from which demands for silencing derive. But, in the present analysis, these structural demands are assumed, not analyzed. Located primarily within classrooms and with individual teachers, this analysis does not aim to place blame on teachers but only to retrieve from these interactions the raw material for a critical examination of silencing. The data derive from a year-long ethnography of a high school in Manhattan (known as Comprehensive High School), attended by three thousand two hundred students, predominantly low-income African Americans and Latinos from central Harlem and run primarily by African-American paraprofessionals and aides, white administrators and teachers, and some Latino paraprofessionals and teachers (see Fine 1985a, 1986b).

An analysis of silencing seems important for two reasons. First, substantial evidence has been accumulated which suggests that many students in this school, considered low in skill, income, and motivation, were quite eager to choreograph their own learning, to generate a curriculum of lived experience, and to engage in a participatory pedagogy (Lather 1991). Every effort by teachers and administrators which undermined such educational autobiographizing violated one opportunity and probably preempted others, to create dialogue and community—that is, to educate—with students, their kin, and their neighborhoods (Bastian et al. 1986; Connell et al. 1982; Lightfoot 1978). Those administrators, teachers, and paraprofessionals who were sufficiently interested and patient did generate classrooms of relatively "alive" participants. More overwhelming to the observer, however, was the silencing that engulfed life inside most classrooms and administrative offices.

Second, this loss of connection has most significant consequences for low-income minority students. These adolescents are fundamentally ambivalent about the educational process and appropriately cynical about the "guarantees" of an educational credential (Carnoy and Levin 1985). The linear correspondence of years of education to income does not conform to their reflections on community life. Most were confident that "you can't get nowhere without a diploma." But most were also mindful that "the richest man in my neighborhood didn't graduate but from eighth grade." And, in their lives, both "truths" are defensible. It is precisely by camouflaging such contradictions that educators advance adolescents' cynicism about schooling and credentials, thereby eroding any beliefs in social mobility, community organizing, or the pleasures of intellectual enlightenment.

The silencing process is but one aspect of what is often, for low-income students, an impoverished educational tradition. Infiltrating administrative "talk," curriculum development, and pedagogical technique, the means of silencing establish impenetrable barriers between the worlds of school and community life. To unearth the possibility of reclaiming students', teachers', and communities' voices, the practices of silencing must be unpacked.

The Impulse to Silence as It Shaped Educational Research

> Lying is done with words and also with silence.
> —Adrienne Rich, *On Lies, Secrets and Silence*

In June of 1984, I began to lay the groundwork for what I hoped would be an ethnography of a public high school in New York City (Comprehensive High School), to begin the fall of 1984 (see Fine 1985a, 1986a, 1986b, and "'The Public' in Public Schools" in this volume). To my request for entry to his school, the principal greeted me as follows:

Field Note: June, 1984
Mr. Stein: Sure you can do your research on dropouts at this school.
   With one provision. You cannot mention the words *dropping out*
   to the students.
MF: Why not?
Stein: If you say it, you encourage them to do it.

Even the research began with a warning to silence me and the imaginations of these adolescents. My field notes continue: "When he said
this, I thought, adults should be so lucky, that adolescents wait for us
to name the words *dropping out*, or *sex*, for them to do it." From
September through June, witnessing daily life inside the classrooms,
deans' and nurses' offices, the attendance room, and the lunchroom, I
was repeatedly bewildered that this principal actually believed that adult
talk could compel adolescent compliance.

The year progressed. Field notes mounted. What became apparent
was a systemic fear of *naming*. Naming involves those practices that
facilitate critical conversation about social and economic arrangements,
particularly about inequitable distributions of power and resources by
which these students and their kin suffer disproportionately. The practices
of administration, the relationships between school and community, and
the forms of pedagogy and curriculum applied were all scarred by the
fear of naming, provoking the move to silence.

The White Noise, or Administrative Silencing

Field Note: September, 1984
We are proud to say that 80 percent of our high school graduates
go on to college.
   —Principal, Parents' Association meeting, September, 1984

At the first Parents' Association meeting, Mr. Stein, the principal,
boasted an 80 percent "college-bound" rate. Almost all graduates of this
inner-city high school head for college: a comforting claim oft repeated
by urban school administrators in the 1980s. Although accurate, this
pronouncement masked the fact that, in this school, as in other comprehensive city high schools, only 20 percent of incoming ninth-graders
ever graduate. In other words, only 16 percent of the 1,220 ninth-graders

of 1978–79 were headed for college by 1985. The "white noise" of the administration reverberated silence in the audience. Not named, and therefore not problematized, was the substantial issue of low retention rates.

Not naming is an administrative craft. The New York City Board of Education, for example, has refused to monitor retention, promotion, and educational achievement statistics by race and ethnicity for fear of "appearing racist" (personal communication, 1984). Huge discrepancies in educational advancement, by race and ethnicity, thereby remain undocumented in board publications. Likewise, dropout estimates include students on the register when they have not been seen for months; they also presume that students who enroll in general equivalency diploma (GED) programs are not dropouts and that those who produce "working papers" are actually about to embark on careers (which involves a letter, for example, from a Chicken Delight clerk assuring that Jose has a job so that he can leave school at sixteen). Such procedures contribute to *not naming* the density of the dropout problem.

Although administrative silencing is, unfortunately, almost a redundancy, the concerns of this essay are primarily focused on classroom- and school-based activities of silencing. By no means universal, the fear of naming was nevertheless commonplace, applied at this school by conservative and liberal educators alike. Conservative administrators and teachers viewed most of their students as unteachable. It was believed, following the logic of social studies teacher Mr. Rosaldo, that, "if we save 20 percent, that's a miracle. Most of these kids don't have a chance." For these educators, naming social and economic inequities in their classrooms would only expose circumstances they believed to be self-imposed. Perhaps these teachers themselves had been silenced over time. It is worth noting that correlational evidence (Fine 1983b) suggests that educators who feel most disempowered in their institutions are most likely to believe that "these kids can't be helped" and that those who feel relatively empowered are likely to believe that they "can make a difference in the lives of these youths."

Disempowered and alienated themselves, such educators see an enormous and inherent distance between "them" and "us," a distance, whether assumed biologic or social, which could not be bridged by the mechanics of public schooling. So, when I presented "dropout data" to these faculty members and suggested that the level of involuntary "discharges" processed through this school would never be tolerated in the schools attended by their children, I was rapidly chastised: "That's an absurd comparison. The schools my kids go to are nothing like this—the comparison is sensationalist!" The social distance between them and us are reified and naturalized. Naming would only be inciting.

The more liberal position of other educators, for whom not naming was also routine, involved their loyalty to belief in a color- and class-neutral meritocracy. These educators dismissed the very empirical data that would have informed the naming process. Here they followed the logic of science teacher Ms. Tannenbaum: "If these students work hard, they can really become something. Especially today with Affirmative Action." They rejected counterevidence: for example, that African-American high school graduates living in Harlem are still far less likely to be employed than white high school dropouts living in more elite sections of New York (Tobier 1984), for fear that such data would "discourage students from hard work and dreams." Enormous energy must be required to sustain beliefs in equal opportunity and the colorblind power of credentials and to silence nagging losses of faith when evidence to the contrary compels on a daily basis. Naming in such a case would only unmask realities, fundamentally disrupting or contradicting educators' and presumably students' belief systems.

Still other educators actively engaged their students in lively, critical discourse about the complexities and inequities of prevailing economic and social relations. Often importing politics from other spheres of their lives, the feminist English teacher, the community activist who taught grammar, or the Marxist historian wove critical analysis into their classrooms, with little effort. These offices and classrooms were permeated with the openness of naming, free of the musty tension that derives from conversations-not-had.

Most educators at this school, however, seemed to survive by not naming or analyzing social problems. They administered and taught in ways that established the school as a fortress for mobility *out* of the students' communities. They taught with curricular and pedagogical techniques they hoped would soothe students and smooth social contradictions. Many would probably have not considered conversation about social class, gender, or race politics relevant to their courses or easily integrated into their curricula. Some would argue that inclusion of these topics would be "political"—whereas exclusion was not. One could have assumed that they benignly neglected these topics.

But evidence of educators' *fear*, rather than *neglect*, grew apparent

when students (activated by curiosity and rebellion) initiated conversations of critique which were rapidly dismissed. A systemic expulsion
of dangerous topics permeated these classrooms. For educators to examine the very conditions that contribute to social class, racial, ethnic, and
gender stratification in the United States, when they are relatively privileged by class usually and race often, seemed to introduce fantasies of
danger, a pedagogy that would threaten, rather than protect, teacher
control. Such conversations would problematize what seem like "natural"
social distinctions, potentially eroding teachers' authority. If not by conscious choice, then, some teachers and administrators actively engaged
in pedagogical strategies that preempted, detoured, or ghettoized such
conversations. Not naming, as a particular form of silencing, was accomplished creatively. Often with good intentions, the practice bore devastating consequences.

Naming indeed subverts or complicates those beliefs that public
schools aim to promote. It is for this very reason essential that naming
be inherent in the educational process, in the creation of an empowered
and critical constituency of citizens (Aronowitz and Giroux 1985). It
was ironic to note that pedagogic and curricular attempts to not name
or to actively avoid such conversation indeed cost teachers control over
their classrooms. Efforts to shut down such conversations were usually
followed by the counting of money by males, the application of mascara
or lipstick by females, and the laying down of heads on desks by students
of both genders: the loss of control over the classroom.

To not name bears consequences for all students, but most dramatically for low-income, minority youths. To not name systematically
alienates, cuts off from home, from heritage, and from lived experience
and, ultimately, severs these students from their educational process.
The pedagogical and curricular strategies employed in not naming are
examined critically below.

Pedagogical and Curricular Muting of Students' Voices

Constructing Taboo Voices: Conversations Never Had

A mechanistic view of teachers terrorized by naming and students passively accommodating could not be further from the daily realities of

life inside a public high school. Many teachers name and critique, although most don't. Some students passively shut down, although most remain alive and even resistant. Classrooms are filled with students wearing Walkmans, conversing among themselves and with friends in the halls, and some even persistently challenging the experiences and expertise of their teachers. But the typical classroom still values silence, control, and quiet, as Jean Anyon (1982), John Goodlad (1984), Theodore Sizer (1984), and others have documented. The insidious push toward silence in low-income schools became most clear sometime after my interview with Eartha, a sixteen-year-old high school dropout.

> *Field Note: January 14*
> *MF:* Eartha, when you were a kid, did you participate a lot in school?
> *Eartha:* Not me, I was a good kid. Made no trouble.

I asked this question of fifty-five high school dropouts. After the third responded as Eartha did, I realized that, for me, participation was encouraged, delighted in, and a measure of the "good student." Yet, for these adolescents, given their histories of schooling, participation meant poor discipline and rude classroom behavior.

Students learn the dangers of talk, the codes of participating and not, and they learn, in more nuanced ways, which conversations are never to be had. In Philadelphia, a young high school student explained to me: "We are not allowed to talk about abortion. They tell us we can't discuss it no way." When I asked a school district administrator about this policy, she qualified: "It's not that they can't *talk* about it. If the topic is raised by a student, the teacher can define abortion, just not discuss it beyond that." The distinction between defining and discussing makes sense only if learning assumes teacher authority, if pedagogy requires single truths, and if classroom control implies silence. Perhaps this is why classroom control often feels so fragile. Control through omission *is* fragile. Fully contingent on students' willingness to collude, such control betrays a plea for student compliance.

Silencing in public schools comes in many forms. Conversations can be closed by teachers or forestalled by student collusion. But other conversations are expressly withheld, never had. Such a policy of enforced silencing was applied to information about the severe economic and social consequences of dropping out of high school. This information was systematically withheld from students who were being discharged. Few, as a consequence, ever entertained second thoughts.

When students are discharged in New York state, they are guaranteed an exit interview, which, in most cases I observed, involved an attendance officer who asked students what they planned to do and then requested a meeting with the parent or guardian to sign official documents. The officer handed the student a list of GED and outreach programs. The student left, often eager to find work, get a GED, go to a private business school, or join the military. Informed conversations about the consequences of the students' "decision" were not legally mandated. As they left, these adolescents *did not learn* the following:

- Over 50 percent of African-American high school dropouts suffer unemployment in cities like New York City (U.S. Commission on Civil Rights 1982).
- Forty-eight percent of New Yorkers who sit for the graduate equivalency diploma test fail (New York State Department of Education 1985).
- Private trade schools, including cosmetology, beautician, and business schools, have been charged with unethical recruitment practices, exploitation of students, earning more from students who drop out than those who stay, not providing promised jobs, and having, on average, a 70 percent dropout rate (see Fine 1986b).
- The military, during "peacetime," refuses to accept females with no high school degree and only reluctantly accepts males, who suffer an extreme less-than-honorable discharge rate within six months of enlistment (Militarism Resource Project 1985).

Students who left high school prior to graduation were thereby denied informed consent. Conversations-not-had nurtured powerful folk beliefs among adolescents: that "the GED is no sweat, a piece of cake"; that "you can get jobs, they promise, after goin' to Sutton or ABI [American Business Institute]"; or that "in the army, I can get me a GED, skills, travel, benefits." Such is a powerful form of silencing.

Closing Down Conversations

Field Note: October 17, Business Class
White teacher: What's EOE?

African-American male student: Equal over time.

White teacher: Not quite. Anyone else?

African-American female student: Equal Opportunity Employer.

Teacher: That's right.

African-American male student (2): What does that mean?

Teacher: That means that an employer can't discriminate on the basis of sex, age, marital status, or race.

African-American male student (2): But wait, sometimes white people only hire white people.

Teacher: No, they're not supposed to if they say EOE in their ads. Now take out your homework.

Later that day:

MF (to teacher): Why don't you discuss racism in your class?

Teacher: It would demoralize the students, they need to feel positive and optimistic—like they have a chance. Racism is just an excuse they use to not try harder.

What enables some teachers to act as if students benefit from such smoothing over (Wexler 1983)? For whose good are the roots, the scars, and the structures of class, race, and gender inequity obscured by teachers, texts, and tests (Anyon 1982)? Are not the "fears of demoralizing" a projection by teachers of their own silenced loss of faith in public education and their own fears of unmasking or freeing a conversation about social inequities?

At the level of curriculum, texts, and conversation in classrooms, school talk and knowledge were radically severed from the daily realities of adolescents' lives and more systematically aligned with the lives of teachers (McNeil 1981). Routinely discouraged from critically examining the conditions of their lives, dissuaded from creating their own curriculum, built of what they know, students were often encouraged to disparage the circumstances in which they live, warned by their teachers: "You act like that, and you'll end up on welfare!" (Most were or had been surviving on some form of federal, state, or city assistance.)

"Good students" therefore managed these dual/duel worlds by learning to speak standard English dialect, whether they originally spoke black English, Spanish, or Creole. More poignant still, they trained themselves to produce two voices. One's "own" voice alternated with an "academic" voice. The latter denied class, gender, and race conflict;

repeated the words of hard work, success, and their "natural" sequence; and stifled any desire to disrupt.

In a study conducted in 1981, it was found that the group of South Bronx students who were "successes"—those who remained in high school—when compared with dropouts, were significantly more depressed, less politically aware, less likely to be assertive in the classroom if they were undergraded, and more conformist (Fine 1991). A moderate level of depression, an absence of political awareness, and a persistence of self-blame, low assertiveness, and high conformity may tragically have constituted the "good" urban student at this high school. They learned not to raise, and indeed to help shut down, "dangerous" conversation. The price of success may have been muting one's own voice.

Other students from the school in Manhattan resolved the "two voices" tension with creative, if ultimately self-defeating, strategies. Cheray reflected on the hegemonic academic voice after she dropped out: "In school, we learned Columbus Avenue stuff, and *I* had to translate it into Harlem. They think livin' up here is unsafe and our lives are so bad. That we should want to move out and get away. That's what you're supposed to learn." Tony thoroughly challenged the academic voice as ineffective pedagogy: "I never got math when I was in school. Then I started sellin' dope and runnin' numbers, and I picked it up right away. They should teach the way it matters." Alicia accepted the academic voice as the standard, while disparaging with faint praise her own voice: "I'm *wise* but not *smart*. There's a difference. I can walk into a room, and I know what people be thinkin' and what's goin' down. But not what he be talkin' about in history."

Finally, many saw the academic voice as the exclusively legitimate, if inaccessible, mode of social discourse. Monique, after two months out of school, admitted: "I'm scared to go out lookin' for a job. They be usin' words in the interview like in school. Words I don't know. I can't be askin' them for a dictionary. It's like in school. You ask and you feel like a dummy."

By segregating the academic voice from students' own voices, public schools do not only linguistic violence (Zorn 1983). The intellectual, social, and emotional substance that constitutes minority students' lives in this school was routinely treated as irrelevant, to be displaced and silenced. Their responses, spanning acquiescence to resistance, bore serious consequences.

Contradictions Folded: Excluding "Redundant" Voices

If "lived talk" was actively expelled on the basis of content, contradictory talk was basically rendered impossible. Social contradictions were folded into dichotomous choices. What does this obscure, and whom does this accommodate? The creation of such dichotomies and the reification of single truths may bolster educators' authority, reinforcing the distance between those who *know* and those who *don't*, often discrediting those who think in complexity (McNeil 1981).

To illustrate: In early spring, a social studies teacher structured an in-class debate on Bernard Goetz—New York City's "subway vigilante." She invited "those students who agree with Goetz to sit on one side of the room and those who think he was wrong to sit on the other side." To the large residual group who remained mid-room, the teacher remarked, "Don't be lazy. You have to make a decision. Like at work, you can't be passive." A few wandered over to the "pro-Goetz" side. About six remained in the center. Somewhat angry, the teacher continued: "OK, first we'll hear the pro-Goetz side and then the anti-Goetz side. Those of you who have no opinions, who haven't even thought about the issue, you won't get to talk unless we have time."

Deidre, an African-American senior, bright and always quick to raise contradictions otherwise obscured, advocated the legitimacy of the middle group. "It's not that I have no opinions. I don't like Goetz shootin' up people who look like my brother, but I don't like feelin' unsafe in the projects or in my neighborhood either. I got lots of opinions. I ain't bein' quiet cause I can't decide if he's right or wrong. I'm talkin'." Deidre's comment legitimized for herself and others the right to hold complex, perhaps even contradictory, positions on a complex situation. Such legitimacy was rarely granted by faculty—with clear and important exceptions, including activist faculty and those paraprofessionals who lived in central Harlem with the kids, who understood and respected much about their lives.

Among the chorus of voices heard within this high school, then, lay little room for Gramsci's (1971) contradictory consciousness. Artificial dichotomies were delivered as natural: right and wrong answers, appropriate and inappropriate behavior, moral and immoral people, dumb and smart students, responsible and irresponsible parents, good and bad neighborhoods. Contradiction and ambivalence, forced underground, were experienced often, if expressed rarely.

I asked Ronald, a student in remedial reading class, why he stayed in school. He responded with sophistication and complexity: "Reason I stay in school is 'cause every time I get on the subway I see this drunk and I think 'not me.' But then I think 'bet he has a high school degree.'" The power of his statement lies in its honesty, as well as the infrequency with which such comments were voiced. Ronald explained that he expected support for this position neither in school nor on the street. School talk promised what few believed but many repeated: that hard work and education breed success and a guarantee against welfare. Street talk belied another reality, described by Shondra: "They be sayin', 'What you doin' in school? Could be out here scramblin' [selling drugs] and makin' money now. That de-gree ain't gonna get you nothing better.'"

When African-American adolescent high school graduates, in the October following graduation, suffered a 56 percent unemployment rate and African-American adolescent high school dropouts suffered a 70 percent unemployment rate, the very contradictions that were amplified in the minds and worries of these young men and women remained unspoken within school (Young 1983).

Conversations Psychologized: Splitting the Personal and the Social Voice

Some conversations within schools were closed; others were dichotomized. Yet a few conversations, indeed those most relevant to inequitable social arrangements, remained psychologized: managed as personal problems inside the offices of school psychologists or counselors. The lived experiences of *all* adolescents, and particularly those surviving city life in poverty, place their physical and mental well-being as well as that of their kin in constant jeopardy. And yet conversations about these very conditions of life, about alcoholism, drug abuse, domestic violence, environmental hazards, gentrification, and poor health—to the extent that they happened at all—remained confined to individual sessions with counselors (for those lucky enough to gain hearing with a counselor in the 800:1 ratio and gutsy enough to raise the issue) or, if made academic, were raised in hygiene class (for those fortunate enough to have made it to twelfth grade, when hygiene was offered). A biology teacher, one of the few African-American teachers in the school, actually integrated creative writing assignments such as "My life as an alcoholic" and "My life as a child of an alcoholic" into her biology class curriculum. Her department chairman reprimanded her severely for introducing "extraneous materials." Teachers too were silenced.

The marginalizing of the health and social problems experienced by these adolescents exemplified the systematic unwillingness to address these concerns academically, in social studies, science, English, or even math. A harsh resistance to name the lived experiences of these teens paralleled the unwillingness to integrate these experiences as the substance of learning. Issues to be avoided at all costs, they were addressed psychologically, individually, and in isolation, and, even then, only after they pierced the life of the adolescent seeking help.

The offices of school psychologists or counselors therefore became the primary sites for addressing what were indeed social concerns, should have been academic concerns, and were most likely to be managed as personal and private concerns. The privatizing and psychologizing of public and political issues served to reinforce the alienation of students' lives from their educational experience.

Democracy and Discipline: Maintaining Silence by Appropriating and Exporting Dissent

The means of maintaining silences and ensuring no dangerous disruptions know few bounds. If silence masks asymmetric power relations, it also ensures the impression of democracy for parents and students by appropriating and exporting dissent. This strategy has gained popularity in the fashionable times of "empowerment."

At this school, the Parents' Association executive board was composed of ten parents: eight African-American women, one African-American man, and one white woman. Eight no longer had children attending the school. At about mid-year, teachers were demanding smaller class size. So too was the president of the Parents' Association at this executive meeting with the principal.

> *President:* I'm concerned about class size. Carol Bellamy (city council president) notified us that you received monies earmarked to reduce class size, and yet what have you done?
>
> *Mr. Stein:* Quinones [school's chancellor] promised no high school class greater than 34 by Feb. That's impossible! What he is asking I can't guarantee, unless *you* tell me what to do. If I reduce class

size, I must eliminate all specialized classes, all electives. Even then I can't guarantee. To accede to Quinones, that classes be less than 34, we must eliminate the elective in English, in Social Studies, all art classes, 11th-year Math, Physics, accounting, word processing. We were going to offer a Haitian Patois Bilingual program, fourth-year French, a Museums program, Bio–Pre-Med, Health Careers, Coop and Pre-Coop, Choreography, and Advanced Ballet. The nature of the school will be changed fundamentally.

We won't be able to call this an academic high school, only a program for slow learners.

Woman: (1): Those are very important classes.

Stein: I am willing to keep these classes. Parents want me to keep these classes. That's where I'm at.

Woman (2): What is the average?

Stein: 33.

Woman (1): Are any classes over 40?

Stein: No, except if its' a *Singleton* class—the only one offered. If these courses weren't important, we wouldn't keep them. You know we always work together. If it's your feeling we should not eliminate all electives and maintain things, OK! Any comments?

Woman (1): I think continue. Youngsters aren't getting enough now. And the teachers will not any more.

Woman (3): You have our unanimous consent and support.

Stein: When I talk to the Board of Education, I'll say I'm talking for the parents.

Woman (4): I think it's impossible to teach 40.

Stein: We have a space problem. Any other issues?

An equally conciliatory student council was constituted to decide on student activities, prom arrangements, and student fees. The council was largely pleased to meet in the principal's office. At the level of critique, silence was guaranteed by the selection and then the invited "democratic participation" of these parents and students.

If dissent was appropriated through mechanisms of democracy, it was exported through mechanisms of discipline. The most effective procedure for silencing was to banish the source of dissent, tallied in the school's dropout rate. As indicated by the South Bronx study referred to above (Fine 1983b) and the research of others (Elliott, Voss, and Wendling 1966; Felice 1981; Fine and Rosenberg 1983), it is often the academic critic resisting the intellectual and verbal girdles of schooling who "drops out" or is pushed out of low-income schools. Extraordinary rates of suspensions, expulsions, and discharges experienced by African-American and Hispanic youths speak to this form of silencing (Advocates for Children 1985). Estimates of urban dropout rates range from approximately 42 percent from New York City, Boston, and Chicago boards of education to 68 to 80 percent from Aspira (1983), an educational advocacy organization.

At the school that served as the site for this ethnographic research, a 66 percent dropout rate was calculated. Two-thirds of the students who began ninth grade in 1978–79 did not receive diplomas or degrees by June, 1985. I presented these findings to a collection of deans, advisors, counselors, administrators, and teachers, many of whom were the sponsors and executors of the discharge process. At first I met with total silence. A dean then explained, "These kids need to be out. It's unfair to the rest. My job is like a pilot on a hijacked plane. My job is to throw the hijacker overboard." The one African-American woman in the room, a guidance counselor, followed: "What Michelle is saying is true. We do throw students out of here and deny them their education. Black kids especially." Two white male administrators interrupted, chiding what they called the "liberal tendencies" of guidance counselors, who "don't see how really dangerous these kids are." The meeting ended.

Dissent was institutionally "democraticized," exported, trivialized, or bureaucratized. These mechanisms made it unlikely for change or challenge to be given a serious hearing.

Whispers of Resistance: The Silenced Speak

In low-income public high schools organized around control through silence, the student, parent, teacher, or paraprofessional who talks, tells, or wants to speak transforms rapidly into the subversive, the trouble-maker. Students, unless they spoke in an honors class or affected the academic mode of introducing nondangerous topics and benign words— if not protected by wealth, influential parents, or an unusual capacity to be critics *and* good students—emerged as provocateurs. Depending on school, circumstances, and style, students' responses to such silencing varied. Maria buried herself in mute isolation. Steven organized students against many of his teachers. Most of these youths, for complex reasons, ultimately fled prior to graduation. Some then sought "alternative contexts" in which their strengths, competencies, and voices could flourish on their own terms:

Hector's a subway graffiti artist: "It's like an experience you never get. You're on the subway tracks. It's 3 A.M., dark, cold and scary. You're trying to create your best. The cops can come to bust you, or you could fall on the electric third rail. My friend died when he dropped his spray paint on that rail. It exploded. He died and I watched. It's awesome, intense. A peak moment when you can't concentrate on nothin', no problems, just creation. And it's like a family. When Michael Stewart [graffiti artist] was killed by cops, you know he was a graffiti man, we all came out of retirement to mourn him. Even me, I stopped 'cause my girl said it was dangerous. We came out and painted funeral scenes and cemeteries on the LL #1 and the N [subway lines]. For Michael. We know each other; you know an artist when you see him. It's a family. Belonging. They want me in, not out, like at school."

Carmen pursued the Job Corps when she left school: "You ever try plastering, Michelle? It's great. You see holes in walls. You see a problem and you fix it. Job Corps lost its money when I was in it, in Albany. I had to come home, back to Harlem. I felt better there than ever in my school. Now I do nothin'. It's a shame. Never felt as good as then."

Monique got pregnant and then dropped out: "I wasn't never good at nothing. In school I felt stupid and older than the rest. But I'm a great mother to Chita. Catholic schools for my baby, and maybe a house in New Jersey."

Carlos, who left school at age twenty, after five frustrating years since he and his parents exiled illegally from Mexico, hopes to join the military: "I don't want to kill nobody. Just, you know how they advertise, the Marines. I never been one of a Few and the Proud. I'm always 'shamed of myself. So I'd like to try it."

In an uninviting economy, these adolescents responded to the silences transmitted through public schooling by pursuing what they considered to be creative alternatives. But let us understand that, for such low-income youths, these alternatives generally *replace* formal schooling. Creative alternatives for middle-class adolescents, an after-school art class or music lessons privately afforded by parents, generally *supplement* formal schooling.

Whereas school-imposed silence may be an initiation to adulthood for the middle-class adolescent about to embark on a life of participation and agency, school-imposed silence more typically represents the orientation to adulthood for the low-income or working-class adolescent about to embark on a life of work at McDonalds, in a factory, as a domestic or clerical, and/or on Aid to Families with Dependent Children (AFDC). For the low-income student, the imposed silences of high school cannot be ignored as a necessary means to an end. They are the present, *and* they are likely to be the future (Ogbu 1978).

Some teachers, paraprofessionals, parents, and students expressly devoted their time, energy, and classes to exposing silences institutionally imposed. One reading teacher prepared original grammar worksheets, including items such as "Most women in Puerto Rico (is, are) oppressed." A history teacher dramatically presented his autobiography to his class, woven with details on the life of Paul Robeson. An English teacher formed a writers' collective of her multilingual "remedial" writing students. A paraprofessional spoke openly with students who decided not to report the prime suspect in a local murder to the police but to clergy instead. She recognized that their lives would be in jeopardy, despite "what the administrators who go home to the suburbs preach." But these voices of naming were weak, individual, and isolated.

What if these voices, along with the chorus of dropouts, were allowed expression? If they were not whispered, isolated, or drowned out in disparagement, what would happen if these stories were solicited, celebrated, and woven into a curriculum? What if the history of schooling were written by those high school critics who remained in school and those who dropped out? What if the "dropout problem" were studied in social studies as a collective critique by consumers of public education?

Dropping out, or other forms of critique, are viewed instead by educators, policymakers, teachers, and often students as individual acts, expressions of incompetence or self-sabotage. As alive, motivated, and critical as they were at age seventeen, most of the interviewed dropouts were silenced, withdrawn, and depressed by age twenty-two. They had tried the private trade schools, been in and out of the military, failed the GED exam once or more, had too many children to care for, too many bills to pay, and only self-blaming regrets, seeking private solutions to public problems. Muting, by the larger society, had ultimately succeeded, even for those who fled initially with resistance, energy, and vision (Apple 1982).

I'll end with an image that occurred throughout the year, repeated across classrooms and across urban public high schools. As familiar as it is haunting, the portrait most dramatically captures the physical embodiment of silencing in urban schools.

Field Note: February 16

Patrice is a young African-American female, in eleventh grade. She says nothing all day in school. She sits perfectly mute. No need to coerce her into silence. She often wears her coat in class. Sometimes she lays her head on her desk. She never disrupts. Never disobeys. Never speaks. And is never identified as a problem. Is she the student who couldn't develop two voices and so silenced both? Is she so filled with anger, she fears to speak? Or so filled with depression, she knows not what to say?

Whose problem is Patrice?

Nurturing the Possibility of Voice in an Improbable Context

To pose a critique of silencing requires a parallel commitment to exploring the possibility of voice in public schools. For, if we are to abandon all hopes that much can be done inside the public school system, we have surely and irretrievably sealed and silenced the fates of children and adolescents like those described in this article. And so the responsibility to unearth possibility lies with the critic of educational institutions (Aronowitz and Giroux 1985).

Indeed, after a year at this public school, I left with little but optimism about these youngsters and little but pessimism about public high schools as currently structured. And yet it would be inauthentic not to note the repeated ways in which students, communities, and parents were, and the more numerous ways in which they could be, granted voice inside schools. Those teachers who imported politics from elsewhere, who recognized that educational work is political work, that to talk about or not to talk about economic arrangements is to do political work, took as their individual and collective responsibility a curriculum that included critical examination of social and economic issues and a pedagogy that attended to the multiple perspectives and ideas inside their classrooms. In vocational education class, Ms. Rodriguez invited students to discuss the conditions of their lives, the relationship of labor market opportunities to their own and their families' survival, and the consequences of giving up, being discouraged, or making trouble at work. Although a thoroughgoing critique of workplace management was not undertaken, a surface analysis was begun, and trust was enabled. Likewise, in hygiene, Ms. Wasserman continually probed the lived experiences and diversity among the students. She integrated writing assignments with curricular and social issues, inviting students to author letters to their mothers—alive or dead—about questions "you wish you could or did ask her about sexuality, marriage and romance." A social studies teacher created a class assignment in which students investigated their communities, conducting oral histories with neighbors, shop owners, and local organizers to map community life historically and currently.

But, of course, much more could be done if all educators saw politics as inherent and the giving of voice as essential to the task of education. To *not* mention racism is as political a stance as is a thoroughgoing discussion of its dynamics; to *not* examine domestic violence bears consequences for the numerous youths who have witnessed abuse at home and feel alone, alienated in their experience, unable to concentrate, so that the effects of the violence permeate the classroom even—or particularly—if not named.

I am not asking teachers to undertake therapy in the classroom nor to present only one political view but, instead, to interrogate the very conditions of students' lives and the very thoughts that they entertain as the "stuff" of schooling.

The good news is that students in public high schools, as thoroughly silenced as they may be, retain the energy, persistence, and even resistance that fuel a willingness to keep trying to get a hearing. They probe teachers they don't agree with, challenge the lived experiences of these authorities, and actively spoof the class and race biases that routinely structure classroom activities:

Field Note: September 18
Social studies teacher: A few years ago a journalist went through

Kissinger's garbage and learned a lot about his life. Let's make believe we are all sanitation men going through rich people's and poor people's garbage. What would we find in rich people's garbage?

Students call out: Golf club! Polo stick! Empty bottle of Halston! Champagne bottle! Alimony statements! Leftover caviar! Receipts from Saks, Barneys, Bloomies! Old business and love letters! Rarely worn shoes—They love to spend money! Bills from the plastic surgeon—for a tummy tuck! Things that are useful that they just throw out 'cause they don't like it! Rich people got ulcers, so they have lots of medicine bottles!

Teacher: Now, the poor man's garbage. What would you find?

Student (1): Not much, we're using it.

Student (2): Holey shoes.

Others: Tuna cans! Bread bags!

Student (3): That's right, we eat a lot of bread!

Others: USDA cheese boxes! Empty no-frills cans! Woolworth receipts! Reused items from rich man's garbage! *Daily News*!

Student (3): *Daily News* from week before.

Others: Old appliances! Rusty toasters!

Student (4): Yeah, we eat lots of burned toast.

Student (5): You know, poor people aren't unhappy. We like being poor.

Teacher: Let's not get into value judgments now. There are people who are eccentric and don't have these things, and poor people who have luxuries, so it is hard to make generalizations.

Student (6): That's why we're poor!

Despite the teacher's attempts to halt the conversation of critique, these students initiated and persisted. The room for possibility lies with the energy of these adolescents and with those educators who are creative and gutsy enough to see as their job, their passion, and their responsibility the political work of educating toward a voice.

Postscript on Research as Exposing the Practices of Silencing

The process of conducting research within schools to identify words that could have been said, talk that should have been nurtured, and information that needed to be announced suffers from voyeurism and perhaps the worst of post hoc academic arrogance. The researcher's sadistic pleasure in spotting another teacher's collapsed contradiction, aborted analysis, or silencing sentence was moderated only by the ever-present knowledge that similar analytic surgery could easily be performed on my own classes.

And yet it is the very naturalness of not naming, of shutting down or marginalizing conversations for the "sake of getting on with learning" that demands educators' attention, particularly so for low-income youths highly ambivalent about the worth of a diploma, desperately desirous of and at the same time discouraged from its achievement. If the process of education is to allow children, adolescents, and adults their voices—to read, write, create, critique, and transform—how can we justify the institutionalizing of silence at the level of policies that obscure systemic problems behind a rhetoric of "excellence" and "progress"; a curriculum bereft of the lived experiences of students themselves; a pedagogy organized around control and not conversation; and a thoroughgoing psychologizing of social issues which enables Patrice to bury herself in silence and not be noticed? A self-critical analysis of the fundamental ways in which we teach children to betray their own voices is crucial.

Beyond Pedestals:
Revisiting the Lives of
Women with Disabilities

Adrienne Asch and Michelle Fine

Despite the prevalence of disability in this society, disabled persons tend to be invisible. Reliable estimates indicate that most people's lives will be touched by disability, but the community avoids the topic in much the same way as it avoids encounters with individuals who have disabling conditions. Indeed, public reluctance to deal with disability as a potential for one's own life or those of loved ones is reflected in the lack of information about it. Despite the penchant for data collection, the community and its major institutions know relatively little about the extent and experience of disability in the population.

In 1980, it was estimated that some thirty-six million citizens of the United States had disabilities: 10 percent of the population under age twenty-one; somewhere between 9 and 17 percent, depending upon studies, of all people of working age; and nearly half of all people over age sixty-five (Bowe 1980; Haber and McNeil 1983). In December, 1986, the *New York Times* reported that one in five adults between the ages of sixteen and sixty-four indicated having a disabling condition that affected life activities ("Census Study" 1986). Of the 51 percent of the nation that is female, we can estimate that perhaps one-sixth have disabilities. How do being female and having a disability interact? How do women with disabilities view their experience? What can we learn about disability from literature, folklore, social science, law, and public policy? Does it matter at what age or stage in life disability occurs? How do race, social class, social circumstances, and sexual orientation influence the lives of women with disabilities?

In 1981, we wrote "Disabled Women: Sexism without the Pedestal," which appeared in a special issue of the *Journal of Sociology and Social Welfare* (Fine and Asch 1981). We reviewed what was then known about the economic, social, and psychological circumstances of women with disabilities and suggested some explanations for why these women found themselves significantly more disadvantaged than either nondisabled women or disabled men. Disabled women, we found, experience much the same oppression as nondisabled women, without receiving the ostensible rewards of the "pedestal" upon which some (white) women traditionally have been placed. We concluded by proposing directions for research, policy, and politics.

The passage of half a decade has seen growth in the new genre of writing on and by disabled women. Jo Campling (1981) brought to public discourse the private lives and stories of British women with disabilities; her book was hailed here, too, because it spoke for long-silent U.S. women. That same year, Duffy (1981) offered a valuable discussion of sexuality as a key arena of both oppression and expression for women with disabilities. More recent works include a report of interviews with forty-five disabled Canadian women (Matthews 1983); the collected essays of an outspoken feminist and disability rights activist (Hannaford 1985); an important collection of research-based chapters on varied spheres of disabled women's experiences (Deegan and Brooks 1985); rich and diverse collections of essays, prose, poetry, and imaginative writing by women, representing a broad range of disabilities and life experiences (Browne, Connors, and Stern 1985; Saxton and Howe 1987). One feminist journal, *off our backs* (1981), and one professional disability publication, *Journal of Visual Impairment and Blindness* (1983), have produced special issues on the situation of disabled women. *The New Our Bodies, Ourselves* (Boston Women's Health Book Collective 1985) attends sensitively and in detail to the concerns of girls and women with disabilities.

Now, six years after the *Journal of Sociology and Social Welfare's* special issue on disabled women, we have attempted to address questions of broad significance within a socialist-feminist framework that acknowledges the importance of class, race, sexual orientation, and disability in understanding and shaping the lives of women. Topics in this essay relate to disabled women's experiences in the "productive," or paid, work worlds; in the reproductive, or motherhood, realm; and in the areas of sexuality, family, friendship, community, and politics. Here we discuss the emergence of disabled women as a group for particular attention; we present data about and interpretation of their economic, social, and psychological circumstances; and we discuss what thinking about disabled women contributes to both theory and politics within the movements of disability rights and feminism.

Before examining the data available on girls and women with disabilities, one must note that there is little to be found. To date, almost all research on disabled men and women seems simply to assume the irrelevance of gender, race, ethnicity, sexual orientation, or social class. Having a disability presumably eclipses these dimensions of social experience. Even sensitive students of disability (for example, Becker 1980; Darling 1979; Davis 1961, 1963; Gliedman and Roth 1980; Goffman 1963; Higgins 1980; Roskies 1972; Wright 1960, 1983) have focused on disability as a unitary concept and have taken it to be not merely the "master" status but apparently the exclusive status for disabled people. Paralleling what Hester Eisenstein (1983) has described as the "false universalism" of feminist writing of the 1970s, the disability rights literature has chosen to stress commonalities among all disabled people rather than differences based on gender.

Although the meaning of gender for either disabled women or men has been neglected by most rehabilitation and medical professionals, social scientists, and disability rights activists, the attentions of such groups has not focused equally on the two sexes. For many years, the thrust of rehabilitation and government study and policy was on the war-wounded or work-injured disabled person, one who was, invariably, a male. Having a disability was seen as synonymous with being dependent, childlike, and helpless—an image fundamentally challenging all that is embodied in the ideal male: virility, autonomy, and independence. Yet this image replicated, if in caricature, all that is embodied in the ideal female: emotionality, passivity, and dependence (Broverman et al. 1972). Concerns with "emasculation" may promote efforts directed toward those at the locus of the *masculinity/dependence* contradiction, not toward those at the redundant intersection of *femininity* and *dependence*. Certainly the social imperative seems to have been to study and rehabilitate the "wounded male" (Rose 1984).

Women with disabilities traditionally have been ignored not only by those concerned about disability but also by those examining women's experiences. Even the feminist scholars to whom we owe great intellectual and political debts have perpetuated this neglect. The popular view of women with disabilities has been one mixed with repugnance. Perceiving disabled women as childlike, helpless, and victimized, nondisabled feminists have severed them from the sisterhood in an effort to advance more powerful, competent, and appealing female icons. As one feminist academic said to the nondisabled coauthor of this essay: "Why study women with disabilities? They reinforce traditional stereotypes of women being dependent, passive, and needy."

Feminist anthologies, including key works that mindfully integrate racial and minority group concerns with gender analyses, continue to exclude women with disabilities (Cox 1981; Eisenstein and Jardine 1985; Freeman 1984; Sargent 1981; Snitow, Stansell, and Thompson 1983). In 1983, Hester Eisenstein chronicled major feminist thought since 1970, noting how feminist writings and politics sought to learn from and unite women of the working and middle classes, married women and single women, mothers and nonmothers, lesbians and heterosexual women, women of color and white women, women of all ages. Yet her otherwise excellent book completely omits comment on the absence of women with disabilities from women's groups and women's writing. Her call for renewed attention to differences among women nowhere recognizes disabled women as a group whose voice needs to be heard. Such omissions by feminists in the mid-1980s are especially distressing when one recalls that disabled women have appeared at political gatherings such as the 1977 Houston conference, the Copenhagen conference on women, and conferences on women and the law since at least 1983. Moreover, despite their presence in anthologies, scholarly publications, and the feminist popular press (in addition to works mentioned above, see Fine and Asch 1982; Finger 1983, 1984; Saxton 1984), nondisabled women scholars have joined men in relegating disabled women to a realm beneath their intellectual and political ken.

Nondisabled academics and activists who have fought hard for women's right to autonomy may fear disability in parents, friends, children, or themselves. Accepting the widespread, if inaccurate, belief that disability inevitably threatens independence, women know that it is they, as women, who will be called upon to care for the disabled individual. As Miller (1976) brought home, it is women who do the culture's nurturing work. Perhaps the conviction that disabled people are inevitably burdensome and that women will be so burdened accounts for feminist resistance to involvement in the disability rights movement.

Disabled Women: "Fact" and Social Construct

Over the past twenty years, feminist researchers have unhooked notions of gender from those of sex. The socially acquired aspects of the female—presumably the loving, caretaking, and cooperative work of women—have been separated from the biological aspects. The maternal instinct, along with women's ostensible inabilities to compete effectively or to be sexually assertive, has been demystified and tracked to socially constructed origins (Chodorow 1978; Ruddick 1980.)

Likewise, in the past twenty years, both the study and the politics of disability have undergone transformation. Activists and scholars have insisted that the *disability* (the biological condition) be conceptually disentangled from the *handicap* (the social ramifications) of the condition. Obstacles to education, community and political participation, independent living, employment, and personal relationships derived not from the incapacities, for example, of individuals in wheelchairs to walk stairs but in the existence of the stairs themselves. If people with mobility impairments could not enter buildings without ramps or ride inaccessible buses, the fault was in the structures and the transportation system, not in their bodies. If people who wished to work could not because of medical standards that barred anyone with a history of heart disease, cancer, epilepsy, or obesity or anyone with diabetes or visual or hearing impairments, the problem might be one of arbitrary medical standards and not of a person's inherent incapacity to perform specific job tasks. If young adults with sensory, motor, or learning disabilities were not attaining a postsecondary education, perhaps the problem lay not in their biology but in the institution's architecture, testing requirements, or admissions standards. If disabled people lived with their parents or in institutions long after their nondisabled age-peers had set up households, perhaps the reason lay not with fears for their independence or their physical well-being but with the lack of accessible buildings in which to live, of affordable support services such as attendants to help with hygiene, or of transportation to nearby stores. If men and women with disabilities suffered social isolation or discovered that former friends no longer had time for them, perhaps the problem was not in their psychology but in others' attitudes toward disability and expectations of friendship.

During the 1970s, grass roots groups of disabled people organized along single- and cross-disability lines, formed statewide and national membership organizations and coalitions, founded legal advocacy centers, and published newsletters. They worked along with parents of disabled children and with nondisabled advocates to obtain laws guaranteeing rights of access to education, employment, government services, and community life. By the end of the decade, although disabled people still had far fewer civil rights than those available to people fighting race or sex discrimination, their situation had begun to improve. (For discussions of civil rights legislation, see Bowe 1980, Funk 1987; for disabled people as a minority group, see Funk 1987, Hahn 1987; and for the disability rights and independent living movements, see Asch 1986a, Crewe and Zola 1983, Scotch 1984.)

Scholars and activists within feminism and disability rights, then, have demonstrated that the experiences of being female or of having a disability are socially constructed; that the biological cannot be understood outside of those contexts and relationships that shape and give meaning to femaleness and to disability. In what follows, we use the tools of feminist and disability scholarship and politics to explore the situation of women who have disabilities. Finding, as we did earlier, that disabled women still are more disadvantaged than either nondisabled women or disabled men, we discuss the relative impacts of sexism and of disability discrimination and examine their interaction.

It is ironic to note that the very category that integrates this text, "disabled girls and women," exists wholly as a social construct. Why should a limb-deficient girl, a teenager with mental retardation, or a blind girl have anything in common with each other or with a woman with breast cancer or another woman who is recovering from a stroke? What they share is similar treatment by a sexist and disability-phobic society. That is what makes it likely that they will be thrown together in school, in the unemployment line, in segregated recreation programs, in rehabilitation centers, and in legislation.

As defined in the Rehabilitation Act of 1973, PL 93-112, as amended by PL 95-602, Section 7, the term *handicapped individual* means

1. any person whose physical or mental impairment substantially limits one or more of the person's major life activities;
2. has a record of such impairment; or
3. is regarded as having such an impairment.

This definition is broad, encompassing conditions not commonly thought of as disabilities but rather as chronic illnesses, health problems, or the like. Disabilities both readily apparent and invisible can interfere with daily activities: mobility, for example, can be affected not only by polio or amputation but by arthritis, a heart condition, or respiratory or back problems. Reading print may be difficult because of vision impairment or the perceptual problems of some types of learning disabilities. People with histories of institutionalization for mental illness or mental retardation may in fact not be hindered in any life task but may carry records that haunt them and impede their access to education and employment. People with cancer in remission, with epilepsy, with cosmetic disfigurements, or with obesity, along with all other people with disabilities, may find themselves regarded as impaired when they can perform in any social role. Thus, the social construction of disability, like that of gender, underscores this fact: It is the attitudes and institutions of the nondisabled, even more than the biological characteristics of the disabled, that turn characteristics into handicaps.

The following data must be preceded by an acknowledgment that, throughout, biology is confounded by the social constructions of disability, gender, and their interaction. If twice as many boys as girls are classified in need of special education services (Gillespie and Fink 1974; Hobbs 1975), the causes cannot be attributed solely to more frequent incidence of biological limitation in boys. Similarly, although it may appear straightforward to determine the numbers of working-age women and men with disabilities, the difficulties in obtaining reliable data are manifold (Asch 1984; *Disability Rag* 1984; Haber and McNeil 1983; Roth 1983).

Obtaining sensitive, accurate data on persons with disabilities requires asking questions that do not confound health status with social role performance. Yet the U.S. census bureau continues to assess disability in the following way: "Does this person have a physical, mental, or other health condition which has lasted for six or more months and which (1) limits the kind or amount of work this person can do at a job? (2) prevents this person from working at a job?" (Haber and McNeil 1983, 6). Not only does such questioning fail to pick up those who do not perceive themselves to be limited in work because of a health condition, but it also fails to obtain any information about people with health impairments who, for whatever reason, do not choose to work. The Health Interview Survey, another often used source of disability data, asks about "usual activities" in the past twelve months. As Haber and McNeil (1983) point out, "The 'usual activity' screen reduces disability reporting for women whose 'usual activity' was keeping house, but should not affect reporting by men" (3). Do women tend not to report themselves as disabled if they can perform what they consider their primary social roles of homemaker and caretaker? Do women overreport because they, more so than men, traditionally are more willing to admit health problems and are more likely to consult health professionals? Notwithstanding these serious qualifications, there is value in outlining the situation of today's disabled female.

The Disabled Girl in Family and School

Growing up in families where they are usually the only one with a disability, disabled girls stand out from peers and even from their intimates. In that disabled youngsters are of all races, cultures, and economic strata, they might be expected to feel connected to others of their class and race rather than to disabled people of another class or race. Yet they may be barred from the intimacy, security, and place that define community. Within what they consider to be their own group, they may feel ostracized, and they may turn to others with disabilities as their only source of acceptance, affirmation, companionship, and strength (Johnson 1987). Disabled boys and young men may appreciate such contact as well, but we suspect that socialization differs somewhat between disabled boys and girls. Accounts of the lives of disabled women and men reveal that boys are more often encouraged to meet the world, whereas girls are more often kept from it. (See Asch and Sacks 1983; Brightman 1984; Hahn 1983b; Heinrich and Kriegel 1961; Roth 1981.) Reactions of the disabled women we have interviewed confirm this.[1]

Maria, age fifteen, testifies: "My brother has the same hearing problem as I do. Growing up, he was encouraged in school, sports, and to learn to work. I was protected and kept at home." We know less than we would like about the familial, educational, and social experiences of today's girls and young women with disabilities. Are Maria's parents typical in sheltering their disabled daughter? Certainly disability will not have the same meaning for all parents, and thus it will differ for their daughters. Class, race, ethnicity, and values of particular parents and the medical professionals with whom they interact powerfully influence parental response to the disabled girl; hanging in the balance are her life chances.

Sara, whose parents were middle-class, was born with cerebral palsy in 1950. Physicians told her parents, "Your daughter has an empty hole in her head." Undaunted, the parents persisted in search of doctors familiar with the mythologies, uncertainties, and possibilities for someone with the condition. Through their efforts, Sara was educated in public schools with nondisabled students before mainstreaming was common. She had access to etiquette and speech lessons, and she enjoyed a climate in which she was encouraged to believe in herself. Today her life as an accomplished economist departs dramatically from that of Patrice, who also was born with cerebral palsy that same year. Patrice now lives in an institution because her welfare mother—having neither the education nor the financial resources to question authority—gave her up on the recommendation of physicians.

Social class, then, can alleviate or exacerbate the impact of a disability, just as class and race influence access to decent housing, schooling, cultural activities, and recreational opportunities for the nondisabled. For the educated and economically comfortable parent willing to assist a disabled youngster, these resources may reduce what could otherwise be serious deprivations. Yet Darling's (1979) literature review of the impact of disabled children on family life, as well as interviews conducted by Rapp (1987), caution against assuming that the disabled child born to middle-class parents will have an easier time in life. Cultures and classes that place high value on autonomy, intellect, or appearance may thwart their disabled child or reject the child altogether. Rapp corroborates the finding of Darling's earlier review, that middle-class and educated parents are more likely to reject cognitive or intellectual disabilities in their children, whereas working-class people and poor people may be more hostile to one whose physical condition may render the child vulnerable. Such findings do not differentiate parental response based on the child's gender. Future research on disabled children and their families needs to examine what it means for a mother or father, rich or poor, to have a son or daughter with a disability.

A decade after the passage of the Education for All Handicapped Children Act mandated access to a free, appropriate public education in the most integrated setting possible, many disabled children still spend far more time in special classes than they do alongside nondisabled students. When parents and teachers create individualized educational plans (IEP's) as required by the act, are girls and boys with comparable impairments equally likely to be given the optimal supplemental services or the greatest opportunity for integrated classroom and social activity? We know that disabled young people still do not benefit from equal opportunities in school (U.S. Department of Education 1987), but we cannot yet say whether and how gender influences the education of disabled youths.

Disabled Women of Working Age

Because the government's efforts on behalf of disabled people historically have been aimed at economic productivity and self-support, more is known about disabled women of working age, and better comparisons can be made with both nondisabled women and disabled men. One must be wary of comparisons between women with and without disabilities, however, because age is a confounding variable. For both sexes, disability increases dramatically with age. Whereas 26.7 percent of all nondisabled women are between the ages of sixteen and twenty-four, for example, only 10 percent of all disabled women fall in that category. More than 70 percent of nondisabled women are under forty-four years of age, but only 38 percent of disabled women are between the ages of sixteen and forty-four. The average age of disabled women is fifty-one, whereas the average age of her nondisabled female counterpart is thirty-three (Bowe 1984; all data not otherwise noted derive from this source, a summary of 1981 and 1982 data obtained from Current Population Surveys conducted by the census bureau in March of both years). Thus, until we learn far more about disabled women by age, we can only speculate that comparisons between disabled and nondisabled women may understate disparities between age-peers. Because the average ages of women and men with disabilities are closer—fifty-one versus forty-nine—such disability/gender comparisons are likely to be more fruitful.

Work disability has been reported by 9 percent of white males, 7.8 percent of white females, 12.9 percent of African-American males, 13.9 percent of African-American females, 7.5 percent of Latino males, and 8.5 percent of Latino females aged sixteen to sixty-four. Disabled men are much more likely than disabled females to participate in the labor force, especially if white or Latino. White disabled men participate at almost twice the rate of white disabled women (44 percent of men, only 24 percent of women). Ninety percent of nondisabled white males and 64 percent of nondisabled white females participate in the labor force, meaning that they either work or are actively seeking work. For whites, then, disabled men are about half as likely as nondisabled men to work, whereas for white disabled women the gap is even greater, with disabled white women only three-eighths as likely to participate as nondisabled white women. For African-Americans, the gender difference is far less significant: 26 percent of disabled men participate, as compared to 20 percent of disabled women. Across groups, fewer than 25 percent of women with disabilities participate in the labor force, and they are unemployed consistently more often than are disabled men.

Employed disabled women tend to be tracked in low-wage, service sector positions. As of 1981, the mean earnings of disabled women fell far below those of disabled men. Including all workers, disabled males averaged $13,863 annually, compared to disabled females, who averaged $5,835. For the disabled person who secured full-time work, her or his earnings approximated those of nondisabled women and men, although, in both instances, they earned less than their nondisabled counterparts. Whatever comfort can be taken from this discovery, however, is small, considering that only 22.3 percent of disabled males and 7.4 percent of disabled females worked year round, full-time in 1981. This is despite the findings of a recent survey of disabled Americans, which showed that, of the three-fourths of all disabled adults out of the labor force, more than two-thirds would prefer to be employed and believe they are capable of doing so (Hill et al. 1986). Thus, we must conclude that relatively few disabled men or women perceive their disabilities as precluding economically productive activity.

Disabled men and women are poorer than those without disabilities. Again, disabled women are at the bottom of the ladder, with African-American disabled women having less income than any other race/ gender/disability category. Income figures are as follows: for *all* white males, $15,832; for white males with work disabilities, $9,394; for white females, $5,912; and for white females with work disabilities, $3,658. For *all* African-American males, $9,621; for African-American males with disabilities, $4,245; for all African-American females, $5,639; for African-American females with work disabilities, $3,520. Using these figures, the median income for African-American disabled females is twenty-two cents to the white nondisabled male dollar (Bowe 1984).

The relationship between disability, unemployment or underemployment, and poverty for disabled women is far from clear, however. We know that, regardless of age or educational attainment, women with disabilities are employed far less than are either nondisabled women or disabled men (Bowe 1984; U.S. Census Bureau 1983). Bowe (1984) reports that, even for disabled women between sixteen and thirty-four, only one-third have jobs, and only slightly more than one-third of disabled women with college educations work. Disabled women are also slightly less likely than disabled men to have college educations. College-educated men with disabilities and women without are considerably more successful than disabled women in obtaining employment. Gender and disability discrimination must interact somehow to exclude these women.

Disabled women's generally low levels of education (five times as likely as nondisabled women to have fewer than eight years of schooling) cannot be ascribed to disability factors, whether inherent in biology or in institutional discrimination. Most women become disabled only *after* education and training have been completed. In fact, it is likely that the women's pre-disability work and living arrangements contribute to disability. Unskilled manual labor, substandard living conditions, poor nutrition, and inadequate medical care all take a toll.

We noted that more African-Americans than whites or Latinos report work disability. Without ascribing cause, Alexander (1985) notes that African-American women confront higher rates of some disabilities than do whites. One in four African-American women will have high blood pressure during her life; rates of cancer for African-Americans have gone up by 34 percent, as compared to 9 percent over the same period of time for whites.

Unfortunately, once she has a disability, a woman is likely to discover that such factors as age, gender, pre-disability education, occupation, and income work to deny her the help she needs. Established to reduce the economic burdens of disabled people, the rehabilitation system disproportionately aids society's haves: those who are male, under forty-five, white, better-educated, middle-class, articulate, aggressive, "motivated" (Kirchner 1987; Stone 1986; U.S. Department of Health, Education and Welfare [HEW] 1975). Rehabilitated women's cases are substantially more likely to be closed in a non–wage-earning capacity (Vash 1982a). Women are more likely to be denied such services entirely (Nagi 1969); they are less likely to be referred to vocational training or on-the-job training, more likely to be trained as homemakers, and more likely to be channeled into traditionally female occupations than are men with equivalent skills and aptitudes (Packer 1983).

Given that disabled women are more likely than disabled men to live in poverty and to rely on government income support, it must be

noted that allocation of public resources provides little relief for either
disabled men or women; still, it does exacerbate gender disparities in
that the amount of a Social Security recipient's benefits under the Disability Insurance program is tied to pre-disability earnings. Mudrick
(1983) further elaborates upon how gender bias and sex stereotyping
work against the woman with a disability whose subsistence depends
upon the Supplemental Security Income program, an "income support"
based on need rather than entitlement.

In this context of extreme educational and economic disadvantage,
worsened for women of color, women with disabilities not only are
systematically cut off from productive work but also are denied access
to the traditional (if now disputed) responsibilities of women: to nurture
and reproduce. In what follows, we offer some hypotheses about the
disabled woman's exclusion from either the productive role of paid work
or the nurturant, reproductive role. To do so, we discuss the meanings
of nurturance, attractiveness and sexuality, and reproduction as they
affect women in the spheres of work and love.

Nurturance, Sexuality, and Reproduction: The Exempt Woman

"Each time I announced I was pregnant, everyone in the family looked
shocked, dropped their forks at the dinner table—not exactly a celebra-
tion" (thirty-five-year-old, white, married woman, mother of two, who
contracted polio at age five).

Disabled Women as Partners

The income-earning opportunities of women with disabilities are severely
constrained. So, too, are their opportunities to be nurtured and to nurture, to be lovers and be loved, to be mothers if they desire. Women
with disabilities are less likely than nondisabled women or disabled men
to fulfill roles customarily reserved for their respective sexes. Exempted
from the "male" productive role and the "female" nurturing one, having
the glory of neither, disabled women are arguably doubly oppressed—
or, perhaps, "freer" to be nontraditional. Should they pursue what has
been thought nontraditional, however, the decision to work, to be a
single mother, to be involved in a lesbian relationship, or to enter politics

may be regarded as a default rather than a preference. We recognize that many women have no desire to marry, mother, or be sexual with men and that marriage and childbearing statistics must not be used to measure "social success." Nonetheless, while many nondisabled and disabled women are choosing nontraditional lifestyles, other disabled women go other routes, not by choice alone.

Franklin (1977) reported that disabled women were less likely than nondisabled women to be married, more likely to marry later, and more likely to be divorced. Bowe (1984) and Hanna and Rogovsky (1986) report similar findings from the Current Population Survey's data of the early 1980s. Whereas 60 percent of men with disabilities and women without them are married, only 49 percent of disabled women are married. As with employment and earnings data, actual disparities between disabled and nondisabled women may be greater when the age factor previously cited is taken into account. Seventy percent of nondisabled women are under forty-four years of age, 26 percent under age twenty-four. It can be expected that many of these nondisabled younger women who show up in census data as unmarried will at some time marry. These data alone do not reveal how much the presence of a woman's disability affects her choices, chances, or inclinations to marry or be involved in a loving relationship with a woman or a man. That more disabled women are unmarried than nondisabled women might be explained by demographic differences alone: Being older, they have had more time for their marriages to sour, just as have millions of others whose relationships dissolve. Many are widowed, as are women of comparable age without disabilities.

When disabled women are compared with nondisabled women and disabled men on rates of divorce and separation, glaring differences again surface between the situation of disabled women and either comparison group. The New York City Affiliate of the National Council on Alcoholism has documented that 90 percent of women alcoholics versus 10 percent of male alcoholics are left by their spouses (National Council on Alcoholism 1980). Hanna and Rogovsky (1986) analyzed 1985 Current Population Survey data on marital status, dividing a subsample of ever-married but not widowed men and women into three categories: nondisabled, mildly disabled, and severely disabled. They found that, of this group, more women than men in all categories were divorced but that significant differences emerged between "severely disabled women" and other groups. Only 14 percent of men termed "severely disabled" were divorced, but 26 percent of severely disabled women were. While men's rates of separation were 3 percent, 5 percent, and 7 percent for each category of disability status, women's rates of separation were 4 percent, 6 percent, and 11 percent. Thirty-seven percent of "severely disabled" women, as contrasted with 22 percent of "severely disabled" men who were once married, are no longer married, for reasons *other* than death of a spouse.

Anecdote, interview, and autobiography corroborate the census data and the stereotype of the disabled woman as alone. For both men and women whose disabilities occur before marriage, literature reveals considerable apprehension about finding a mate. Hahn (1983b) and Asch and Sacks (1983) reviewed large numbers of published autobiographies and noted how little could be found about intimate relationships; of those who did live with adult partners, nearly all were men.

In personal accounts and interviews reported in Bowe (1981), Brightman (1984), Duffy (1981), Heinrich and Kriegel (1961), Matthews (1983), and Roth (1981), we discover how relatively difficult it is for disabled men or women to find a partner relationship. Nonetheless, many more men than women eventually established relationships they found satisfying. Matthews (1983) found that only five of the forty-five women she interviewed were married, and more than half reported no sexual relationship since becoming disabled. Only half of the seventy-five orthopedically disabled women who responded to Duffy's (1981) questionnaire had ever been married. Bonwich (1985) recounts that twenty-nine of the thirty-six rural, spinal cord–injured women she interviewed had been romantically involved or married prior to their becoming disabled; of these twenty-nine, fifteen saw the end of these relationships soon after onset of disability. Only one of the more than sixty pieces in Browne, Connors, and Stern's (1985) collection of disabled women's writing mentions marriage. Although many of the women represented are lesbians, none discusses an ongoing intimate relationship or provides a glimpse of the trials and pleasures of meeting a lover and maintaining a valued partnership.

In conferences of disabled girls and women in which the topic of relationships comes up at all, discussion centers around the difficulty of meeting men who pay them any notice. The only group of disabled adults in which women are *more* likely than men to be married is women who are labeled retarded. Safilios-Rothschild (1977) has suggested that the retarded wife may fit all too well the criteria of the "good wife": one who is docile, passive, loyal, and dependent, not likely to show her husband up.

How can we explain these data? If disability is thought to reinforce the customary female characteristics of passivity, compliance, and good nature, why should women with disabilities frequently be without partners?

A look at the literature on the views of the nondisabled toward persons with disabilities reveals that the attitudes of nondisabled women and men are overwhelmingly negative. Men's attitudes, however, are the more extreme (Siller et al. 1976). These researchers found that disabled children and adults were more likely to be rejected as family members than as acquaintances or workmates by both men and women, but rates of rejection were greater for nondisabled men. Hanna and Rogovsky (1986) suggest that the disabled woman may be more negatively viewed by both women and men than the similarly disabled man. In surveying nondisabled college students at an Eastern public university, they found that images of "disabled woman," "disabled man," and "woman," differed markedly. When asked how women and men using wheelchairs became disabled, nondisabled students attributed male disability to external situations such as war, work injury, or accident. They attributed female disability to internal causes, such as disease. The authors suggest that attributing disability to disease may foster more negative attitudes because disease stimulates primitive fears of contagion or of the person's inherent moral badness. Thus, the disabled woman may be viewed as more dangerous than a similarly disabled male, more morally suspect, or more deserving of her fate.

When these same students were asked to draw associations for "woman" and "disabled woman," the associations cited for the two could not have been more different. "Woman" drew associations of worker (intelligent, leader, career); of sexuality (soft, lovable, orgasm); of mother or wife (wife, mother, mom, married, childbearer). When asked to associate to "disabled woman," students described her in terms of dependence and impairment (crippled, almost lifeless); of age (gray, old, white hair); of despair (someone to feel sorry for, pity, sorry, lonely, ugly). She was virtually never depicted as wife, mother, or worker by the more than one hundred students questioned.

Attractiveness and Nurturance

To understand these phenomena and their consequences for disabled women, we speculate about the implications for disabled women of cultural views of attractiveness and of nurturance. First, it is important to note that a pervasive "attractiveness stereotype" enables people to believe that those who are attractive are also "more sensitive, kind, interesting, strong, poised, modest, sociable, outgoing, and exciting, sexually warm and responsive," and will "hold better jobs, have more successful marriages, and happier and more fulfilling lives" (Berscheid and Walster 1972, 46, 74). In short, attractiveness is linked to virtue, to all that is desired, especially by men of women. In the cultural imagination, beauty is linked to goodness and nurturance, the traits most sought after in women both as lovers and as workers. Ample evidence substantiates that perceptions of women's attractiveness influence women's educational and work opportunities (Unger 1985; Unger, Hilderbrand, and Mardor 1982). Unfortunately for the disabled woman, only a few attributes count toward attractiveness in the United States, and a woman's bodily integrity is one such requirement (Hahn 1983a; Lakoff and Scherr 1984). Furthermore, a woman's beauty is seen as a reflection of a male partner's social status. As Lakoff and Scherr (1984) note in *Face Value: The Politics of Beauty:* "The message we are given daily by the myriad images of beauty is that women must look a certain way to be loved and admired, to be worth anything" (114).

In a discussion of male notions of attractiveness, these authors note that physical grace and ease are also important in the assessment of what is desirable in women. The woman with a disability, whether apparent or invisible, may display less than the norm or the fantasied ideal of bodily integrity, grace, and ease. The very devices she values for enhancing free movement and communication (braces, crutches, hearing aids, or canes) may repel men seeking the fantasied flawlessness. Even those with "intact" bodies, such as Mary, a woman with a severe perceptual/motor problem stemming from a learning disability, can find themselves deemed clumsy and therefore unattractive. Given that disabled women are found unattractive by college students as well as by clinicians (Hanna and Rogovsky 1986; Unger 1985; Unger, Hilderbrand, and Mardor 1982), and given that men value physical attractiveness in a partner significantly more than women do, it is little wonder that heterosexual women with disabilities are more likely than disabled men to be alone.

The argument of women's attractiveness as a display of male status is not sufficient, however, to explain the underinvolvement of disabled women in intimate relationships with men (and women). To pursue the heterosexual question first and more extensively, it appears that men's unacknowledged needs and dependencies—satisfied often in relationships with women—reduce men's desire to become connected in work or in love with disabled women. Drawing on the writing of Miller (1976), we contend that, if a woman's role in heterosexual relationships has been to accommodate a man emotionally while not exposing his vulnerabilities, the disabled woman may be thought unfit. If men desired only the passive, doll-like female of the stereotype, disabled women might do, but the doll must be functional as well as decorative. Feminist theorists such as Hartmann (1981) and Zillah Eisenstein (1984) have argued that the smooth functioning of advanced capitalism requires the illusion, if not the reality, of a heterosexual nuclear home warmed and nurtured by an all-giving and all-comforting woman.

Brownmiller (1984) characterizes nurturance when applied to women as

> warmth, tenderness, compassion, sustained emotional involvement in the welfare of others, and a weak or nonexistent competitive drive. Nurturant labor includes child care, spouse care, cooking and feeding, soothing and patching, straightening out disorder and cleaning up dirt, little considerations like sewing a button on a grown man's raincoat, major considerations like nursing relationships and mending rifts, putting the demands of family and others before one's own, and dropping one's work to minister to the sick, the troubled, and the lonely in their time of need. (221–22)

Men may assume incorrectly that a disabled woman could not contribute either physical or emotional housekeeping to a spouse and children. If a woman cannot sew on a button because she cannot use her hands, she may be thought unfit to help with the mending of emotional fences as well.

Disabled persons (men and women) often elicit in nondisabled others powerful existential anxieties about their own helplessness, needs, and dependencies (Hahn 1983a). For a man who may have such emotional residues well buried, their activation in the presence of a disabled woman may stimulate reflexively his rejection of her. Even if a man believed that a particular disabled woman could manage to run her own life and master the details of helping him with his, how could he accept help from an unwhole, "sick" woman? How can she minister to his needs when a disabled woman epitomizes all that is needy herself? Might it be that taking help from such a presumably helpless woman arouses guilt or shame in any man who might consider it? If men can accept emotional sustenance only from women who can provide the maximum in physical caretaking, the woman with limitations may be viewed as inadequate to give the warmth, companionship, and shelter men traditionally expect from their mates. If men fear both their own and another's dependency and intimacy to the extent that Chodorow (1978) and Gilligan (1982) have argued, if disabled persons awaken such feelings, and if men desire women who can satiate their own emotional needs without either publicly acknowledging them or requiring reciprocity, disabled women are likely to be rejected forcefully as lovers/partners.

Disabled women who have partners, especially if they are nondisabled men, are likely to discover that they and their partners are subjected to curiosity, scrutiny, and public misunderstanding. Ubiquitously perceived as a social burden, the disabled woman evokes pity that spreads to her partner. "Whenever my husband and I are shopping, and he is pushing my wheelchair, people stop us and say [to him], 'You must be a saint.' What about me? Do you think it's easy to live with him?" The public assumption is that this woman is a burden and her husband is either saintly or a loser himself.

The view of the disabled woman as limited emotionally because she may be limited physically may account for the acknowledged preference of disabled men for nondisabled partners. In their review of the autobiographies of blind women and men, Asch and Sacks (1983) discovered that the men sought sighted wives to complement them; to confer upon them a status of normal, successful, integrated; and to ensure their smooth navigation literally and figuratively through the world. In a study of the coping strategies of disabled scientists, a group that was overwhelmingly male, many reported that one major strategy was acquisition of a woman/wife (H. Redden, pers. com., 1985). In a *New York Times* article enshrining negative stereotypes about nondisabled women who marry disabled men and the men they marry, Rose (1984) postulated that the disabled man is the perfect outlet for nurturance and competence for nondisabled women who could not fulfill themselves or demonstrate their full capacity in a relationship with a truly competent male. Here disabled men are perceived as lacking all capacities for self-direction merely because they cannot walk or see; nondisabled women are pictured as dominating their disabled spouses. The reverse situation of a disabled woman with a nondisabled male partner is omitted altogether from the discussion.

Male commitment to narrow conceptions of attractiveness and nurturance also may illuminate the rejection of disabled women as workers. The presumed costs of hiring disabled workers have been refuted elsewhere (Hill et al. 1987; U.S. Department of Labor 1982); the resistance to hiring women with disabilities stems from sources more primitive and unrecognized than either fiscal conservatism or aesthetic and existential anxiety (Hahn 1983a). To the extent that women are employed in ways that sustain male domination, the "neutered" disabled woman fails to fill the bill (Rich 1980). We assert that the resistance to employing disabled women derives in part from the unacknowledged forms of heterosexual male privilege sustained in the workplace. Sheehy (1984) reminds us that male judges sometimes have awarded workers' compensation benefits to women with disabilities deemed so unattractive that future employment was highly unlikely!

We contend that men spurn disabled women as workers and partners because they fail to measure up on grounds of appearance or of perceived abilities in physical and emotional caretaking. Although this argument aids understanding of her marginality in the arenas of heterosexual love and male-controlled work, it fails to fully explain the situation of disabled lesbians. We have found no data on the numbers of lesbians with disabilities or on their acceptance by nondisabled lesbians as partners, but comments made by many disabled lesbians indicate that, within the community of lesbians, the disabled woman is still in search of love. Disabled lesbians have described being dismissed, shunned, or relegated to the status of friend and confidante rather than lover, just as have heterosexual disabled women.

Chodorow (1978) and Gilligan (1982) have much to say about women's capacity for relatedness. At its best, that relational potential renders women well suited to cooperate, empathize, affiliate, examine the interpersonal dimensions of moral questions, anticipate others' needs—all those qualities current feminists at once struggle against and delight in. Cultivated by the culture to perpetuate male dominance and now seen as the source of women's potential strength for our own and the world's betterment (Eisenstein 1983; Miller 1976), these very qualities may be stimulated when a woman confronts a disabled woman as a potential lover. If the dark, problematic side of a capacity for relatedness is a too-ready potential for merger with another, stereotypes about the presumed dependency and neediness of a disabled woman could easily send women scurrying in the other direction. So long as nondisabled women hold the stereotypes that the disability rights movement fights against, the thought of a disabled woman as a lover may engender fears of merger, exaggerate lack of boundaries, and spawn fantasies of endless responsibility, of unremitting and unreciprocated care. Until nondisabled men and women recognize that disabled people can contribute to others' well-being, contemplating "taking on" such a woman as friend or lover will tend to activate such fears.

These arguments, admittedly, are speculative. Whether or not these dynamics operate in intimate heterosexual or lesbian couples involving a disabled partner remains to be explored. Whether or not heterosexual and lesbian relationships are characterized by similar patterns must be discovered. So, too, must we inquire about interdependence, reciprocity, and gender roles in couples where both partners have disabilities. Although many disabled people shun other disabled people as intimates, not all do. From our interviews, observations at disability conferences, and conversations with scores of women, we suspect that disabled women who marry *after* onset of disability are more likely than similarly disabled men to have a disabled spouse. Becker (1980) reports that 75 percent of deaf women marry deaf men. Because disability, unlike race or ethnicity, has not created natural cultures or communities wherein people customarily look to one another to create intimacy and family, one wonders whether those women whose partners are also disabled consider this a positive choice, a default option, or an irrelevant characteristic. What is crucial is that readers understand that *why* disabled women encounter difficulty in establishing nurturing relations is a significant question and not one with an "obvious answer."

Why disabled women are alone is an important question. That they are has complicated consequences. For example, Kutner (1985) and Kutner and Gray (1985) have specified how the condition of "aloneness" interacts with access to medical care and social support. In their investigations of people with renal failure who used various forms of dialysis, Kutner and Gray learned that maintenance of a home dialysis regimen (which is considered optimal for people with this condition) was substantially affected by marital status. Home dialysis requires a partner ready to assist the user for four to six hours three times a week. As a consequence of gender-stratified aloneness, men are more likely than women to receive home dialysis (and white women are more likely to receive it than African-American women). Supportive people, of course, need not be spouses, but, for those Kutner and Gray surveyed, lack of such a spouse often resulted in less than the best medical care.

When Kutner surveyed 332 Atlanta-area residents with cardiac, kidney, and mobility disabilities regarding their perceptions of social support, she found that married people received help from more sources than did their never-married or formerly married peers. The gap in help received between married and nonmarried, however, was greater for women than for men. As is all too often true, the woman getting the least help was the one most likely to need it: She was more likely than an unmarried man to head a household with dependent children and thus to face the combined stresses of single parenthood and disability.

Sexuality and Motherhood

Often deprived of the chance for long-term intimacy, disabled women also are commonly considered unfit as sexual partners and as mothers. Many women speak angrily of the unavailability of adequate counseling on sexuality, birth control, pregnancy, and childbirth from either gynecologists or rehabilitation professionals. Ignorant of the adverse consequences of some birth control devices for women with particular conditions, many gynecologists prescribe unsafe methods. Safilios-Rothschild (1977) notes that, since coronary research has been conducted almost exclusively on men, it has produced data relevant only to men. Women who seek information about resuming sexual activity after a heart attack have been provided with male standards or with no answers at all. So astonishing is it to some physicians that disabled women might be sexual that Galler (1984) reports completely unnecessary abdominal surgery for one woman because no one believed that someone with cerebral palsy could have the symptoms of venereal disease.

One woman with spina bifida described a preadolescent encounter with her gynecologist this way:

"Will I be able to have satisfying sexual relations with a man?"

"Don't worry, honey, your vagina will be tight enough to satisfy any man."

Her satisfaction probably didn't cross his mind.

Motherhood, the institution and experience that perhaps has dominated all cultural conceptions of women—eclipsing even expectations of beauty, softness, or ever-present sexuality—often has been proscribed for a woman with a disability. Many states have had laws forbidding people with histories of epilepsy, mental retardation, and psychiatric disability from marrying. Fears that disabled women would produce children with similar conditions (nearly always groundless since the vast majority of disability is not hereditary) have mingled with convictions that they would harm, deprive, or burden children they attempted to rear. As a result, many medical professionals still urge or coerce women into being sterilized (Finger 1984; Macklin and Gaylin 1981; U.S. Commission on Civil Rights 1983). Women in interviews cite recent sessions with gynecologists who urged them not to bother with birth control by saying, "Get your tubes tied. You couldn't take care of a child yourself." Women with diabetes, epilepsy, and spinal cord injuries report difficulty in finding obstetricians or midwives willing to help them through what they view as "high-risk" pregnancies (Asrael 1982; Collins 1983).

Problems in mothering for disabled women are not limited to the medical aspects of reproduction. Regardless of marital status or the disability status of any partners, disabled women report discrimination in adopting, in being permitted to provide foster care, and in winning child custody after divorce. Sadly and perversely, Gold (1985) reports, a 1978 amendment to the California welfare and institutions code intended to prevent discrimination against disabled parents has, in fact, been used to sanction unannounced home visits and the removal of children simply on the grounds that mothers were blind. In 1986, a Colorado social service agency took custody of a thirteen-month-old girl, alleging that the underweight child was malnourished because her blind, single mother could not feed her properly. Even after two doctors testified that the child, though small, was not malnourished, the social service agency would not permit the child to be returned to her mother ("Legalized Kidnapping" 1986).

Exemption of exclusion from voluntary sexuality and reproduction has not exempted disabled females from sexual abuse and victimization. Perhaps even more than nondisabled women, disabled women confront serious psychological and social problems in ending abusive or exploitative relationships. Galler (1984) and *Disability Rag* (1986) relate instances in which women with cerebral palsy or mental retardation have been ignored by professionals when they report rape. If women without disabilities hesitate to give up abusive relationships because they cannot imagine how they will survive economically, disabled women in abusive homes may feel even more trapped. Melling (1984) discusses the problem of wife abuse in the deaf community, noting a battery of factors that conspire against deaf women standing up for themselves in degrading or even dangerous situations. Even more than the nondisabled girl, a disabled girl is an easy victim of abuse by male relatives. Unfortunately, even personal care attendants employed by the disabled woman are not infrequently reported to abuse the women they have been hired to assist. One counselor of disabled women in a Denver domestic violence project has commented that many disabled women, like their nondisabled counterparts, return to the abusive relationships because "it is the only thing they have had. As bad as it is, for many it is better than living in an institution or going back to their families" (*Disability Rag* 1986, 9–10).

Disabled girls and women, in numbers hard to estimate, are raped at home, in institutions, or on the streets. We know of women whose stay in long-term care institutions or rehabilitation facilities included sterilization with official approval because, they were told, there was danger of molestation in the institution. An inquiry into California's community care facilities for the mentally and physically disabled and for the elderly found that "daily, throughout this state, residents of community care facilities are being sexually abused, beaten, fed spoiled food, forced to live with toilets that don't work" ("Panel Details" 1984). We wonder how many of these same women have been sterilized to keep the effects of rape from the public eye. That such exploitation frequently occurs outside of institutions as well is demonstrated by one study conducted by the Seattle Rape Relief Center. The center found that, between May, 1977, and December, 1979, more than three hundred cases of sexual exploitation of physically or mentally disabled women came to its attention (Bellone and Waxman 1983). Extrapolating to the State of Washington, the center estimated that perhaps thirty thousand rapes of such women occur annually.

Self-esteem, Resistance, and Identity

If our culture views being female and disabled as "redundant," whereas being male and disabled is a contradiction, we must ponder on the effects of such role definitions and social options on the self-concept of the disabled woman. Some women accommodate societal projections, becoming the dependent creatures their parents, teachers, and others expected. In fact, the psychological literature suggests this response to be the norm.

Consider this in relation to findings that disabled girls and women perceive themselves and are perceived by others more negatively than is the
case with disabled boys and men. They report more negative self-images
(Weinberg 1976), are viewed in less favorable ways (Miller 1970), and are
more likely to be victims of hostility than are disabled men (Titley and
Viney 1969). The Asch and Sacks (1983) analysis of autobiographies of
blind women and men indicated that the women internalized negative
messages much more than did the men, seeing themselves as burdensome,
unwanted, and unlovable, whereas men rarely did.

Weinberg's (1976) self-concept research found that negative self-
concept was less related to one's level of disability than to one's gender—
with women reporting more negative feelings than either disabled or
nondisabled males. In a review of the self-esteem literature on disability,
Darling (1979) found that—contrary to predictions of much psychoanalytic and labeling theory discussions—disabled children and adolescents demonstrated levels of self-esteem not substantially different from
those of their nondisabled counterparts. Nonetheless, she reports, disabled girls evidence lower self-esteem than disabled boys and either
nondisabled girls and boys.

Such findings about self-esteem need to be analyzed. It may be that
males with disabilities can escape some of the trap of the disability role
by aspiring to male characteristics of mastery, competence, and autonomy; disabled women and girls, however, forsake their gender role if
they seek to escape from disability-imposed dependence by such means.
We believe that such role contradictions can plague the female seeking
to affirm her identity in the presence of a disability. Particularly for the
disabled girl (and the self-esteem literature generally concentrates on
children and adolescents) becoming socialized in a family and school
unclear about what norms to suggest or what hopes to give her for her
future, self-esteem may be a serious problem.

A look at current discussions of male and female paths of development suggests ideas about the sense of self and of socialization of the
disabled girl. Many of these are elaborated upon by Harris and Wideman
(1988). What happens to a disabled girl growing up in a family where
her mother perceives that, because the daughter is disabled, she is fundamentally different from the mother and thus is not expected to develop
into the kind of woman the mother aspired to be? Friedman (1980)
suggests that a mother's major task is to "hand down the legacy of
womanhood . . . to share it and be an example of it" (90). If the mother's

definition of womanhood is based upon being attractive to and caring for a mate, she may inculcate in her daughter the belief that disability renders such a life impossible.

Thus, the disabled girl's best hope may be to turn to the traditionally male norms of achievement for establishing a sence of herself. Although she may acquire many skills and psychological resources to assist her in the productive world, she is not becoming the typical girl and young woman for whom establishing affiliative ties is of paramount importance (Person 1982). Autobiographies of many disabled women emphasize their quest for independence, work, and escape out of the stereotype of disability as helplessness. As one disabled woman put it to us: "I was raised to be a nondisabled son." However proud she may be of her accomplishments, the disabled girl knows she is not becoming like other women. Unless she likes that difference, it may lead to the lowered self-esteem found in psychological studies and in the autobiographical literature (Asch and Sacks 1983).

We have said that her "best" hope is to turn toward male standards of achievement. Like the fifteen-year-old Maria quoted earlier, however, many disabled girls are sheltered, kept from activities and opportunities where they might manage mastery of skills or acquiring of friends. In such a sad and too-common situation, the disabled girl may have no sense of identity with her mother or other girls and women and no validation for accomplishments beyond the home. Little wonder, then, that there are trapped and demoralized girls and women.

At the other end of the spectrum are disabled females who resist all the gender-based and disability-based stereotypes and take pride in the identities they forge. Because of or despite their parents, they get an education and a job. They live independently, enjoy sex with men or women, become pregnant and carry to term, if they choose, or abort, if they prefer. They relish their friendships, intimacies, lovers, activities. Some determine that they will play by the rules of achievement and succeed at meeting standards that are often deemed inaccessible to them. Some accept societal norms of attractiveness and enjoy the challenge of living up to them, disability notwithstanding. Others choose to disregard anything that seems like "passing" (Goffman 1963). Like Sarah in *Children of a Lesser God*, they demand that the world accept them on their terms, whether those terms be insisting upon signing rather than speaking, not covering their burn scars, not wearing clothing to hide parts of their bodies others may see as "ugly" or "deformed," or rejecting prostheses that inhibit and do not help.

Following her mastectomy, Lorde (1980a) refused to wear a prosthetic breast: "On the day after the stitches came out . . . I got so furious with the nurse who told me I was bad for the morale of the office because I did not wear a prosthesis" (52). Diane, a quadri-amputee interviewed by Gelya Frank, refused her prosthesis because, she said, "I knew it was going on my body. And that would add more sweat, and more asthma, because I would have to work harder with it. So I always saw my body as something that was mine, and something that was free, and I hated anything kind of binding" (Frank 1981, 84). Michele, a seventeen-year-old Hispanic high school student, told us that she wore her prosthetic arms only to her doctor's appointments. They are clumsy, she said, and she could manage to do things much more easily without them; she was perfectly comfortable having people see her short and "deformed" arms.

Having, as a child, incorporated her disability into her identity, Harilyn Rousso (1984) resisted her mother's attempts to make her appear more typical. She explains: "She [her mother] made numerous attempts over the years of my childhood to have me go for physical therapy and to practice walking more 'normally' at home. I vehemently refused all her efforts. She could not understand why I would not walk straight. . . . My disability, with my different walk and talk and my involuntary movements, having been with me all of my life, was part of me, part of my identity. With these disability features, I felt complete and whole. My mother's attempt to change my walk, strange as it may seem, felt like an assault on myself, an incomplete acceptance of all of me, an attempt to make me over" (9).

From these and many other examples, we know that some disabled girls and women flourish in spite of the pressures from family and the distortions and discrimination meted out by society. We need to know much more than we do about what helps some disabled girls and women resist, but this chapter testifies to both the travails and the victories of these women.

Disabled Women: Implications for Disability Rights and Feminism

The struggles of feminism and of disability rights have much in common. In order to pursue gender and disability equality, activists have argued for the elimination of laws, institutional structures and practices, and social attitudes that have reduced women or disabled people to one biological characteristic. Although both movements have borrowed and profited from the civil rights movement, these later movements share the indisputable fact that, in some situations, biology *does* and *should* count. Feminism and disability rights advocates insist, however, that instances where biology matters are extremely rare, and such cases can be minimized by changing society to better incorporate all its citizens.

In the writings of such socialist-feminists as Hester Eisenstein (1983; Eisenstein and Jardine 1985), one discovers a fine understanding of the differences among women. Also present are continued commitment to economic and political freedom as well as to psychological liberation and a balanced appreciation of women's attributes of nurturance and cooperation that neither glorifies women nor denigrates men. She and others, such as many of the contributors to the Sargent (1981) discussion of the "unhappy marriage" of Marxism and feminism, maintain that women's situation will not and cannot improve substantially until they gain full economic, political, sexual, reproductive, and psychological recognition. Recognition in their terms includes appreciation of both sameness *and* difference, and it entails social transformation in order for diversity to be tolerated and not punished. They understand that some differences, even if culturally created, are acceptable and perhaps even valuable, not only for women but for men and for social and political institutions.

We believe such an analysis can readily incorporate the particular issues of disability rights and of disabled women. That portion of the disability rights movement calling for societal change along with equality of opportunity should also be able to address concerns particular to disabled women. We suggest that progress for disabled people will not be achieved through stress on equality of opportunity alone, no matter how crucial such equality is, and we believe that disability rights theorists and activists can borrow from socialist-feminists who call for societal transformation in addition to equality of opportunity within existing arrangements.

Although we would not now assess the relative contributions of race, sex, or disability discrimination to any one woman's life experience or to that of disabled women in general, we can cite areas of theory and politics in disability rights and feminism that will benefit from specific attention to the concerns of today's disabled women. In thinking about the barriers to disabled women's full social, economic, and political participation, we also seek to recognize which ones are most amenable to work through disability rights activity, which ones through feminism, and which ones through both.

Omolade (1983) and Joseph (1981) have argued that, in certain instances, African-American women share more commonalities with African-American men than they do with white women. To ignore that fact and look to white feminists to embrace "all women's" concerns violates political and psychological realities. The same can be said for women with disabilities—including racial/ethnic minority women with disabilities—who may need to look to feminists, to their ethnic or racial group, and to the disability rights movement for support. One must recall the crucial difference between relations of disabled women and men and relations of women and men of color commented upon earlier: Many disabled men reject disabled women as intimates based on their own feelings about nurturance and attractiveness. African-American men, however, may be intimate with African-American women even if sexism persists within family and community relations. While we in no way suggest that disabled women and men should look only to one another for intimacy, that disabled people often reject one another for such intimacy may make genuine political struggle together for all disabled people's rights especially difficult.

Nonetheless, access to transportation, to housing, and to public places is a concern of all disabled people in which disabled women's best hope probably hinges on their joining and broadening the existing disablity rights movement. As we have said, independent living for disabled women may raise special problems in the training and supervision of personal care attendants and assistants. Independent living centers will need to pay attention to reports of abuse and domestic violence, perhaps modifying recruitment, training, and supervision of attendants; assisting disabled women with assertiveness training and self-defense classes; and pressuring domestic violence projects and battered women's shelters to reach out to disabled women.

Disabled girls and women confronting the separate, nearly always inferior special education and vocational rehabilitation systems must ally themselves with the disability rights movement to improve (or abolish) these bureaucracies that so profoundly affect disabled people's access to knowledge and employment. To make these systems less biased against disabled people—the very people they purport to serve—and less perpetuating of disability stigma and stereotype, disabled women must act in consort with the disability rights movement. Some sectors of that movement are male-dominated and may, without persistent pressure from women, ignore the gender and racial biases pervading these institutions. The mission of compelling regular educational, vocational training, and employment services to properly assist disabled people—thus abolishing or circumscribing the need for special services altogether—is one for the disability rights movement as a whole.

If we can generalize from our interviews, conference participation, and reading of the stories of disabled women, disability dominates gender in their discussions about education and employment opportunity, not-withstanding the disparities between disabled women and men noted earlier. Although they may object to being channeled into traditionally female occupations by the vocational rehabilitation system or to being kept from sports and adventures by parents and schools, disabled women focus on how their disability affects their access to education and jobs. Whether disabilities are apparent or invisible, they focus on fielding the humiliating and non-job-related disability questions of the employment interviewer or the medical examiner and not on questions about marital status, dependents, or sexual harassment on the job. Perhaps this lack of concern stems from their awareness that they are not viewed as sexual beings or perhaps from an accurate assessment that their disability obscures everything else about them to the employer or the college admissions officer. (We wonder, though, if forty-year-old disabled men are asked if they live with their parents, as forty-year-old disabled women are asked by men and women who should know better.)

While getting jobs for disabled women may be a disability problem impeded only secondarily by sexism, what happens on the job is as likely to be influenced by gender as by disability. Earnings and benefits for disabled women are far less than for disabled men, and thus disabled women must join with other women workers in struggles for comparable worth, for an end to job segregation by sex, and for an end to tying disability, pension, and Social Security benefits exclusively to earnings. Thus, for disabled women, equal access to education, to jobs, and to economic security depends on work with both disability rights and feminist groups.

Women with disabilities have not been "trapped" by many of the social expectations feminists have challenged. They have not been forced to get married or to subordinate paid work to child rearing or house-keeping. Instead, they have been warned by parents that men only "take advantage"; they have been sterilized by force or "choice," rejected by disabled and nondisabled heterosexual and lesbian partners, abandoned by spouses after onset of disability, and thwarted when they seek to mother.

Such contradictions and tensions emerged at the First National Conference on Disabled Women and Girls in Baltimore in 1982. As such, they demonstrate disabled women's challenge to feminism. In a keynote dialogue between a major feminist speaker and a major disability rights activist, nondisabled and disabled women witnessed gaps as well as similarities:

> *Letty Cottin Pogrebin:* The concerns about sexual harassment affect all women.
> *Judy Heumann:* You know, I use a wheelchair, and when I go down the street I do not get to be sexually harassed. I hear nondisabled women complaining about it, but I don't ever get treated as a sexual object.
> *Pogrebin:* You would hate it.

Throughout that weekend, and running through all our interviews, conversations, and conferences since that time, has been the response of disabled women: "Try two weeks or thirty years without that sexual attention. Then tell us if you would hate getting some, even in the form of harassment!" Denied the basic, if oppressive, gender-role prescriptions and offered nothing to replace them but often the worst of deadend jobs, disabled women have been without social role or gender-based value. Their anger at such deprivation uncomfortably reminds nondisabled women that sexual objectification is one vehicle by which at least heterosexual confirmation may be conveyed—a vehicle about which these women may feel more ambivalence than they choose to admit.

Indeed, a valuable effort to begin such conversations among women (disabled and not) and among disabled persons (women and men) to introduce women with disabilities into feminism and to incorporate a feminist perspective into disability rights is *Building Community,* a book of discussion, questions, readings, and exercises produced by the Women and Disability Awareness Project (1984), New York City.

More recently, disabled women have challenged feminism on yet another bedrock position: that of the alleged contradictions between women's rights to reproductive freedom and parental autonomy over the lives of disabled newborns. Not only do disabled women confront non-disabled women with that they prize about themselves in the areas of beauty and nurturance, but they compel these same women to examine what they expect of mothering and of the kind of children they choose to bear, rear, and love. What are women saying to disabled people when they choose to abort fetuses with Down's syndrome or spina bifida because "it would be better for the fetus. It would have been a vegetable"? If some disabled women challenge such decisions as based on inaccurate information available about the potential of such people, are they eroding women's fragile reproductive freedoms currently under severe attack? If women do not wish to mother such a child, are they expressing realistic concerns that such children will drain them financially or emotionally? Are they responding to fears about what would await such a child in the larger world or to fears that they will not receive what they prize about being mothers? Does a woman's right not to bear a child known to be disabled extend to her right to end medical treatment to an infant born with a disability?

Feminists struggling to maintain reproductive choice and disabled people struggling to assert their rights to existence, support, and opportunity have been confronting one another about these issues in the past five years. These tangled questions of women's reproductive rights versus disabled newborns' rights to treatment, of women's rights to decide what types of children they will mother versus disabled women's conviction that they deserve to be mothered and to mother, have sparked passionate and soul-searching panels and writings. (In addition to Asch and Fine, 1988, see Asch 1986b, 1986c; Fine and Asch 1982; Finger 1984; Harrison 1986; Rapp 1984; Rothman 1986; Saxton 1984.) This continuing dialogue promises an enriched feminism. Feminism will be strengthened by appreciation of disabled women and by a recognition that feminist commitments to nurturance, diversity, and inclusiveness can be used to create a society that provides opportunity for all people, without consigning certain people to the role of unending caretakers to others.

In these pages, we have taken a risk in trying to unearth the complexities of gender and disability. Our goal has been to introduce the former into disability scholarship, the latter into feminist thought, and both into the mainstream of social science. Beyond this, we demand attention to the lives and experiences of women with disabilities, be it on the street, at work, in bed, in maternity wards, at feminist rallies, within the ranks of the disability rights movement, or across progressive grass roots movements. We further seek it in psychology and sociology texts, legal casebooks, folklore, popular literature, and film. We demand that the images of helplessness, passivity, need, and longings for care be projected no longer onto disabled women but be redistributed throughout all of society, rich in fear, need, desire, and hope.

NOTES

We would like to thank Richard K. Scotch and Irving Kenneth Zola for comments that have assisted us in developing this article, and Janet Francendese and Tina Trudel for thorough reading, suggestions, and wording that have clarified and sharpened our ideas.

1. Since 1982 and the First National Conference on Disabled Women and Girls, the authors have participated in more than twenty conferences in the Northeast and Midwest on disabled women and girls. Many have been sponsored by the Networking Project for Disabled Women and Girls or by the Women and Disability Awareness Project. Others have been held by colleges and universities, state or local offices for the handicapped, independent living centers, feminist groups, disability organizations, professional rehabilitation or service organizations, the National Women's Studies Association, and the Association for Women and Psychology. We have heard the stories of hundreds of women with a range of disabilities, including many whose disabilities occurred before adulthood and others who have discovered its meaning during adulthood. Unless otherwise cited, our examples come from conversations at these conferences, from formal interviews, and from our participation in many meetings with the Women and Disability Awareness Project.

PART 3

Within Feminist Talk

In *Whose Science? Whose Knowledge?* Sandra Harding argues for feminist scholarship that is, at once, centered in women's daily experiences and committed to liberatory social interests. Harding writes of the tainted politics of "legitimate" research:

> The history of science shows that research directed by maximally liberatory social interests and values tends to be better equipped to identify partial claims and distorting assumptions, even though the credibility of the scientists who do it may not be enhanced during the short run. After all, antiliberatory interests and values are invested in the natural inferiority of just the groups of humans who, if given real equal access (not just the formally equal access that is liberalism's goal) to public voice, would most strongly contest claims about their purported natural inferiority. Antiliberatory interests and values silence and destroy the most likely sources of evidence against their own claims. That is what makes them rational for elites. (1991, 148).

This final set of essays takes us toward this next generation of feminist psychology, in which feminist activism explicitly constitutes our political work.

The first essay in this section, "Over Dinner: Feminism and Adolescent Female Bodies," chronicles a set of conversations Pat Macpherson and I held with a group of adolescent women about gender, politics, bodies, cultures, and their daily lives. Through a feminist methodology we call "collective consciousness work," we sculpted, quite literally over dinner, a way to theorize consciousness, moving from stridently individualist feminism (Fox-Genovese 1991) to a collective sense of women's

solidarity among differences. As Terry Eagleton has written, consciousness grew around and with us: "To put the point differently, consciousness is less something 'within' us than something around and between
us, a network of signifiers which constitute us through and through"
(Eagleton 1991, 194). This essay talks through the four adolescent women
about their bodies, sexualities, and gender politics, and it displays the
consciousness work we six did as feminist methodology.

The final essay in this collection, "Passions, Politics, and Power:
Feminist Research Possibilities" weaves bodies, silences, and feminist talk
together to challenge the narrative stances that feminist psychologists
have been willing to take (and not) and depicts an image of what feminist
psychologists could be writing if we took our own politics, our activism,
and our talk seriously.

And, so, with this set of essays, I invite feminist psychologists, in
the 1990s, to celebrate our numbers, our power, and our passions through
narratives in which the radical edge of feminism nestles sweetly within
our texts. Always critically engaged with women's representations, experiences, and differences, our work must interrupt traditional silences,
lighten shadows, disrupt dualisms, and provoke delicious feminist movements for social change. In times when the Supreme Court has determined
that federally funded clinics *must* deny women information about abortions; when the well-endowed National Association of Scholars is scan-
ning our campuses urging censorship of feminism, Third World studies,
and lesbian and gay studies; when every popular magazine is on its
front page mocking the intellectual work that seeks to open the canon
to all women and men of color; when today's generation of undergraduates has most intimately experienced politics under only Reagan and
Bush, feminist research needs to become a safe and outraged space for
voices too long silenced and for activism too long individualized. Few
others will—or can—speak. And, so, we must.

Over Dinner: Feminism and Adolescent Female Bodies

Michelle Fine and Pat Macpherson

> The experience of being woman can create an illusory unity, for it is not
> the experience of being woman but the meanings attached to gender,
> race, class, and age at various historical moments . . . that [are] of strate-
> gic significance.
> —Chandra Mohanty, "Feminist Encounters" (1987, 123)

When we invited four teenagers—Shermika, Damalleaux, Janet, and
Sophie—for a series of dinners to talk with us about being young women
in the 1990s, we could not see our own assumptions about female adolescence much more clearly than we saw theirs. By the end of the first
dinner, we could, though, recognize how old we were, how dated the
academic literatures were, how powerful feminism had been in shaping
their lives and the meanings they made of them, and yet how inade-
quately their feminism dealt with key issues of identity and peer relations.

Only when we started to write could we see the inadequacies of
our feminism to understand the issues of female adolescence they struggled to communicate. In this space of our incredulity, between our
comprehension of their meanings and our *incomprehension* of "how they
could call themselves feminist," we are now able to see the configuration
of our own fantasies of feminism for female adolescents. The re-vision
that is central to feminist process gets very tricky when applied to
adolescence, because our own unsatisfactory pasts return as the "before"
picture, demanding that the "after" picture of current adolescent females
measure all the gains of the women's movement. Our longing is for
psychic as well as political completion. Michael Payne (1991, 18)
describes the fantasy of the Other: "What I desire—and therefore lack—

175

is in the other culture, the other race, the other gender"—the other generation, in our case. In the case of these four young women, to our disbelief, the desired Other is "one of the guys."

We grew convinced that we needed to construct an essay about these young women's interpretations of the discourses of adolescence, femininity, and feminism in their peer cultures. Barbara Hudson explains the incompatibility of femininity and adolescence:

> femininity and adolescence as discourses [are] subversive of each other. All of our images of the adolescent—the restless, searching teen; the Hamlet figure; the sower of wild oats and tester of growing powers—these are masculine figures. . . . If adolescence is characterized by masculine constructs, then any attempt by girls to satisfy society's demands of them qua adolescents is bound to involve them in displaying notably a lack of maturity but also a lack of femininity. 1984, 35)

Adolescence for these four young women was about the adventures of males and the constraints on females, so their version of feminism unselfconsciously rejected femininity and embraced the benign version of masculinity that allowed them to be "one of the guys." They fantasized the safe place of adolescence to be among guys who overlook their (female) gender out of respect for their (unfeminine) independence, intelligence, and integrity. For them, femininity meant the taming of adolescent passions, outrage, and intelligence. Feminism was a flight from "other girls" as unworthy and untrustworthy. Their version of feminism was about equal access to being men.

When we scoured the literatures on adolescent females and their bodies, we concluded that the very construction of the topic is positioned largely from white, middle-class, nondisabled, heterosexual, adult women's perspectives. The concerns of white elite women are represented as *the* concerns of this age cohort. Eating disorders are defined within the contours of what *elite* women suffer (e.g., anorexia and bulimia) and less so what nonelite women experience (e.g., overeating, obesity, etc.). The sexual harassment literature is constructed from *our* age perspective—that unwanted sexual attention is and should be constituted as a crime—and not from the complicated perspectives of the young women involved. The disability literature is saturated with images produced by *nondisabled* researchers of self-pitying or embarrassed "victims" of biology and is rarely filled with voices of resistant, critical, and powerfully "flaunting" adolescents who refuse to wear prostheses, delight in the passions of their bodies and are outraged by the social and family discrimination they experience (Fine and Asch 1988; Frank 1988; Corbett 1989).

We found that women of all ages, according to this literature, are allegedly scripted to be "good women," and that they have, in compliance, smothered their passions, appetites, and outrage. When sexually harassed, they tell "his stories" (Brodkey and Fine 1988; see also "Presence of Mind in the Absence of Body" in this volume). To please the lingering internalized "him," they suffer in body image and indulge in eating disorders (Orbach 1986). And to satisfy social demands for "attractiveness," women with and without disabilities transform and mutilate their bodies (Bordo 1990).

We presumed initially that the three arenas of adolescence in which young women would most passionately struggle with gendered power would include eating, sexuality, and outrage. And so we turned to see what these literatures said and to unpack how race, class, disability, and sexuality played with each of these literatures. In brief, within these literatures, we saw a polarizing: (1) eating disorders appear to be a question studied among elite white women in their anticipated tensions of career vs. mother identities; (2) sexuality is examined disproportionately as problematic for girls who are African-American and underprivileged, with motherhood as their primary identity posed as "the problem"; and (3) finally, young women's political outrage simply does not exist as a category for feminist intellectual analysis. The literature on adolescent women had thoroughly extricated these categories of analysis from women's lives. So, in our text, we decided to rely instead upon the frames that these young women offered as they narrated their own lives and the interpretations we could generate through culture and class.

Our method was quite simple, feminist, and, ironically, anti–eating disorder. We invited the six of us to talk together over pizza and soda, while Sam—Michelle's four-year-old—circled the table. We talked for hours, on two nights two months apart, and together stretched to create conversations about common differences—about the spaces in which we could delight together as six women; the moments in which they bonded together as four young women who enjoy football, hit their boyfriends, and can't trust other girls (not ever!); and, too, the arenas in which the race, class, and cultural distances in the room stretched too far for these age-peers to weave any common sense of womanhood. Collectively, we created a context that Shermika and Sophie spontaneously considered "the space where I feel most safe." We were together, chatting, listening, hearing, laughing a lot, and being truly interested in understanding our connections and differences, contoured always along the fault lines of age, class, race and culture, bodies, experiences, and politics.

But we each delighted in this context differently. For Michelle and Pat, it was a space in which we could pose feminist intellectual questions from our generation—questions about sexuality, power, victimization, and politics—which they then turned on their heads. For Shermika (African-American, age fifteen), it was a place for public performance, to say outrageous things, admit embarrassing moments, "practice" ways of being female in public discourse, and see how we would react. For Damalleaux (African-American, age fourteen), it was a place to "not be shy," even though the room was integrated by race, a combination that had historically made her uncomfortable. For Sophie ("WASP," age seventeen), it was a "safe place" where, perhaps for the first time, she was not the only "out" feminist in a room full of peers. And for Janet (Korean-American, age seventeen), like other occasions in which she was the only Asian-American among whites and African-Americans, it was a time to test her assimilated "sense of belonging," always at the margins. In negotiating gender, race/ethnicity, and class as critical, feminist agents, these four women successfully betrayed a set of academic literatures written by so many of us only twenty years older. Our writings have been persistently committed to public representations of women's victimization and structural assaults and have consequently ignored, indeed misrepresented, *how well young women talk as subjects*, passionate about and relishing their capacities to move between nexus of power and powerlessness. That is to say, feminist scholars have forgotten to take notice of how firmly young women resist—alone and sometimes together.

The four young women began their conversation within this space of gendered resistance. Shermika complained, "Boys think girls cannot do *any*thing," to which Sophie added, "So we have to harass them." Shermika explained, "[Guys think] 'long as they're takin' care of 'em, [girls will] do anything they want. And if I'm in a relationship, I'm gonna take care of you just as much as you take care of me. You can't say 'I did this'—No: 'We did this.'. . . Guys think you're not nothin'—anything—without them." Janet sneered, "Ego." Shermika recruited her friend into this conversation by saying, "Damalleaux *rule* her boyfriend [Shermika's brother]." Damalleaux announced her governing principle: "Boys—they try to take advantage of you. . . . As far as I'm concerned, I won't let a boy own me." Janet provided an example of the "emotionally messed up guys" she encounters: "I didn't want to take care of him. I didn't want to constantly explain things to him. . . . I want to coexist with them and not be like their mother. . . . It happened to me twice." And Sophie explained: "I'm really assertive with guys [who say sexist stuff]. If they have to be shot down I'll shoot them down. They have to know their place."

The four expressed their feminism here as resistance to male domination in their peer relations. They applied the same principle in discussing how they saw careers and marriage, when Michelle asked about men in their future plans. Shermika laid it out in material terms: "I imagine bein' in my *own* house in *my name*. And then get married. So my husband can get out of *my house*." Sophie chimed in, "Seriously," and Shermika nodded, "Yes, *very important*. So I won't end up one of them battered women we were talkin' about. I'm not going to have no man beatin' on me." Sophie offered her version: "You have to like be independent. You have to establish youself as your own person before some guy takes you—I mean." Janet asserted her standard of independence: "I wouldn't follow a guy to college." Their feminism asserted women's independence from men's power to dominate and direct.

Class and cultural differences entered the conversations with their examples of domination and resistance. Shermika's example of guys materially "takin' care" of girls to establish dominance and Damalleaux's resistance to male "ownership" reflected the practice of gift giving as ownership, a norm of their local sexual politics (see Anderson 1990). Damalleaux explained that respect could interrupt this dominance structure: "How much respect a guy has for you—especially in front of his friends? . . . If a boy finds out you don't care how they treat you, and you don't have respect for your*self* . . . they won't have respect for you." Damalleaux turned to Shermika and said, "You try to teach me." Shermika's talk was full of lessons learned from her mother and examples of their closeness. "My mom and me like this. 'Cause she understands." Not talking "*leads* to problems. My mom tells me so much about life."

Sophie and Janet defined their resistance within their "professional class," peopled by "individuals," not relationships, who suffer from the dilemmas of "independence," typically explained in terms of psychology.

Their isolation from their mothers and female friends enabled them to frame their stories alone, as one-on-one battles across the lines of gender and generations.

Ways of Talking: On Cultures of Womenhood

> Herein lies a cautionary tale for feminists who insist that underneath or beyond the differences among women there must be some shared identity—as if commonality were a metaphysical given, as if a shared viewpoint were not a difficult political achievement.... Western feminist theory has in effect ... [demanded that] Afro-American, Asian-American or Latin American women separate their "woman's voice" from their racial or ethnic voice without also requiring white women to distinguish being a "woman" from being white. This double standard implies that while on the one hand there is a seamless web of whiteness and womanness, on the other hand, Blackness and womanness, say, or Indianness and womanness, are discrete and separable elements of identity. If ... I believe that the woman in every woman is a woman just like me, and if I also assume that there is no difference between being white and being a woman, then seeing another woman "as a woman" will involve me seeing her as fundamentally like the woman I am. In other words, the womanness underneath the Black woman's skin is a white woman's, and deep down inside the latina woman is an Anglo woman waiting to burst through the obscuring cultural shroud. As Barbara Omolade has said, "Black women are not white women with color."
>
> —Elizabeth Spelman, *The Inessential Woman* (1988, 13)

At this moment in social history, when the tensions of race, class, and gender couldn't be in more dramatic relief, social anxieties load onto the bodies of adolescent women (Fine 1991; Halson 1990). Struggles for social control attach to these unclaimed territories, evident in public debates over teen pregnancy, adolescent promiscuity, parental consent for contraception and abortion, date rapes, and stories of sexual harassment, as well as in women's personal narratives of starving themselves or binging and purging toward thinness. For each of these social "controversies" there is, however, a contest of wills, a set of negotiations. Young women are engaged with questions of "being female"; that is, who will control, and to what extent can they control, their own bodies?

Threaded through our conversations at the dining room table, culture and class helped to construct (at least) two distinct versions of womanhood. It became clear that the elite women, for instance, constructed an interior sense of womanhood out of oppositional relations with white men. They positioned white men as the power group White Men (H. Baker, pers. com., 1989). And they positioned themselves in an ongoing, critical, hierarchical struggle with these men. Sophie, for example, often defined her feminism in relation to white boys; instead of "reinforcing guys all the time, I BUST on guys. Because if you don't bust 'em they'll get ahead. You have to keep 'em in their place."

It was quite another thing to hear the sense of womanhood constructed horizontally—still in struggle—by African-American women, situated with or near African-American men. Given the assault on African-American men by the broader culture, it was clear that any announced sense of female superiority would be seen as "castrating" and unreconcilable with cross-gender alliances against racism (Giddings 1984; hooks 1984). So, the construction of African-American womanhood was far less dichotomized and oppositional toward men and far richer in a sense of connection to community.[1] In the context of being "deprived," then, of the traditional (oppositional to White Men) feminine socialization, women of color, like women with disabilities, may construct womenhoods less deeply repulsed by the traditional accoutrements of femininity, less oppositional to the cardboard White Male, and less assured that gender survives as the primary, or exclusive, category of social identity.

Among these four, then, we heard two quite distinct constructions of "being female." From the African-American women, both living in relatively impoverished circumstances, we heard a "womanhood" of fluid connections among women within and across generations; maturity conceived of as an extension of self with others; a taken-for-granted integration of body and mind; a comfortable practice of using public talk as a place to "work out" concerns, constraints, and choices; and a nourishing, anchored sense of home and community. bell hooks describes "home" as the site of nurturance and identity, positive in its resistance to racist ideologies of African-American inferiority:

Despite the brutal reality of racial apartheid, of domination, one's homeplace was the one site where one could freely confront the issue of humanization, where one could resist. Black women resisted by making homes where all black people could strive to be subjects, not objects, where we could be affirmed in our minds and our hearts despite poverty, hardship and deprivation, where we could restore to ourselves the dignity denied us on the outside in the public world. (hooks 1990)

As the words of Damalleaux and Shermika reveal to us, however, the drawback of this centeredness in community is in its fragility, its contingent sense of the future, terrors of what's "across the border," and the lack of resources or supports for planned upward mobility.

Indeed, when we discussed future plans, Shermika "joked" that she'd be a custodian or bag lady. She joked that she'd like to be dead, to see what the other world was like. She said she'd like to come back as a bird—"Not a pigeon, I hope," said Sophie. "Dove or peacock," Shermika decided, "something nobody be kickin' around all the time." Shermika finally confided—in an uncharacteristic whisper—that she'd like to be a lawyer, even the D.A. (district attorney). What Shermika can be, could be, would like to be, and will be constitutes the terrain of Shermika's and Damalleaux's dilemma. Shermika doesn't worry that education would defeminize her or that her parents expect more or different from her career than she does. She quite simply and realistically doubts she'll be able to get all the way to D.A.

Nevertheless, Damalleaux and Shermika, on the other hand, expressed the connections with and respect for mothers found in Gloria Joseph and Jill Lewis's African-American daughters: "A decisive 94.5% expressed respect for their mothers in terms of strength, honesty, ability to overcome difficulties, and ability to survive" (1981, 94). Shermika's many examples of respect for her mother and Damalleaux's mother calling her "my first girl" suggest "the centrality of mothers in their daughters' lives" (Joseph and Lewis 1981, 79). In their stories, active female sexuality and motherhood are everywhere "embodied," while "career" is a distant and indistinct dream—marginal, foreign, and threateningly isolated.

In contrast, from the two privileged women, both living in relatively elite circumstances, we heard a womanhood struggling for positive definition and safe boundaries; a sharp splitting of body and mind; maturity as a dividing of self from family and school to find individual identity; and an obsessive commitment to using privacy—in body, thought, and conversation—as the only way to "work out" one's problems. All nourished a highly individualized, privatized, and competitive sense of home and community as sites from which they would ultimately leave, unfettered, to launch "autonomous" lives as independent women. Materially and imaginatively these two women recognized an almost uninterruptable trajectory for future plans. Their womanhood was built on the sense of *self as exception,* "achievement" meritocratically determining how exceptional each individual can prove herself (away) from the group. Self-as-exception, for women, involves transcending gender. Rachel Hare-Mustin describes the illusion of gender-neutral choices:

> The liberal/humanist tradition of our epoch assumes that the meanings of our lives reflect individual experience and individual subjectivity. This tradition has idealized individual identity and self-fulfillment and shown a lack of concern about power. Liberalism masks male privilege and dominance by holding that every (under-gendered) individual is free. The individual has been regarded as responsible for his or her fate and the basic social order has been regarded as equitable. Liberal humanism implies free choice when individuals are not free of coercion by the social order. (Hare-Mustin 1991, 3)

The invisibility of women's "coercion by the social order" came out most clearly in Janet's and Sophie's relationships with their working mothers. They did not analyze their mothers' lives for power.

Sophie said, "My mom doesn't like her job but she has to work so I can go to college." Janet and Sophie said they were afraid of becoming their mothers, unhappy and overworked in jobs they hate, their workloads doubled with domestic responsibilities. "I fear I might be like her. I want to be independent of her," white, middle-class women said of their mothers in the research of Joseph and Lewis (1981, 125). Janet and Sophie said they didn't talk much, or very honestly, to their mothers and didn't feel they could ever do enough to gain their mothers' approval. Janet said, "My mother [says] I really have to go to college . . . be a doctor or lawyer. . . . That's her main goal . . . job security . . . then she wants me to get married and have a nice family . . . preferably Catholic. . . . Mom's got my life mapped out." Ambition and career embody this mother-daughter relationship, in a sense, while the daughter's problems with sexuality and power and the mother *as woman* are absent in the relationship Janet describes.

When discussing who they'd tell if they had a problem, Shermika immediately said, "My mom," and Damalleaux said, "I tell Shermika almost everything before I tell my mother." Sophie and Janet agreed only in the negative. It wouldn't be their mothers: "Don't talk to my mom."

> *Janet:* I can't tell my mother anything. If I told her something she
>   would ground me for an entire century.
> *Sophie:* Once you tell them one thing, they want to hear more, and
>   they *pry.* I keep my home life and school—social—life so separate.
> *Janet:* I'll be noncommittal or I won't tell her the truth. I'll just tell
>   her what she wants to hear.
> *Sophie:* I wish I could talk to my mom. It'd be great if I could.
> *Shermika:* It's the wrong thing to do [not talking], though. . . . It
>   always *leads* to problems. My mom tells me so much about life.

Janet said her mother stares at her complexion [her acne] and says, "You're not going to get married, you're not going to have a boyfriend." "I get so mad at her," Janet says. She tells her mother either "I'm leaving, I'm leaving" or "Stop it! Stop it!" Later, when Pat asked whether self-respect was learned from the mother, Janet said her self-respect had "nothing to do with my mother. I used to hate myself, partly because of my mother. But not anymore. My mother's opinion just doesn't matter to me." Sophie said,

> My mother . . . nitpicks. . . . I'm sure it was like her mom [who] never
> approved anything about her. I get self-respect from my mom
> because she wants me to respect myself. . . . I don't think she respects
> herself enough. I respect her more than she respects herself. Her
> mother belittled her so much.

Later Sophie said, "I have the feeling that no matter what I do, it's not enough." Janet said her mother makes her and her sister feel like her mother's "racehorses":

> My mom *lives* through her kids. Two daughters: two *chances.* My
> sister wants to be an actress and my parents hate that [dykey] way she
> looks. . . . My mom: "You're just not *feminine* enough!" I'm just like,
> "Mom, grow up!". . . She compares her daughters to everyone else's.
> [One example is] a straight-A student on top of all her chores. . . .

I know there's things in her personality that are part of myself. . . .
We're just like racehorses. . . . "My daughter has three wonderful children and a husband who makes a million dollars a year."

For Janet and Sophie, their mothers were supports to get over, central to
the life these daughters wished to escape, and to revise, in their own
futures. Within their liberal discourse of free choice, the inequalities of
power determining their mothers' misery were invisible to them—and
their own exceptional futures also unquestioned.

The Body: Boundaries and Connections

Over our dinners, we created a democracy of feminist differences. That
is, all four, as an age/gender cohort, introduced us to the female body
in play with gendered politics. These young women consistently recast
our prioritizing of sex at the center of feminist politics into *their* collective
critique of gender politics. Using a language that analyzed dominance
and power, they refused to separate sex from other power relations.
Perhaps even more deeply Foucauldian than we assumed ourselves to
be, they deconstructed our voyeurism with examples of sexuality as only
one embodied site through which gendered politics operate. All four
shared a distrust of men ("they think they have power"), but they also
distrusted female solidarity ("they backstab you all the time"). Their
examples overturned our notions of sisterhood by showing us that both
young women and young men proficiently police the borders, and tenets,
of masculinity and femininity among today's teens. They are often
reminded of their bodies as a public site (gone right or wrong), commented on and monitored by others—male and female. But as often,
they reminded us, they forcefully reclaim their bodies by talking back
and by talking feminist. "It'd be harder not to talk," Sophie thinks. "It'd
be harder to sit and swallow whatever people are saying."

Resonating with much of feminist literature, when these four young
women spoke of their bodies, it was clear that they found themselves
sitting centrally at the nexus of race, class, and gender politics. Gender
determines that the young women are subject to external surveillance
and responsible for internal body management, and it is their gender
that makes them feel vulnerable to male sexual threat and assault. Culture
and class determine how—that is, the norms of body and the codes of

surveillance, management, threat, assault, and resistance available to them.

Susan Bordo (1990) writes about body management as a text for "the controlling" / "controlling the" middle class. Reflecting both elite material status and a pure, interior soul, this fetish of body management, operated by the "normalizing machinery of power," produces a desire to control flesh otherwise out of control, as it positions individuals within an elite class location. The tight, svelte body reflects material and moral comfort, while the loose, sagging body falls to the "lumpen." Bordo's cultural analysis of the representations and experiences of women's bodies, and women's revulsion at sagging fat, captures, and yet too narrowly homogenizes, what the four young women reported.

Each of the four, as Bordo would argue, was meticulously concerned with her body as the site for cataloging both her own and others' "list" of her inadequacies. Indeed, each body had become the space within which she would receive unsolicited advice about having "too many pimples," "being too chocolate," "looking chubby," "becoming too thin," "looking like a boy," or, in the case of a sister, dressing "very butch." The fetish to control, however, was experienced in ways deeply classed and raced. While the elite women were familiar with, if not obsessed by, eating disorders now fashionable among their status peers, the African-American women were quite literally bewildered at the image of a young woman binging on food and then purging. Therein lies a serious problem in white feminist literatures: class and culture practices are coded exclusively as gender, reinforcing hegemonic definitions of (white) womanhood, while obscuring class/culture contours of the body.

For these women, the female body not only signified a site of interior management vis-à-vis male attention/neglect. It was also a site for gendered politics enacted through sexual violence. Celia Kitzinger (1988), in an analysis of how two thousand young women and men frame their personal experiences with "unfairness," found that 24 percent of interviewed girls spontaneously volunteered instances of body-centered unfairness, including sexual harassment, rape, and/or abuse. So, too, violence stories were offered by all four of the young women, each particular to her social context:

When I got my first boyfriend [he] pressured me to have sex with him. That's why I didn't never go over his house. (Damalleaux)
I feel safe nowhere. (Sophie)

When he pulled a gun on me, I said, "This is over." (Shermika)
I know it's unlikely, but I am terrified of someday being date raped.
It's always been something I've been afraid of. (Janet)

For Janet, violence is imagined as possible because of the stories of her friends. For Sophie, violence is encountered as harassment on the street. For Damalleaux and Shermika, violence is encountered or threatened in relations with boyfriends.

*   *   *

Michelle: Is there any place where guys have more power than you?
Damalleaux: In bed.
Shermika: In the street. In the store, when he has all the money.
Damalleaux: And all the guys can beat girls. But I don't think it's true.

*   *   *

Michelle: Are you ever afraid that the hitting will get bad?
Shermika: Yeah, that's why I don't do so much hitting.
Damalleaux: When I go out with a boy I hit him a lot to see if he's going to do anything. . . . You hit me once, I don't want anything to do with you.

*   *   *

Shermika: Sometimes you can get raped with words, though. You feel so slimy. . . . The guy at the newspaper stand, I speak to him every morning. Then one day he said, "How old is you? I can't wait till you sixteen." And I told my mom, and she came [with me and told him off]. He lost respect. He didn't give me none. And that day I felt bad, what was I, bein' too loose? . . . You just can't help feelin' like that [slimy].

Liz Kelly (1988, 41) offers this definition of sexual violence:

Sexual violence includes any physical, visual, verbal or sexual act that is experienced by the woman or girl, at the time or later, as a threat, invasion or assault, that has the effect of degrading or hurting her and/or takes away her ability to control intimate contact.

We found that the impression and/or experience of surviving male violence was indeed central. But its expression was, again, classed and raced. These fears and experiences were deeply traumatic to all the women, and yet the African-American women more frequently and more publicly, if uncomfortably, related them in the context of conversation. For the elite women, the assaults and fears were more privatized and so left relatively unanalyzed, unchallenged, and in critical ways "buried." For example, Janet's story of a friend's date rape contrasts radically with Shermika's stories of male violence and female resistance.

> *Janet:* That happened to one of my friends.
> *Sophie:* A date rape?
> *Janet:* Sort of.... He'd been pressuring her for a long time, and she's just "no no no no." She's at this party, her [girl] friend says, "Why don't you just do it?" and she says, "Because I don't *want* to."... She was drunk, puking. She fell asleep, and the next thing she knows she wakes up and he's on top of her and she's not really happy about it but she didn't do anything about it so she just let it happen. And... she was upset about it, she was really angry about it, but there was nothing she could *do* about it? [Janet's voice rises to a kind of question mark.] It didn't really bother her, but after that she totally knew who her friends were...
> *Sophie:* She could've done something about it.
> *Janet:* I guess we didn't talk about how she really felt about it. She seemed really comfortable with it after it. She was upset for a while. After she—
> *Sophie:* There's no way she was *comfortable* with it.
> *Janet:* She's dealt with it in a way. She's gotten to the point where it doesn't really make her cry to talk about it.

Earlier in the conversation, Sophie complained that the popular crowd got drunk at parties and had one-night stands. Somewhat defensive, Janet said as an aside to Sophie, "Hey, *I've* done that." Janet's story of the rape included Janet's anger at the girl's girlfriend: "Her *friend* was the hostess of the party and gave her the condoms and told her to go do it." Betrayal by the girlfriend and the boyfriend, a rape Janet calls "sort of" a date rape, in a party situation Janet has been in many times, anger and helplessness, talking about it finally without tears: this worst-case scenario of women's sexuality and powerlessness is "dealt with" by *not* "talk[ing] about how she really felt about it." Janet's story was about the social and interior limits on one girl's control, before and after "sex" she didn't want.

In sharp contrast, Shermika offered a story of embodied resistance through public talk. Michelle asked, "Have you ever been in a relationship where you felt you were being forced to do what you didn't want to do?" Shermika's answer was immediate and emphatic, "Yeah, I quit 'em, I quit 'em." She followed with a story about what happened when she "quit" the boyfriend who was getting possessive:

> *Shermika:* I almost got killed. Some guy pulled a gun on me. . . .
>   He put the gun *to my head.* I said, "You'd better kill me 'cause
>   if you don't I'm gonna kill you." Then he dropped the gun. . . . I
>   kicked him where it hurts . . . hard. He had to go to the hospital.
>   I was scared . . .
> *Janet:* What happened—have you ever seen him again?
> *Shermika:* I see him every day.
> *Michelle:* Did you call the cops?
> *Shermika:* Yeah. . . . he had to stay in jail [two weeks] till I decided
>   not to press charges. . . . Don't nobody around my way playin'
>   like that with them guns . . .

Shermika's examples of male threat and violence all show her and her mother talking back, striking back, or disarming the man. The woman is embodied as her own best protector. Shermika followed up her first story (which stunned her audience into awed silence) with a second, another jealous boyfriend: "He told me if I went with anybody else he'd kill me. And he pulled a knife on me. . . . 'Stab me. Either way, you ain't gonna have me.'" Later she told a story about her mother:

> My stepfather and my mother were fightin'—it's the only time they
> ever fought. And he stepped back and hit my momma with all his
> might. And he thought she was gonna give up. She stepped back
> and hit *him* with all *her* might—and he fell asleep. She knocked
> the mess outta him. He never hit her again.

And another about herself, with her mother as model: "A guy tried to beat me with a belt, and I grabbed it and let him see how it felt to get beat with that belt. My mom wouldn't even take that." The scars of actual and/or anticipated sexual violence were clear for each of the young women, and always culturally specific as encounter, resistance, and recounting.

As with the violence of gender, the violence of racism on the female body was painfully voiced by the three women of color. Fears of attending a white prep school "where they'll ignore me," stories of fleeing an integrated school after three weeks, and retrospective outbursts of anger at being "the only woman of color in my class!" showed a kind of agoraphobia that kept Shermika and Damalleaux in their wholly African-American communities, and, inversely, created in Janet deep assimilative wishes to disappear into the white suburbs. For Janet the "white church" in her elite suburban neighborhood—not the Korean church her parents attend—was the "safest place" she could imagine.

For Damalleaux and Shermika, the neighborhood and its school are clearly the only safe place. Damalleaux reported that she'd lasted three weeks at an integrated school: "It was OK, but I didn't feel right. I didn't know anybody. I don't like introducing myself to people, I'm too shy. . . . I came back to the neighborhood school."

Shermika was offered a scholarship to go to a fancy private school in a white suburb. When discussing what scares us about the future, Shermika admitted she fears "being neglected. Not fitting in. . . . One time I'm goin' in and nobody likes me." When Michelle asked if that was her fear about the prep school, Shermika said, "Not as far as the people. But I don't like traveling. And I'm not staying on the campus. . . . I ain't stayin' away from home, though." By the time of our second interview, Shermika had convinced her mother to delay her going to prep school, from mid-year until the next fall. Shermika said she feared she would not be able to keep her grades up in the new school. Shermika's reliance on nonstandard English meant she would have to manage a major cultural shift both academically and socially. Her only envy of Sophie and Janet's school was what she called its "socializing" function, which taught them "how to get along, socialize, fit in, knowin' the right thing to say and do." Shermika said that, when she has a job, she wants to stay in her neighborhood, "where it all happenin', [not] where you won't fit in." Racial identity, segregation, and racism combine to reinforce the boundaries of Shermika's and Damalleaux's lives and futures by defining where and who is "safe."

Shermika evidently decided our dinner table was a "safe" enough place to explore our own racial (and maybe racist) differences. Shermika asked Janet, "Are you Chinese?" and Janet said, "No, Korean," and launched into a story about Japanese racism, including the sale of "Sambo" dolls in Japan, and then a story about the four-thousand-year-old hatred of Koreans for the Japanese. Shermika responded, "Well I don't understand that. I mean, I'm supposed to hate somebody white because somebody I know was a slave?" Then Shermika put race and racism right on our dinner table:

> *Shermika:* I walk into a store and Chinese people be starin' at me.
>   [Shermika was mistaking Korean for Chinese for the third time.]
> *Janet:* My *mother* does that—I hate that, my *mother* does it. [Her
>   mother runs a dry cleaner.] And I'm just like, "Mom, *stop* it."
> *Damalleaux:* I leave [the store].
> *Janet:* How do you feel when you're the only minority in a room?
> *Damalleaux:* I don't care.
> *Shermika:* I make a joke out of it. I feel like a zebra.

Unlike Janet's experience, the assaultive nature of Shermika's and Damalleaux's encounters with the white world had given them little encouragement to isolate themselves among a white majority. Shermika said her "darkness" meant she "looked like a clown" when they put on make-up for her local TV interview about the scholarship program she's in; then her pride and excitement about the video of herself on TV was clouded by family jokes about her dark skin making her "invisible" to the camera. Shermika reported plenty of harassment about her dark skin from girlfriends and boyfriends, even those as dark as herself. *Choclate!* was the common, hated term, and Shermika was troubled by its implied racial hierarchy and self-hatred. Atypically, she had no easy comeback for that one.

Race in Sophie's (WASP) experience is about being privileged and feeling harassed for her blonde and blue-eyed good looks. Janet, for instance, annoys Sophie by calling her the "Aryan Goddess." Sophie is harassed on public transportation on her daily commute, where she is in the minority as a white woman. (Janet, in contrast, drives from suburb to school.) Sophie became exasperated in our interview when she felt targeted for white racism and said she didn't "notice" race half as often as race identified her in public situations in which she is made to represent WASPhood or white womanhood.

Just as these women cocreated for us a shared, if negotiated, sense of body politics, they separated along culture lines in their expressed reliance on social connections and surveillance of bodily borders. The African-American women, for instance, detailed deeply textured and relational lives. They not only care for many, but many also care for them. They give much to others and receive much in return, but they don't call it volunteer or charity work—simply "what I do." When they receive favors (from mothers and boyfriends), they feel neither "guilty" nor "obligated." Held in a complex web of reciprocal relations, they contribute, easily assured that "what goes around comes around." They echo the writings of Robinson and Ward:

> Nobles' conception of "the extended self" is seen in the value structure of many black families. Willie (1985) argues that many African American children are encouraged to employ their own personal achievements as a means to resist racism. The importance of hard work and communalism is viewed threefold: as a personal responsibility, as an intergenerational commitment to family, and as a tie to the larger collective. A resistant strategy of liberation, in keeping with African American traditional values, ties individual achievement to collective struggle. We maintain that in the service of personal and cultural liberation, African American adolescent girls must resist an individualism that sees the self as disconnected from others in the black community and, as it is culturally and psychologically dysfunctional, she must resist those who might advocate her isolation and separation from traditional African American cultural practices, values and beliefs. (Robinson and Ward 1991, 9)

The elite women, in contrast, deployed a language of bodily integrity, patrolled borders, social charity, obligation, and guilt. As for any favors of gifts or time from mothers and boyfriends, they felt a need to "pay back." Bearing often quite deeply hostile feelings toward their mothers, they nevertheless both feel obligated to repay her sacrifices by fulfilling her expectations, often a professional career in return for a gigantic tuition bill. As vigilantly, they monitor their social and bodily boundaries for what and how much comes in and leaves—food, drink, drugs, exercise, money, sacrifices, and gifts. And they give back to community in the form of "charity." They live their connections almost contractually.

Related to these contrasting forms of body-in-relation, these two groups performed quite differently within our public talk. That is, they parted sharply in terms of how they hibernated in privacy and how they revealed themselves through public talk. In numerous instances the white and Korean teens deferred to a cultured privacy in which "personal problems" were rarely aired, "personal grievances" were typically suffocated, "personal disagreements" were usually revealed "behind our backs." They often withheld juicy details of life, safe only in diaries or other private writings. Their bodies absorbed, carried, and embodied their "private troubles." These elite girls made it quite clear that their strategies for survival were interior, personal, and usually not shared. The costs of "privilege," as they revealed them, were in the internalizing, personalizing, and depoliticizing of gender dilemmas. Research makes evident these costs in anorexia, bulimia, depression, "talking behind each other's back," and even the "secrets" of rape or abuse survival stories. Socialized out of using public talk to practice varied forms of womanhood, while these women recognized collective gender power struggles, they retreated from women, and they embodied their resistance alone, through feminist individualism.

The individualism from which modern feminism was born has much to answer for but much in which to take pride. Individualism has decisively repudiated previous notions of hierarchy and particularism to declare the possibility of freedom for all. In so doing, it transformed slavery from one unfree condition among many into freedom's antithesis—thereby insisting that the subordination of one person to any other is morally and politically unacceptable. But the gradual extension of individualism and the gradual abolition of the remaining forms of social and political bondage have come trailing after two dangerous notions: that individual freedom could—indeed must—be absolute, and that social role and personal identity must be coterminous.

Following the principles of individualism, modern Western societies have determined that the persistence of slavery in any form violates the fundamental principle of a just society. But in grounding the justification in absolute individual right, they have unleashed the specter of a radical individualism that overrides the claims of society itself. To the extent that feminism, like antislavery, has espoused those individualistic principles, it has condemned itself to the dead ends toward which individualism is now plunging. (Fox-Genovese 1991, 240–41)

In contrast, the African-American women were publicly playful as well as nasty to each other and about others—"because we love each other." Shermika told wonderful, vivid, outrageous tales, in part to "test" what the others would do, including, we believe, testing whether she was being classified as exotic/sexualized/Other/specimen for the white women and the evening's analysis. Their school context made their bodies a matter of public talk, exposed.

> *Shermika:* I don't like my rear end. Guys are so ignorant. "Look at all that cake."
> *Pat:* Maybe it's their problem.
> *Shermika:* No, it *is* my problem. Because you see my butt before you see me.

Public talk could be aggression as well:

> *Damalleaux:* I wouldn't talk to him [a stranger] and he got mad.
> *Shermika:* I hate when they constantly talk to you and they get closer and closer.

The African-American women used and experienced conversation, public disagreements, pleasures, and verbal badgerings as ways to "try on" varied ways to be women.

During the second evening, the four young women discovered and explored these differences through the metaphor of the "private" and "public" schools they attend.

> *Janet:* I've got a question. At [your school, Shermika], are there kids who are like by themselves? Loners . . . who don't sit with anyone else? . . . who nobody wants to sit with?
> *Shermika:* Yeah, but they can't because there's somebody always messin' with 'em, tryin' to get 'em to do something. So if they wanted to be by themselves they couldn't.

*   *   *

> *Janet:* At our school it's so easy to get shut out when you're by yourself.
> *Sophie:* You just kind of—disappear.

*   *   *

Janet: They don't say it [criticism or insult] in front of your face.

Sophie: You insult someone by not considering them. . . . You don't consider their existence . . .

Shermika: Sometimes people need you to tell them how you feel . . .

Janet: . . . for the most part when I'm mad at someone I don't say it to them.

Sophie: Only one on one. You don't say it to them in front of others unless you're joking. It's more private.

Shermika: But if you say it *to* the person, you avoid fights. . . . If they hear you saying it behind they back, they wanna fight.

The four pursued this discovered difference between the private and the public school.

Shermika: Ain't nothin private at my school. If someone got gonorrhea, everyone knows it.

Sophie: Everything's private at my school.

Janet: 'Cause nobody really cares about each other at our school . . .

Shermika: In our school, when I found out I had cancer, I heard about it on the loudspeaker. And everybody come and offer me help. When you're havin' problems in our school, people talk. That's why they're more mature at my school—excuse me. Say somebody poor, need name-brand sneaks, they'll put they money together and give 'em some sneaks. And teachers do that too, if someone need food.

Sophie: We like to pretend that we're good to the neighborhood and socially conscious.

Over time, we came to see that the "facts" of these young women's lives were neither what we had invited them to reveal in our conversations, nor what they were giving us. Rather, we were gathering their interpretations of their lives, interpretations that were roaming within culture and class.

On Good and Bad Girls: Prospects for Feminism

I consider myself a bad girl, but in a good sorta way.

—Shermika

Feminist scholars as distinct as Valerie Walkerdine (1984), Carol Gilligan (1990), and Nancy Lesko (1988) have written about polarizations of good girls and bad ones—that is, those who resist, submit, or are split on the cultural script of femininity. Gilligan's recent essay "Joining the Resistance" (1990) argues that at the outset of adolescence, young women experience a severing of insider from outsider knowledge, such that "insider knowledge may be washed away." Gilligan and her colleagues have found that young women at early adolescence begin to submerge their interior knowledge, increasingly relying on "I don't know" to answer questions about self. They say "I don't know" at a rate amazingly greater the older they get—an average of twice at age seven, twenty-one times at age twelve, and sixty-seven times at age thirteen. Gilligan and colleagues conclude: "If girls' knowledge of reality is politically dangerous, it is both psychologically and politically dangerous for girls not to know . . . or to render themselves innocent by disconnecting from their bodies, their representations of experience and desire" (33).

Nancy Lesko (1988) has written a compelling ethnography of gendered adolescents' lives inside a Catholic high school, where she unpacks a "curriculum of the body" mediated by class distinctions. In this school, female delinquency was sexualized and embodied. The genders segregated in high school by class and created categories of behaviors to hang onto within these class groups. The rich and popular girls at her school paraded popular fashions, spoke in controlled voices, muted their opinions, and worked hard at being "nice." If they pushed the boundaries of wardrobe, it was always in the direction of fashion, not "promiscuity." The "burnouts," in contrast, were young women who fashioned their behaviors through smoking and directness. They rejected compulsions toward being "nice" and excelled at being "blunt." Refusing to bifurcate their personal opinions and their public stances, they challenged docility and earned reputations as "loose" and "hard" (like Leslie Roman's [1988] working class women, who displayed physicality and sexual embodiment). Social class, then, provided the contours within which a curriculum of the body had its meaning displayed, intensifying within gender oppositions and undermining possibilities for female solidarity.

Departing somewhat from Gilligan and Lesko, Walkerdine (1984) sees adolescence for young women as not a moment to *bury* the questioning female self, but a time in which young women must negotiate their multiple selves, through struggles of heterosexuality and critiques of gender, race, and class arrangements. In an analysis of popular texts read by adolescent women, Walkerdine finds that "heroines are never angry; most project anger onto others and suppress it in self, yielding the active production of passivity" (182). She asks readers to consider the notion that "good girls are not always good," and asks, "[but] when and how is their badness lived?" Interested in the splitting of goodness and badness, we, like Walkerdine, asked these young women that question. When Shermika said, "I consider myself a bad girl, but in a good sorta way," she was positioning herself in our collectively made feminist context where good girls follow femininity rules, and bad girls don't. This good kind of bad girl plays by male rules of friendship, risk, danger, and initiative.

Within five minutes of our first meeting, the four girls discovered they all liked football—*playing* football—and they eagerly described the joys of running, catching the ball, tackling, and being tackled. Only Janet drew the line at being tackled, citing a "three-hundred-pound boy" in her neighborhood. As an explanation for their preferred identities as "one of the guys," they suggested that football exemplifies "masculine" values of gamesmanship. It is a game with rules and space for spontaneous physicality, with teamwork and individual aggression in rule-bound balance, and with maximum bodily access to others of both sexes, without fear about sexual reputation or reproductive consequences. When asked why they trust and like boys over girls, they cited boys' risk-taking as making them more fun, their ability to "be more honest" and not backstab and to "be more accepting": "You can tell when a guy's lyin'." "First of all they won't even notice what you're wearing and they won't bust on you." Shermika bragged that all of her boyfriends said they valued her most as a friend, not merely a girlfriend. The behavior, clothing, and values associated with such identification with boys and sports suggests both a flight from the femininity they collectively described as "wearing pink," "being prissy," "bein' Barbie," and "reinforcing guys all the time"—*and* an association of masculinity with fairness (vs. cattiness), honesty (vs. backstabbing), strength (vs. prissiness, a vulnerability whether feigned or real), initiative (vs. deference or reactionary comments), and integrity (vs. the self-doubt and conflicting loyalties dividing girls). The four's risk-taking behaviors—driving fast, sneaking out at night—reinforced identities as "one of the guys." Such are the Bad Girls.

But being "one of the guys" makes for a contradictory position of self versus "other girls." Sophie mocked the femininity of good girls at its worst when she said dismissively, "You should sit and wait in your little crystal palace" rather than "chase after guys." This constructed difference between self (the good kind of bad girl) and other girls (the bad kind of good girl) is an essential contradiction of identity that all four girls were struggling with. Valerie Hey, in her study of adolescent female friendships, calls this "deficit dumping": "all the 'bad' bits of femininity, social and sexual competitiveness, placed upon the 'other,'" that is, other girls (1987, 421). Sophie, like the girls in Hey's study, excepted her best friend along with herself from the generality of femininity: "It's different, though, with best friends. I mean like girls in general." Shermika, likewise, excepted Damalleaux when Michelle asked whether *no* other girls were to be trusted. "She a boy," Shermika countered, raising a puzzled laugh. But when Shermika's boyfriend likened her to a bodybuilder when she was running track, she felt ashamed to "feel like a boy . . . like a muscle man."

Sophie confessed ruefully, "I'm certainly no bad girl," and Janet taunted her, "Sophie has a little halo." Certainly Sophie's good grades, good works, politeness, friendliness, and trustworthiness were acceptably "good" to both adults and peers, even if the popular crowd had not approved or welcomed her. "I don't want that image," Sophie told Janet about the halo. Goody-goodyism would be unacceptable to *all* peers. Good-*girl*ism—Sophie's uncomfortable state—seems good for her conscience and adult approval but bad for approval by the popular set, whose upper-class drink- and drug-induced party flirtations and sexual liaisons Sophie disapproves of.

The meaning of Sophie's good girl image is, however, quite class-specific, as Mary Evans describes in her analysis of middle-class schooling, *A Good School*:

> as far as possible a 'good' girl did not have an appearance. What she had was a correct uniform, which gave the world the correct message about her—that is, that she was a well-behaved, sensible person who could be trusted not to wish to attract attention to herself by an unusual, let alone a fashionable, appearance. (1991, 30–31)

Signaling her acceptance of the career-class uniform, Sophie could not also signal her interest in boys. Indeed, she walked away from her body, except at an athletic court. "Other girls" dressed either "schleppy" (the androgynous or indifferent look) or "provocative." Sophie's neat, "sporty" look—tights and a lean body made her miniskirt look more athletic than hooker-inspired—seems designed to be comfortable and competent as one of the guys while ever so casually gesturing toward femininity (no dykey trousers). Her dress is designed to bridge the contradiction of middle-class education and femininity, as Evans describes it in her own schooling in the 1950s:

> To be a successful [prep] school girl involved, therefore, absorbing two specific (but conflicting) identities. First, that of the androgynous middleclass person who is academically successful in an academic world that is apparently gender blind. Second, that of the well-behaved middleclass woman who knows how to defer to and respect the authority of men. (1991, 23)

Over the course of history, feminism has altered these young women's terms of deference to men, their ability to name sexism and resist. But their feminism does not seem to have revised the categories of gender or body at all. What seems intact from the 1950s are their terms of respect for the authority of men as superior and normal forms of human being. What seems distinct in the 1990s is that these young women think they have a right to be young men too.

Damalleaux's example of her own good-girlism shares some of Sophie's dilemma of being a good student at the expense of peer popularity. But Damalleaux resolved this tension differently, as Signithia Fordham (1988) would argue is likely to happen among academically talented, low-income African-American students:

> *Damalleaux:* I used to be a straight-A girl and now I'm down to B's and C's. I used to be so good, it's a shame . . .
>
> *Pat:* What changed?
>
> *Damalleaux:* I couldn't help it any more. . . . When I got straight A's they'd call me a nerd and things. But I'd be happy because my mother would give me anything I want for it. . . . Mom [would say to teasing brothers], "Leave my first girl alone!" . . . [Then] I got around the wrong people, I don't study so much . . .
>
> *Pat:* Is it uncool to be a girl and get good grades?
>
> *Damalleaux:* Yes it is. . . . I'll do my work and they'll say "Smarty Pants! Smarty Pants!"

Janet gave an example of "acting stupid" with peers, which seemed to be her manner of flirtation. Sophie pointed out that Janet could afford to because everyone already knew she was smart. Sophie clearly felt more trapped by being smart and a good girl.

Girls can be good, bad or—best of all—they can be boys. This version of individualized resistance, or feminism, reflects a retreat from the collective politics of gender, and from other women, and an advance into the embattled scene of gender politics—alone, and against boys, in order to become one of them.

On Closings, or, The End of the Second Pizza

We heard these four women struggling between the discourses of feminism and adolescence. Perhaps *struggling* is even too strong a word. They hungered for a strong version of individualistic, "gender-free" adolescence and had rejected that which had been deemed traditionally feminine, aping instead that which had been deemed traditionally masculine. Delighted to swear, spit, tell off-color jokes, wear hats, and trash other girls, they were critical of individual boys, nasty about most girls, rarely challenging of the sex/gender system and ecstatic, for the most part, to be engaged as friends and lovers with young men. But we also heard their feminism in their collective refusal to comply with male demands, their wish for women friends to trust, their expectations for equality and search for respect, their deep ambivalence about being "independent of a man" and yet in partnership with one, and their strong yearnings to read, write, and talk more about women's experiences among women. They appreciated our creation of a context in which this was possible. "The women of Michelle's place," Shermika called us at the end of one evening, prizing our collectivity by re-using an African-American woman writer's novel title.

> The public terms of the discourse of femininity preclude the expression of deviant views of marriage, motherhood, and the public terms are the only ones to which girls have access. Part of the task of feminist work with girls is thus, I would suggest, giving girls terms in which to express their experiential knowledge, rather than having to fall back into the stereotyped expressions of normatively defined

femininity in order to say anything at all about areas of life which vitally concern them. (Hudson 1984, 52)

Through critical and collaborative group interview, we evolved a form of conversation with these four young women that allowed us to engage in what we might consider collective consciousness work, as a form of feminist methodology. Our talks became an opportunity to "try on" ways of being women, struggling through power, gender, culture, and class.

With Donna Haraway's (1989) notion of "partial vision" firmly in mind, we realized that in our talk, no one of us told the whole truth. We all occluded the "truth" in cultured ways. The conversation was playful and filled with the mobile positionings of all of us women. While we each imported gender, race, class, culture, age, and bodies to our talk, we collectively created an ideological dressing room in which the six of us could undress a little, try things on, exchange, rehearse, trade, and critique. Among the six of us we were able to lift up what had become "personal stories," raise questions, try on other viewpoints, and re-see our stories as political narratives.

As a critique of the excesses of individualism, feminism potentially contributes to a new conception of community—of the relation between the freedom of individuals and the needs of society. The realization of that potential lies not in the repudiation of difference but in a new understanding of its equitable social consequences. (Fox-Genovese 1991, 256)

We could recount together how alone and frightened we have each felt as we have walked, and are watched, down city streets; how our skin tightens when we hear men comment aloud on our bodies; how we smart inside with pain when we learn that other women define themselves as "good women" by contrasting themselves with our feminist politics; how we fetishize those body parts that have betrayed us with their imperfection. Within the safety of warm listening and caring, yet critical, talk, we attached each of these "secret" feelings to political spaces defined by culture, class, and gender contours of our daily lives. This method moved us, critically and collectively, from pain to passion to politics, prying open the ideologies of individualism, privacy, and loyalty that had sequestered our personal stories.

After our last dinner, stuffed and giggly, tired but still wanting just one more round of conversation, we—Pat and Michelle—realized that the four young women were getting ready to drive away. Together and without us. Before, Pat had driven Shermika and Damalleaux to Michelle's and back home. But now they were leaving us behind. Stunned, we looked at each other, feeling abandoned. We thought we were concerned about their safety. Four young women in a car could meet dangers just outside the borders of Michelle's block.

We turned to each other, realizing that even our abandonment was metaphoric, and political. These four young women were weaving the next generation of feminist politics, which meant, in part, leaving us. We comforted ourselves by recognizing that our conversations had perhaps enabled this work. No doubt, individual interviews with each of the four would have produced an essay chronicling the dangers of femininity— eating disorders, heterosexual traumas, perhaps some abuse or abortion stories; that is, deeply individualized, depoliticized, and atomized tales of "things that have happened to me as an adolescent female." What happened among us, instead, was that a set of connections was forged— between personal experiences and political structures, across cultures, classes, and politics, and within an invented space, cramped between the discourses of a rejected femininity, an individualized adolescence, and a collective feminism as resistance.

> Resistance is that struggle we can most easily grasp. Even the most subjected person has moments of rage and resentment so intense that they respond, they act against. There is an inner uprising that leads to rebellion, however short-lived. It may be only momentary, but it takes place. That space within oneself where resistance is possible remains: It is different then to talk about becoming subjects. That process emerges as one comes to understand how structures of domination work in one's own life, as one develops critical thinking and critical consciousness, as one invents new alternative habits of being and resists from that marginal space of difference inwardly defined. (hooks 1990, 15)

In our finest post-pizza moment, we—Pat and Michelle—realized that as these women drove off, they were inventing their own feminist legacy, filled with passions, questions, differences, and pains. We were delighted that we had helped to challenge four young women's versions of individualistic feminism without solidarity by doing the consciousness work of our generation. We taught, and relearned, feminism as dialectical and historical discourse about experience and its interpretation, a collective reframing of private confessions. As we yelled, "Go straight home!" to their moving car, for a moment we felt like the world was in very good hands.

NOTES

Many thanks to Elizabeth Sayre for her patient assistance.

1. And, although not at the table, it is still another thing to construct a sense of womanhood by and for women whose disabilities socially and sexually "neuter" them, propelling them out of any presumed relation with men and depriving them of the many burdens of being female, including the privileges that come with those burdens, in experiences such as sexual harassment, motherhood, sexuality, having others rely on you, etc. Disabled women's identities are rarely positioned under, against, or with men's. As Kathryn Corbett, Adrienne Asch and Michelle Fine, Harilyn Rousso, and others have written (Asch & Fine 1988), it is no blessing for the culture to presume that because you are disabled, you are not female; not worth whistling at, not able to love an adult man or woman; not capable of raising a child; not beautiful enough to be employed in a public space.

Passions, Politics, and Power: Feminist Research Possibilities

Michelle Fine

Foreplay

The essays in this volume have served as a sampling of feminist psychologies. They have developed across the text largely as my own work developed, moving from relatively detached "collecting" of women's embodied stories as in "Sexuality, Schooling, and Adolescent Females," "Presence of Mind in the Absence of Body," "Coping with Rape," and "Beyond Pedestals," to a "living" essay such as "Over Dinner," in which Pat Macpherson and I co-constructed our conversations, as critics, participants, and interpreters of a two-generation women's collective. Across these essays, my narrative stance has grown more self-consciously activist and more textually embedded.

This final essay, "Passions, Politics, and Power," presses hard on the question of stances—where do feminist psychologists situate ourselves within the texts we produce? In the first half of the essay, I articulate three possible stances—ventriloquy, voices, and activism—and invite feminist researchers to commit to activism, particularly today when so many in the academy have drifted to the conservative Right; the Supreme Court has decided that free speech about abortion and reproductive freedoms *will* be curtailed in public settings; as scholarships and financial aid have been cut; and as multiculturalism and feminism are being framed as violations of white men's freedom of speech. It seems to me that feminist researchers have little choice and much responsibility to shape our research through an activist stance, in collaboration with community-based political women. Not only are we among the few who are free and legitimated to speak, but feminist research itself is most alive and intellectually rich when nested inside a movement. As Sandra Harding has written:

> [F]eminist politics is not just a tolerable companion of feminist research but a necessary condition for generating less partial and perverse descriptions and explanations. In a socially stratified society, the objectivity of the results of research is increased by political activism by and on behalf of oppressed, exploited and dominated groups. Only through such struggles can we begin to see beneath the appearances created by an unjust social order to the reality of how this social order is in fact constructed and maintained. (1987, 127)

If feminist researchers do not take critical, activist, and open stances on our own work, then we collude in reproducing social silences through the social sciences. This final essay worries aloud about the history of feminist psychology, imagines vividly its future, and invents political stances we could indulge in passionately as activist feminist psychologists.

Passions Muffled

Through the 1980s and into the 1990s, feminist psychologists have been chatting busily in the kitchen of the social sciences, delighted by the vivid and disruptive possibilities of our scholarship on women's lives and yet as voyeurs, primarily, to the deep and radical transformations washing through the humanities and social sciences. As we sit, we worry, collectively and alone, about how best to unleash ourselves from our central contradiction—being research psychologists and activist feminists (Crawford and Gentry 1989; Crawford and Marecek 1989a, 1989b; Fine and Gordon 1989; Flax 1990; Hare-Mustin and Marecek 1990a, 1990b; Kahn and Yoder 1990; Lykes and Stewart 1986; Morawski 1990; Parlee 1990; Payton 1984; Russo 1984; Stewart and Healy 1989; Unger 1990; Wittig 1985). Within the discipline of psychology, we document at once the depths of violence and discrimination embedded in the lives of women (Amaro 1989; Belle 1990; Blackman 1989; Brown 1987; Gilkes 1988; Golden 1987; Lykes 1989; Smith 1987) and the complex maneuvers by which women deny such oppression (Childers and hooks 1990; Crosby et al. 1989; Gilligan 1990; Majors et al. 1990; Taylor, Wood and Lichtman

1983). Harvesting substantial evidence of gender, race/ethnic, class disability, and sexuality based oppression, we also know how meticulously women take care, make nice, and rarely, in our research, express outrage or critique power embedded in the gendered politics of their lives (Brodkey and Fine 1988).

> In failing adequately to conceptualize and explore the subject of power, feminist psychology, then, reflects *psychology's* failings. But it also, I think reflects *feminism's*. . . . There is a profound ambivalence about power within feminist theory. On the one hand, feminists have often relied upon a characterization of power as something evil, dangerous and corrupting—a male activity or preoccupation with control and domination which results in violence, rape, the stockpiling of nuclear weapons and the destruction of the planet. "Power" here clearly carries negative connotations: it is not something any self-respecting feminist would want to get involved with. (Kitzinger 1991, 113)

We, as feminist psychologists, report women's stories, girdled in by "professional" notions of objectivity and positivism, denuding the role of power in their stories and in their telling. Like the women we study, we smuggle our knowledge of social injustice into a discourse of science which fundamentally contains, and painfully undermines, the powerful politics of feminism. As is often the case with moments of *social containment*, women within psychology, and feminists in particular, carry weighty evidence for a passionately disruptive transformation of the discipline. And yet we also carry domesticating responsibilities to keep this social science dispassionately detached. Valerie Walkerdine narrates this problem when she writes,

> I want . . . to demonstrate that women, positioned as teachers, mothers, carers and caring professionals . . . are held absolutely necessary for the moral order: they are responsible. This responsibility places women as at once safe, yet potentially dangerous (the bad mother). It places them as responsible for ensuring the possibility of democracy, and yet as deeply conservative. . . . My argument is that, quite simply, women of all classes have been placed as guardians of an order from which it is difficult to escape. (1986, 63)

Feminist psychologists have sat, and continue to sit, as guardians of this political and intellectual order from which it is most difficult to escape or survive with integrity. It is within this order that we have made, and continue to make, decisions about how explicitly feminist politics should (and should not) pepper our texts. That is, how deeply we tame the shrew, in the language of "neutrality" and "science." This essay is an attempt to unravel our feminist psychological contradiction—the stances we do and don't take, as feminists, within the narratives we construct as psychologists (Aronowitz 1988).

Containing the Contradiction

Mainstream psychology, perhaps more than any of the other social sciences, stubbornly refuses to interrogate how researchers create our texts (see Becker 1986; Brodkey 1988; Reinharz 1988; Rosaldo 1989; Semin and Gergen 1990). It is typically presumed that psychological theories and methods simply neutralize personal and political influences. When psychologists write about "laws" of human behavior, our political stances seemingly evaporate. That we are human inventors of some questions and repressors of others, shapers of the very contexts we study, coparticipants in our interviews, interpreters of others' stories and narrators of our own, are somehow rendered irrelevant to the texts we publish.

Donna Haraway caricatures this epistemological fetish with detachment as a "God trick . . . that mode of seeing that pretends to offer a vision that is from everywhere and nowhere, equally and fully" (1988, 584). Such narrative removal seeks to front universal truths while denying the privileges, interests, and politics of researchers. With Haraway and Sandra Harding (1986), feminist scholars have interrupted, across the academy and in their respective disciplines, refusing containment, and asking how feminist politics can and do play, explicitly and subversively, in our intellectual lives.

Feminist psychologists have been somewhat timid to engage in this debate. Clearly, where we have gained the most ground is in the rethinking of our relationships with "subjects" and of the politics that gather between us. British psychologist Sue Wilkinson characterizes feminist research in the following way:

First, there is its reflexive and self-reflective quality . . . an emphasis on the centrality of female experience directly implies its corollary: "ourselves as our own sources." Similarly, du Bois has emphasized the way in which the knower is part of the matrix of what is known; and Reinharz has required the researcher to ask her/himself how s/he has grown or changed in the process of research.

Second, the relationship between the researcher and the researched will evidently be very different from that of the traditional "experimenter" and "subject." In feminist research, at the very least, both are to be regarded as having the same status: as participants or collaborators in the same enterprise. (1986, 13)

Like Wilkinson, Leonore Tiefer (1987) invites feminist psychologists to adopt "a collaborative stance, using participants' subjective perceptions to enrich objective measurements and planning research to benefit the participants as well as the researchers." Indeed, she invites researchers to design our work toward "improv[ing] the situation of women in the world" (1987, 24).

And, as an early advocate of advocacy-based research, Carolyn Payton has long prodded psychologists about the bankruptcy of our "professional" social commitments. Almost ten years ago, she wrote:

Please keep in mind that almost two decades ago the APA [American Psychological Association] grappled with the question of the propriety of psychologists as a group advocating social change or taking part in political advocacy, and a process for dealing with such matters are suggested. Yet, here we are in 1983 still denying that we have any responsibility for or obligation to the society in which we live. We behave as if, along with study in this discipline, we inherit a dispensation from considering all matters concerning social consciousness barring those related to guild issues (1984, 392).

Wilkinson, Tiefer, and Payton, like feminist scholars across disciplines, situate themselves proudly atop a basic assumption that all research projects are political and that researchers who represent themselves as detached only camouflage their deepest, most privileged interests (Rosaldo 1989).

But, if feminist research is directed toward social transformations and if presumptions of "neutrality" serve primarily to laminate deeply conservative interests of social scientists, then feminist psychologists sit on a central dilemma. That dilemma concerns the self-conscious role our politics can play as we pursue our intellectual work. To this dilemma,

Donna Haraway offers us *passionate detachment* through which she believes: "we are bound to seek perspectives from those points of view which can never be known in advance, that promise something quite extraordinary, that is, knowledge potential for constructing worlds less organized by axes of domination" (1988, 585). Feminist psychologists are today beginning to seek such perspectives and ask intriguing questions about the disruptive possibilities of our research. These questions shape this essay.

Carving a Space: Feminist Psychologists Refuse to Guard the Order

Within feminist psychology, we have begun to witness the deep immersion of our scholarship into the waters of feminist politics. Nancy Henley (1989) has studied not the neutrality of masculine generic pronouns but their documentable damage to girls and women. Faye Crosby researches not women's access to "equal opportunity" but women's refusal to acknowledge personal discrimination, "imag[ing] ostrich-like a personal exemption from the rule of generalized sex bias" (Crosby et al. 1989). Brinton Lykes (1989) gathers compelling, cross-cultural stories of resistance narrated by Guatemalan women refugees. Althea Smith and Abby Stewart (1983) investigate not the individual personalities of women of color but, instead, construct theoretical arguments about the dense webbing of sexism and racism as structural forces seeping within the minds and bodies of African-American women. Hortensia Amaro not only documents women's vulnerability to and experiences with AIDS but argues for a particular politic of research in which "clinicians and policy makers alike have the responsibility to take a leadership role in the development of medical care and policies related to HIV testing and to ensure that the application of policies do not undermine women's reproductive rights" (1989, 44).

And, so, feminist psychologists have meandered deeply and explicitly into political waters. But, now, in the midst of a rapid and expansive rise of the New Right on our campuses, in the broader culture and at the federal funding agencies, we have to interrogate the internal politics of this work. Rich with powerful stories of injustice and strengths, we live within a disciplinary heritage that reifies not only denuded notions of objectivity, dispassion, and researcher neutrality but also holds psychological methods to be value-free, social contexts to be essentially distracting, and the properties of individuals to be the basis for what psychologists need to study (see Mishler 1979; Stewart and Healy 1986).

Knowing what we know and sitting where we sit, the early 1990s offers a perfect time to reflect, from within feminist psychologies, on the political stances that we can, do, don't, won't, and must take with respect to our work; on the transgressions we are and are not willing to advance within the conversations of feminist psychology; and on the epistemological, methodological, and narrative consequences that unfold once these stances are assumed. This essay traces three such stances on the politics of research. All of these stances can be found within the academy, all comingle on occasion, and all affect our work deeply.

Reflecting on Stances

This essay presumes that all research psychologists, like all other social scientists, choose from among a set of political stances and epistemologies. Most psychologists deny these choices within veils of "objectivity," describing behaviors, attitudes, and preferences as if these descriptions were static and immutable, "out there," and unconnected to political contexts, and representing these texts as if they were constructed without authority. Such texts typically neglect to discuss why one research question or interpretation prevailed over others or why this researcher selected this set of questions over others. Such texts render oblique the ways in which we, as researchers, construct our analyses and narratives. Indeed, these texts are written as if researchers were simply vehicles for transmission, with no voices of their own. Such researchers position themselves as ventriloquists (Rosaldo 1989).

Other researchers, in their texts, assume a dis-stance, importing to their work the voices of Discarded Others, who offer daily or local meanings in contrast with hegemonic discourses and practices. With voices as the vehicles for social representation, these researchers typically claim little position for self.

Finally, some researchers position themselves self-consciously, as participatory activists. Their work seeks to unearth, disrupt, and transform existing institutional arrangements. Here the researcher's stance frames the texts produced and carves out the space in which intellectual surprises surface. These writers position themselves as political and inter-rogating, fully explicit about their original positions and where their research has taken them.

I paint these three stances—ventriloquy, voices, and activism—that feminist researchers can take in our research. It seems crucial in the 1990s that social researchers who seek to be explicitly political (e.g., feminists, African Americans, poststructuralists, neo-Marxists), as well as those who refuse to so acknowledge, consider the kinds of political decisions we have always made and continue to make in, through, and with our research.

Ventriloquy

> Once upon a time, the introduction of writings of women and people of color were called politicizing the curriculum. Only *we* had politics (and its nasty little mate, ideology), whereas *they* had standards.
> —Lillian Robinson, "What Culture Should Mean" (1989, 76)

Ventriloquy relies upon Haraway's God trick. The author tells Truth, has no gender, race, class, or stance. A condition of truth telling is anonymity, and so ventriloquy. Dramatizing ventriloquy as an academic stance, I offer a snip of institutional biography from an institution with which I've had some intimacy, the University of Pennsylvania.

The Scene
In 1985, the University of Pennsylvania denied tenure to Dr. Rosalie Tung, then associate professor at the Wharton School of Business. While Wharton justified the decision to not tenure Tung on the grounds that the Wharton School was allegedly not interested in China related research, Tung maintained that her department chairman had sexually harassed her and that, after she insisted on a professional and not sexual relationship, he submitted a negative letter to the university's Personnel Committee, adversely influencing her tenure decision.

Tung brought the case to the Equal Employment Opportunity Commission (EEOC), which undertook an investigation, requesting documents from Penn. When the university refused to provide these documents, the commission subpoenaed for Tung's tenure review file as well as those of the five male faculty members who had been tenured just prior to Tung. Penn argued the need to exclude all "confidential peer review information" and failed to provide: (1) confidential letters written by Tung's evaluators; (2) the department chairman's letter of evaluation; (3) documents reflecting the internal deliberations of faculty committees considering applications for tenure; and (4) comparable portions of the tenure review of the five males. The commission denied the university's application for these exclusions.

The case made its way to the Supreme Court. Four years after denial of tenure, in a 9–0 vote, the Supreme Court found against Penn in a decision in which the justices wrote:

> We readily agree with the petitioner regarding that universities and colleges play significant roles in American society. Nor need we question, at this point, petitioner's assertion that confidentiality is important to the proper functioning of the peer review process under which many academic institutions operate. The costs that ensue from this disclosure, however, constitute only one side of the balance. As Congress has recognized, the costs associated with racial and sexual discrimination in institutions of higher learning are very substantial. . . . disclosure of peer review material will be necessary in order for the Commission to determine whether illegal discrimination has taken place. Indeed, if there is a "smoking gun" to be found that demonstrates discrimination in tenure decisions, it is likely to be tucked away in peer review files. (*University of Penn. v. EEOC*, 58 U.S.L.W. 4096 [1990])

Penn sought relief on the basis of that well-known precedential exemption for questions of confidentiality, *United States of America v. Nixon*, with Penn positioning itself with Nixon. Characterizing its First Amendment claim as one of "academic freedom," Penn argued that tenure-related evaluations have historically been written by scholars who have been provided with assurances of confidentiality. Such provisions of confidentiality, they argued, could enable evaluators to be candid and institutions to make tenure decisions on the basis of "valid academic criteria." Disclosure of documents or names, Penn continued, would undermine the existing process of awarding tenure and instigate a "chilling effect" on candid evaluations and discussions of candidates. They wrote:

This will work to the detriment of universities, as less qualified persons achieve tenure causing the quality of instruction and scholarship to decline ... and also will result in divisiveness and tension, placing strain on faculty relations and impairing the free interchange of ideas that is a hallmark of academic freedom. (*University of Penn. v. EEOC*, 58 U.S.L.W. 4093 [1990] [No. 88-493])

To which the justices responded:

Although it is possible that some evaluations may become less candid as the possibility of disclosure increases, others may simply ground their evaluations in special examples as illustrations in order to deflect potential claims of bias or unfairness. Not all academics will hesitate to stand up and be counted when they evaluate their peers. (58 U.S.L.W. 4097 [1990])

Following the Supreme Court decision, Penn submitted to the EEOC a set of redacted documents from the Tung file in which all names and identifiers were removed from the texts. Penn maintained that, if faculty were forced to commit their names to their judgments, they would cower from "true" evaluations. The university took the terrifying position that only when authorship is obscured will truth prevail among academics.

Penn spoke for (but not with) its faculty. The position taken reminded many of Donna Haraway's God trick, in which researchers pronounce truths while whiting out their own authority, so as to be unlocatable and irresponsible. Penn's position vis-à-vis the Supreme Court embodies institutionally researchers' refusal to acknowledge their personal involvements as they construct the very worlds we write about.

Ventriloquy is perhaps most bold when a university mandates the whiting out of authorship but can be found in all research narratives in which researchers' privileges and interests are camouflaged. Ventriloquy means never having to say "I" in the text (Clark 1990)—treating subjects as objects, while calling them subjects. And ventriloquy requires the denial of all politics in the very political work of social research (see also *Noble v. Massachusetts Institute of Technology* 1986).

In the aftermath of this Supreme Court decision, it becomes clear why the academy is so distressed when feminists, African-Americanists, and others on the Left write and speak through critical intellectual discourses. We autograph them, specify authors, knowers, and the conditions for our admittedly very partial and transitory perspectives. By refusing to ventriloquize, we reveal the everyday practices of academic ventriloquy.

Voices

It's easy to be glib about the ventriloquism of researchers who seek asylum behind anonymous texts or texts in which they deny their authorial subjectivities. Somewhat closer to home, however, is a critical analysis of the ways in which scholars—critical ethnographers, in particular—have used voices to accomplish a subtler form of ventriloquism. Within such texts, while researchers appear to let the Other speak, just under the covers of those marginal—if now "liberated" voices—we hide, unproblematical. As Shulamitz Reinharz has written:

> By dealing in voices, we are affecting power relations. To listen to people is to empower them. But if you want to hear it, you have to go hear it, in their space, or in a safe space. Before you can expect to hear anything worth hearing, you have to examine the *power dynamics of the space and the social actors.*
>
> Second, you have to be the person someone else can talk to, and you have to be able to create a context where the person can speak and you can listen. That means we have to *study who we are and who we are in relation to those we study.*
>
> Third, you have to be willing to hear what someone is saying, even when it violates your expectations or threatens our interests. In other words, *if you want someone to tell it like it is, you have to hear it like it is.* (1988, 15–16; emphasis added)

Voices offer a qualitative opportunity for scholars interested in generating critical, counterhegemonic analyses of institutional arrangements. But they also offer a decoy. Through such work, many of us have been fortunate. We've collected rich and multisituated voices from adolescents—dropouts in my case, teen parents for others (see Lesko 1988; McDade 1988; Sullivan 1990; Tolman 1990; Willis 1981). When I have spoken with adolescents, particularly low-income adolescents, it's been consistently easy to gather up *their* stories of critique, dissent, contradictory consciousness, and quite vivid counterhegemonic commentary in order to tell *my* story. Low-income adolescents easily criticize their schools, challenge the relation of education credentials to labor market participation, and name the hypocrisies that fuel societal terrors of sexualities (Fine and Zane 1989).

The ease with which such adolescents reflect (somewhat outrageous) versions of my own political stances diminished, however, as my work moved from gathering adolescent voices to soliciting those of adults. The stories of adults—be they teachers, parents, students, or workers—constitute a much more dense mass of critical insights cast, typically, within "ruling class" scripts (Smith 1987). A romantic reliance on these voices—as though they were rarified, innocent words of critique—represents a sophisticated form of ventriloquy, with lots of manipulation required. Unlike with teens, here I have struggled in the shadows of the voices of Others.

The complexities of relying upon adult voices are revealed in an evaluation research project involving low-income mothers of sixth-grade students living in Baltimore. Conducted collaboratively with Dr. Donnie Cook of the University of Maryland, this evaluation focuses on a Parent Empowerment Project developed by an advocacy organization for a randomly selected sample of one hundred fifty sixth-grade students and their parents/guardians. The project initially rested upon a loose set of assumptions:

1. The social alienation of low-income parents/guardians from public schools furthers the academic alienation of low-income students, worsening their academic outcomes.

2. Conversely, the engagement of low-income parents/guardians by public schools will reduce the alienation and increase the engagement of low-income students, enhancing their academic outcomes.

3. Parents/guardians can be encouraged to see their individual problems as grounds for collective action toward transforming schools.

4. The project staff will "empower" but should not presume to "represent" parents/guardians. At the heart of the push for empowerment lies parents'/guardians' ability to represent themselves and their children and not be represented by advocates.

Interviews with parents/guardians illuminate that these early assumptions fit well with organizing theory but poorly with life in contemporary urban low-income America. Simply put, the narratives spoke directly to and authentically from the women's lived conditions, in which they sought desperately to be represented (more than empowered) and in which they often advocated interventions and strategies that the organizers didn't feel they could support. While these women varied much from each other, as a group, they did not carry institutional critique anywhere as "pure" as that of their organizers. With all their suspicions of public education (and they expressed many), they still saw public schooling as the only possible vehicle for their children's futures. For many, the risks of voicing critique were simply seen as too great.

The interviews with these mothers convinced us that, for instance, many of these mothers were extremely (and realistically) hesitant to "raise sand" [make trouble] at school for fear that any complaint would "come back on my child." Some desperately sought a set of educational interventions which many advocates would consider "conservative" (e.g., special education testing, uniforms, or tracking), hoping these interventions could at least provide personal attention and small classes. Indeed, quite a few empathized deeply with teachers and did not see themselves as having anything like adversarial interests. And, finally, most firmly trusted the organizers to represent them and explained that they had neither the resources nor the sense of entitlement to advocate at school about every transgression they witnessed concerning their children's education.

The Baltimore women gave us (researchers and project staff) considerable pause about community organizing in the 1990s, but they also gave us a chance to consider epistemological troubles with voices as a "raw form" of social science evidence. When I was interviewing dropouts and pregnant teens, I could reproduce, almost unaltered, large chunks of their narratives to extract new frames and critique "from below," which could easily be contrasted with authoritative frames gathered "from above." The words of dropouts and teen parents could easily be framed political resistance.

But when I moved to adults—particularly parents/guardians, educators, or other adults who sit between oppressive institutional arrangements and the lives of children—I collected far more nuanced analyses. Neither monolithic voices of critique nor single voices of institutional praise. These women were multiply-situated, and their perspectives were stuffed with social contradictions. The braiding of their commentary was rich but not easily captured with the categories familiar to social analyses. Laced with perspectives of dominant classes, they wanted desperately to believe in public institutions, and, at the same time, they routinely witnessed the institutional inadequacies of these schools and felt absolutely responsible for the lives of children, who lived at levels of substantial economic disadvantage. These women set forth rich, complex, and hard-to-code voices (Condor 1986; Scott 1991).

These interviews forced me to come clean, to reinsert self-consciously my interpretive self into my writings. Researchers cannot write about/ with/through adults' (or adolescents') voices as if they had "said it all." I/we do not sit where they sit. White, privileged, and at Penn, I am simply not sandwiched between the same forms of institutional oppressions they are. I have the luxury of voicing critique risk-free—with few adverse consequences. Even our common status—motherhood—is raced and classed. I can afford private child care, leave my house safely to represent myself and/or my child, and critically comment to any institution I please, without worrying about retaliation for either of us.

As a researcher, I find myself struggling to contextualize why some mothers, some teachers, and some adults say what they say. But I have rarely felt so compelled to contextualize the words of dropouts. My troubles, then, with voices are many. First, social research cast through voices typically involves carving out unacknowledged pieces of narrative evidence that we select, edit, and deploy to border our arguments. In precisely the ways that quantitative social scientists edit before, during (in survey design, sampling, questions asked and not asked), and after (in analytical strategies pursued and not pursued) they collect data, reporting on oral or written narratives involves a delicate tailoring of texts. The problem is not that we tailor but that so few researchers reveal *how* we do this work.

A second problem arises when we rely on individual voices to produce social interpretations of group behavior. This often means repoliticizing perspectives narrated by people who have tried hard to represent themselves as nonpolitical. Our interpretations as researchers often betray the very concerted "individualism" and "apolitical nature" insisted on by narrators (Fox-Genovese 1991). This betrayal may well be essential analytically, but it nevertheless reflects the usually unacknowledged stances of researchers who navigate and camouflage theory through the richness of "native voices."

A third issue involves the popular romancing of the voices of women in poverty. Those of us who work to unearth personal stories tend to privilege contradiction, polyvocality, and subjugated voices. And then we often reproduce these voices as though they were relatively uncontaminated, free of power relations. As Michel Foucault has argued, all voices contain and negotiate power relations. Oppressed informants are neither "free" from nor uncontaminated by dominant perspectives. Indeed, Jill Morawski, in her essay "Impasse in Feminist Thought?" reminds feminists that, as we listen to the voices of Others, our work, as psychologists, is to critically interpret what we hear:

> The current political climate must be met not with anxiety or retrenchment, but by working through the dialectic of oppression to generate alternatives. Mired language and disciplinary boundaries require us to continue resistance and to redouble our interpretive cunning. Likewise, the construction of feminist theory needs reflexive self-consciousness and constant reminders of the force of knowledge structures. We *must not forget why experience became a central focus of feminist analysis, yet we must simultaneously recall how experience itself is structured by the social relations and language of patriarchal culture.* Feminist analysis of experience can account for these conditions while experimenting with even more imaginative and powerful interpretations. (1990; emphasis added)

This critique of voices is by no means advanced to deny the legitimacy of rich interview material or other forms of qualitative data. On the contrary, it is meant for us to worry collectively that when voices—as isolated and innocent moments of experience—organize our research texts, there is often a subtle slide toward romantic, uncritical, and uneven handling and a stable refusal by researchers to explicate our own stances and relations to these voices.

As such, researchers mystify the ways in which we select, use, and exploit voices. That we use them, I am delighted. That we fail to articulate how, how not, and within what limits is a failure of methodology and a flight from our own political responsibilities to tell tough, critical, and confusing stories about the ideological and discursive patterns of inequitable power arrangements.

Activist Feminist Research

The third research stance constitutes activist, feminist research, committed to positioning researchers as self-conscious, critical, and participatory analysts, engaged with but still distinct from our informants. Such research commits to the study of change, the move toward change, and/or is provocative of change (Fine and Vanderslice 1992).

Activist research projects seek to unearth, interrupt, and open new frames for intellectual and political theory and change. Researchers critique what seems natural, spin images of what's possible, and engage in questions of how to move from here to there. In such work, researchers are clearly positioned within the domain of a political question or stance, representing a space within which inquiry is pried open, inviting intellectual surprises to flourish. The text itself is conceived and authored with a critical eye toward "what is," attending seriously to local meanings, changes over time, dominant and suppressed frames, and contextual contradictions. And researchers, within these texts, carry a deep responsibility to assess critically and continually our own as well as informants' changing positions. The strength of feminist activist research lies in its ability to open contradictions within collaborative practices. Essential to an activist stance is that researchers, activists, informants, and other audiences are engaged as critical participants, as we did in *Over Dinner,* in what Donna Haraway calls "power-sensitive conversations."

> Above all, rational knowledge does not pretend to disengagement: to be from everywhere and so nowhere, to be free from interpretation, from being represented, to be fully self-contained or fully formalizable. Rational knowledge is a process of ongoing critical interpretation among "fields" of interpreters and decoders. *Rational knowledge is power-sensitive conversation.* Decoding and transcoding plus translation and criticism; all are necessary. So science becomes the paradigmatic model, not of closure, but of that which is contestable and contested. Science becomes the myth, not of what escapes human agency and responsibility in a realm above the fray, but, rather, the accountability and responsibility for translations and solidarities linking the cacophonous visions and visionary voices that characterize the knowledge of the subjugated. (1988, 590)

Below, I try to capture some images of activist scholarship, all of which share three distinctions. First, the author is explicit about the space in which she stands politically and theoretically—even as her stances are multiple, shifting, and mobile. Second, the text displays critical analyses of current social arrangements and their ideological frames. And, third, the narrative reveals and invents disruptive images of what could be (Lather 1986).

Breaking the Silence

As the essays on silencing represent, research that breaks social silence(s) fractures the very ideologies that justify power inequities. In such work, researchers pry open social mythologies that others are committed to sealing. And in two pieces of such scholarship described below, we can hear the costs of breaking the silence for researchers at the margins.

In "Hispanics, AIDS and Sexual Practices," Ana Maria Alonso and Maria Teresa Koreck wedge open a political analysis of women and AIDS in the Latina community. In their writings, they write about contradictory community loyalties:

> The implications of denial are particularly deadly for Latina women. . . . Because of every way in which gender and sexuality are constructed, Latino men are not held accountable. . . . We almost did not write this paper. After much discussion, we decided that maintaining the silence is to cede terrain . . . is to let dominant discourse define the politics of ethnicity, disease, sexuality and morality. . . . We can contest the power of the dominant discourses to define not only who we are and how we live, but also how we die. (1989, 57)

These women resist, in their narrative, the culture that both threatens and protects them. As border crossers, holding membership in multiple communities (Rosaldo 1989), Alonso and Koreck refuse to collude in either cultural or gendered betrayal. But, as they remind us, while their project seeks to interrupt the silences that assault them as Latinas, the work of desilencing is costly and dangerous to them.

In an equally compelling way, critical legal scholar Regina Austin's essay "Sapphire Bound!" problematizes the legal silence surrounding African-American women's bodies within white men's law. Austin talks of the price of breaking the silence when she asks:

When was the last time someone told you that your way of approaching problems . . . was all wrong? You are too angry, too emotional, too subjective, too pessimistic, too political, too anecdotal and too instinctive? I never know how to respond to such accusations. How can I legitimate my way of thinking? I know that I am not just flying off the handle, seeing imaginary insults and problems where there are none. I am not a witch solely by nature, but by circumstance and choice as well. I suspect that what my critics really want to say is that I am being too self consciously black (brown, yellow, red) and/or female to suit their tastes and should "lighten up" because I am making them feel very uncomfortable, and that is not nice. And I want them to think that I am nice, don't I? or "womanish"? . . . The chief sources of our theory should be black women's critiques of a society that is dominated by and structured to favor white men of wealth and power. We should also find inspiration in the modes of resistance black women mount, individually and collectively. (1989)

Austin describes a case in which an African-American adult woman, single and pregnant, was fired from Omaha Girls' Club because, as the justices argued, "while a single pregnant woman may indeed, provide a good example of hard work and independence, the same person may be a negative role model with respect to the girls' club objective of diminishing the number of teenage pregnancies" (551). Austin continues:

A black feminist jurisprudential analysis of Chambers must seriously consider the possibility that young, single, sexually active, fertile and nurturing black women are being viewed ominously because they have the temerity to attempt to break out of the rigid, economic, social and political categories that a racist, sexist and class stratified society would impose upon them. . . . Like a treasonous recruit, Crystal turned up unmarried and pregnant. As such, she embodied the enemy. If the Club could not succeed in shaping and retraining the workers whose economic welfare it controlled, how could it expect to win over the young members and supplant their mothers' cultural legacy? The requirement that one allows one's self to be modeled in order to keep one's job is not limited to blacks who are young, fertile females. To a certain extent, the trouble Crystal Chambers encountered is a generic infliction suffered by black role models of both sexes and all ages who reject the part and become rebellious renegades or traitors to the cause of black cultural containment. (1989, 555)

Austin explodes her own rage, wedges a conversation within the law, and, with the body of Crystal Chambers, levers a critical analysis of African-American women's bodies as they embody social disgrace. Like Alonso and Koreck, Austin has fractured the seamless discursive webs that surround, contain, and oppress women of color within their communities and within the courts. And readers can feel the strength, and the pain, of that fracture.

Denaturalizing What Appears So Natural

As the essays on women with disabilities and adolescent sexuality reflect, critical theorists interested in race, class, gender, sexuality and disability have noted how easily biologic explanations seem to explain away perceived "differences." These explanations float within an almost uninterruptible language of the natural. If there is no other task that feminist activist researchers can accomplish, we must provoke a deep curiosity about, indeed an intolerance for, that which is described as inevitable, immutable, and natural. Two examples may capture the task.

Frigga Haug, in an edited text, *Female Sexualization*, writes with a German Marxist-feminist women's group committed to "collective memory work," on the sexualization of their bodies (1987). Sexualization, for the collective, involves the reduction and subjugation of women's bodies to a constant requirement to arouse male desire and, at the same time, to be normal. Haug and colleagues write the stories of their bodies with chapters focusing on hair, thighs, buttocks, cleavage, and parts that have grown to be sexually charged. These women track the sexual reconstruction of body parts once considered asexual. They spin histories of their bodies, and, by doing so, they denaturalize that which appears to be so natural, so female, so in the body and not in the body politic. Their work forces another look at the social production of gender, sexuality, nature, and, finally, desire.

Moving from bodies to classrooms but still inside the unpacking of the "natural", Patti Lather, in her recent book, *Getting Smart: Feminist Research and Pedagogy within the Post-Modern*, invites researchers to consider how researchers package the stories we tell about Others. She seeks to "explore what it means to write science differently" by framing and reframing interviews, reports, journal entries, and personal "musings" from her introductory women's studies course. Interested in why women resist feminism, Lather refused to tell *the* story about these women. Instead, she spins four possible "tales" from her data:

> Each of the four tales I shall spin will be grounded in words generated via journals and interviews from students across varied sections of this introductory women's studies class. Borrowing loosely from Van Maanen (1988), I call these a realist tale, a critical tale, a deconstructive tale, and a reflexive tale. By "realist," I mean those stories which assume a found world, an empirical world knowable through adequate method and theory. By "critical," I mean those stories which assume underlying determining structures for how power shapes the social world. Such structures are posited as largely invisible to common sense ways of making meaning but visible to those who probe below hegemonic meaning systems to produce counter-hegemonic knowledge, knowledge intended to challenge dominant meaning systems. By "deconstructivist," I mean stories that foreground the unsaid in our saying, "the elisions, blind-spots, loci of the unsayable within texts" (Grosz, 1989:184). Deconstruction moves against stories that appear to tell themselves. It creates stories that disclose their constructed nature. And, finally, by "reflexive," I mean those stories which bring the teller of the tale back into the narrative, embodied, desiring, invested in a variety of often contradictory privileges and struggles. (1990, 224–25)

By forcing readers to recognize the promiscuity of intellectual frames around our data, Lather invites researchers and educators to "begin to understand how we are caught up in power situations of which we are, ourselves, the bearers [and to] foreground the limits of our lives and what we can do within those boundaries" (1990, 25). By text end, we can enjoy the freshness of Lather's questions: Who speaks? for what and to whom? who listens? And we can recognize the partiality of any one interpretive frame.

Whether the text is armpit hair or the story of women's resistance to feminism, both Haug and Lather ask researchers/educators to engage critically in the process of interrogating how we have settled on the stories we tell; how else these stories could be told; how we can organize disruptively for what could be within these stories.

Attaching What Is to What Could Be

Today there is a flurry of writing on what could be, advancing the social critiques of what has been. By pressing readers to imagine what could be, a collection of writers has taken readers to the boundaries of current intellectual debates in order to conceive beyond, in order to provoke political possibilities. Such work is best exemplified by Lois Weis in her recent text, *Working Class without Work: Adolescence in Deindustrializing America* (1990b), and by Derrick Bell in *And We Are Not Yet Saved* (1987).

In *Working Class without Work*, Weis produces an ethnography of white male and female students attending high school in a recently deindustrialized working-class town. Weis analyzes working-class, white male development as it is carved in opposition to young white women and adolescents of color, and she examines working-class, white female development as an instance of incipient feminist awareness. Weis weaves critical analyses of *what seems to be* with speculative theorizing about *what could be*. In so doing, she connects adolescent consciousness [male and female] to the erosion of labor markets and movements, and she anticipates theoretically that these young, white, working-class men could find comforting political respite within the New Right, while these young, white, working-class women could nestle comfortably within an emergent feminist politic. Thus, Weis attaches her analyses of adolescent development to activist movements past and future and achieves enormous theoretical advance by repoliticizing psychological development and inviting readers to notice how systematically schools work to depoliticize students from the social movements and events that have shaped their lives.

As a talented critical ethnographer, Weis closely documents the ways in which schools not only reproduce but actually refuse to interrupt oppositional white, male development. As a theorist of possibility, Weis advances these insights toward a rich melding of what is with a powerful sense of what could be. She breaks silences and denaturalizes what is, but, even further, she provokes readers to imagine multiple, postmodern possibilities of what could be, nurturing the social responsibilities among educators/readers to create that which is not yet.

Like Weis, Derrick Bell reframes what has been and what could be through a radical jolt of perspective. In *And We Are Not Yet Saved*, a series of legal chronicles, Bell writes through the voice and wisdom of fictitious Geneva Crenshaw. Each chronicle revisits a "racially based" judicial decision and shifts the historic discourse by forcing readers to tour U.S. history through a self-consciously African-American vantage. The chronicles on desegregation, housing, and Affirmative Action force multiple readings of these decisions rendered ostensibly *for* people of color.

In the final chronicle, Bell tells the story of the "Black Crime Cure." A group of young African-American boys find some rocks, which they eat, and, in so doing, they stop participating in criminal activities. Now, he notes, whites can no longer reason that African Americans don't have housing, education, health care, or adequate living conditions because African Americans bring crime and the poverty on themselves. With the Black Crime Cure, the white liberal explanation is removed. And he is relieved. These young boys pass the rocks onto their friends. All indulge and pass them onto their children. Bell writes:

> Time does not permit a full recounting of how the Black Crime Cure was distributed across the country. While the stones seemed to give indigestion to whites who took them, they worked as they had in the cave for anyone with a substantial amount of African blood. Black people were overjoyed and looked forward to life without fear of attack in even the poorest neighborhoods. Whites also lost their fear of muggings, burglary and rape.
>
> But, now that blacks had forsaken crime and begun fighting it, the doors of opportunity, long closed to them because of their "criminal tendencies," were not opened more than a crack. All-white neighborhoods continued to resist the entry of blacks, save perhaps a few professionals. Employers did not hasten to make jobs available for those who once made their living preying on individuals and robbing stores. Nor did black schools, now models of disciplined decorum, much improve the quality of their teaching. Teachers who believed blacks too dangerous to teach continued their lackadaisical ways, rationalized now because blacks, they said, were too dumb to learn.
>
> Moreover, the Black Crime Cure drastically undermined the crime industry. Thousands of people lost jobs as police forces were reduced, court schedules were cut back and prisons closed. Manufacturers who provided weapons, uniforms and equipment of all forms to

law enforcement agencies were brought to the brink of bankruptcy. Estimates of the dollar losses ran into the hundreds of millions.

And most threatening of all, police—free of the constant menace of black crime and prodded by the citizenry—began to direct attention to the pervasive, long neglected problem of "white collar crime" and the noxious activities of politicians and their business supporters. Those in power, and the many more who always fear that any change will worsen their status, came to an unspoken but no less firm conclusion: fear of black crime has an important stabilizing effect on the nation. (1987, 246–47)

Bell, throughout this text, unhooks the past, present, and future from traditional, taken-for-granted notions. Working backwards (like Haug) and forward (like Weis and Austin), Bell explodes "commonsense" (white?) notions of justice, entitlement, and progress and forces readers to reconsider explanations that have for so long suited, legitimized, and even perpetuated racist hierarchies.

Both Weis and Bell position narratives inside intellectual spaces heretofore uncharted. They capture readers' imaginations with portrayals of adolescent identity and racial history cast historically, and futuristically, in terms of what could be—full of impending doom and rich in possibilities.

Engaging in Participatory Activist Research

The fourth strategy for feminist research concerns participatory, activist research. In the tradition of Kurt Lewin (1948) and later Carolyn Payton (1984), this fourth strategy assumes that knowledge is best gathered in the midst of social change projects—that the partial perspectives of participants and observers can be collected by researchers in "power sensitive conversations" (Haraway 1988). This work is at once disruptive, transformative, and reflective; about understanding and about action; not about freezing the scene but always about change (Gitlin, Siegel, and Boru 1989).

To illustrate: For over a decade, feminist psychologist Brinton Lykes has been engaged in political activism/research with Guatemalan Indian women in their struggles against political repression. Combining activist politics with feminist psychological research, Lykes has created a collaborative work with these women in which:

> we ... shared an interest in better understanding the conditions under which people come to understand themselves as actors constructing their future, as active participants in the social and political development of their people. We agreed that a project that documented the processes by which women, beginning with their immediate concerns, develop a political consciousness that is accompanied by action and gives social meaning to their activity, would contribute both to a better understanding of Guatemalan women's resistance efforts and, more generally, to our knowledge about the development of political self-consciousness among women. The project was conceived thus as a concrete resource for existing Guatemalan communities, as a vehicle for exploring a more theoretical problem of interest to theorists and to breaking the silence surrounding Guatemala's recent history. (1989, 171)

In her writings, Lykes is the exemplary poststructural narrator. Positioned multiply, and often contradictorily, she describes herself as an activist, collaborator, and researcher; as a naive North American, a critical psychologist, and an overly "ethical" researcher (Lykes documents some telling negotiations over her construction of an "informed consent" form). A reflective interviewer and an anxious interviewee. Engaged over a decade with a set of activist refugees and psychologists, Lykes considers her project to be explicitly about liberatory struggle and its documentation. And she writes, beautifully and reflectively, about the consequences of such an agenda for psychological research practices.

One particularly compelling essay from this project concludes with a detailed analysis of the politics of collaborative research:

> The decision to engage in collaborative research does not *de facto* resolve competing interests. Nor does it minimize the importance of developing strategies for ensuring, for example, the anonymity of our informants, concerns that are even more critical in research with members of oppressed groups than in university-based work with college sophomores. Rather it affirms a commitment on the part of both researcher and participant to engage the research process as subjects, as constructors of our own reality. (1989, 179)

With Lykes, this piece of social research constructs a gendered archive of political resistance which would otherwise be buried within the deep history of repression which characterizes these women's lives.

To illustrate participatory activist work quite differently, from my own involvement in an entirely other area, since 1987, I have been involved as consultant to the Philadelphia Schools Collaborative, an $8.3 million project for restructuring the comprehensive high schools in Philadelphia. Working with secondary school educators to nurture radically transformed organizational structures, governance bodies, instructional practices, and relationships with community, we collaborate with teachers, administrators, students, and parents on the politics, practices, and policies of urban schooling. The collaborative sits both inside and out of the district and shares all work with the district and the Philadelphia Federation of Teachers. The work commits to flattening and democratizing "downtown" bureaucratic structures as well as decentralizing the practices of individual schools.

Our goals are to engage schools in teacher-driven, school-based change such that large anonymous high schools can be transformed into relationship-rich, teacher-designed, intellectual communities for the long-term working together of students, parents, and educators. While tensions at the hyphen of consultant-activist-researcher are numerous, the gains of being *in* the change—for knowing, "eavesdropping," gathering varied points of view, and being able to orchestrate conversations around multiple stances—are enormous.

Like the work of James Comer (1980), Linda Darling Hammond (1988), Hank Levin (1989), Anne Lieberman (1988), and Ted Sizer (1989), this work within the collaborative addresses issues of structure, instruction, assessment, governance, and community. It is constantly reflective, transformative, and educational—for all of us. To take a static picture of these schools at one point in time and call it research would be absurd. To write a simple story from afar or even alone would fly in the face of the democratic and participatory terms of the project and would produce inadequate data. To assume that *I* know all that must be told, or that *all* I know must *all* be told, would simply be naive. I have never been so deeply embedded in that which I am studying; never been as keenly aware of all the ways in which my stance is always personal and collective, sustained, and transitory, remote and revealing; and never has it been so hard to commit a text to paper.

Scholars who participate in facilitating and documenting social change projects sit in the midst of the richest data possible on the politics of organizational and individual transformations (Fine and Vanderslice 1992). Having said that, however, I have to acknowledge the emergence of a new generation of epistemological dilemmas: What makes this research? When does intervention stop and reflection begin? How do I/ we "know" what I/we "know"? What are our grounds for disproof? What are the limits of collaboration? And what are the bases for shared censorship? Herein grows the delicious next generation of feminist research dilemmas/possibilities.

Reframing Feminist Psychologies

It is essential for feminist psychologists, in the 1990s, to come "out" about the political spaces in which we pursue our work. We now know that ventriloquism, popular though it may be, cannot survive even the Supreme Court and shouldn't survive the academy. We now know that the voices of Others can no longer sit as innocent texts behind which researchers hide. And we now know that social researchers can engage in facilitating and documenting social inequities and enabling struggles of resistance without sacrificing the quality of our research.

One might say it's unfair to ask those who have elected to work in spaces already marginal to the academy—women's studies, African-American studies, or cultural studies—to pursue scholarship explicitly within political praxis. And yet, in this essay, I have argued that research-ers always take positions within politics, if typically unacknowledged and conservative, and that the only way to do activist research is to be positioned explicitly with questions but not answers; as mobile and multiple, not static and singular; within spaces of rich surprise, not predetermined "forced choices"; surrounded by critical conversation, never alone.

The central dilemma for feminist psychologists is how to reconcile, with integrity, our adjective (feminist) with our noun (psychologist). Because we acknowledge that politics saturates all research but are usu-ally the only ones who "come clean," we run the risk of being portrayed as distinctly "biased" and thus discounted. Of course, we could refuse to confront this question and hide within the space separating feminist from psychologist. But, by so doing, we would systematically compro-mise our adjective and become the detached and dispassionate noun so many of us repel. Mary Parlee has written to this dilemma.

It is by now very clear, I think, that the inertia of the routine practices of traditional psychology excludes the subversive potential of feminism; other organization routines, embodying and enacting different goals and values are needed to counter this inertia. A body in motion maintains its speed and trajectory unless an external force is applied. (Parlee 1991, 46)

And so, as Parlee has provoked us toward the subversive, this book has displayed a set of possibilities, chronicling my own work and inviting feminist researchers to resuscitate our politics through our scholarship. I have asked you to dip with me across these essays to spin possibilities for activist feminist research and to raise questions that will incite the next generation of our work. While the official academy cowers behind what it calls neutrality, and progressive researchers are drowning in voices collected over the past five years, feminist scholars can today braid activist feminist politics with compelling theoretical work to take back the bodies, silences, and shadows—to fill them with feminist talk. As the gag orders move forward on abortion, Affirmative Action recedes, and the Right stomps through the academy, I wish us all the collective outrage and the political will to produce disruptive feminist research.

Works Cited

Advocates for Children. 1985. Report of the New York hearings on the crisis in public education. New York.

Alexander, V. 1985. Black women's health concerns. *National Campaign to Restore Abortion Funding*, Fall, 8–9.

Alonso, A., and Koreck, M. 1989. Silences: Hispanic and Latina women and AIDS. *Sexual Practices* 1, no. 1:101–24.

Amaro, H. 1989. *Women's reproductive rights in the age of AIDS: New threats to informed choice*. Article drafted from paper presented at the 97th annual convention of the American Psychological Association, New Orleans, 1988.

Amaro, H.; Fried, L.; Cabral, H.; and Zuckerman, B. 1990. Violence during pregnancy and substance use. *American Journal of Public Health* 80:575–79.

Amaro, H., and Russo, N. F. 1987. Hispanic women and mental health: An overview of contemporary issues in research and practice. *Psychology of Women Quarterly* 11:393–407.

Anderson, E. 1990. *Streetwise: Race, class and change in an urban community.* Chicago: University of Chicago Press.

Angelou, Maya. 1969. *I know why the caged bird sings.* New York: Random House.

Antonucci, T., and Depner, C. 1982. Social support and information helping relationships. In *Basic processes in helping relationships,* ed. T. Wills. New York: Academic Press.

Anyon, J. 1980. "School curriculum: Political and economic structure and social change. *Social Practice* 16:96–108.

———. 1982. Intersections of gender and class: Accommodation and resistance by working-class and affluent females in contradictory sex-role ideologies. In *Gender, class and education,* ed. L. Barton and S. Walker. London: Fatimer Press.

Apfelbaum, E. 1979. Relations of domination and movements for liberation: An analysis of power between groups. In *The social psychology of intergroup relations,* ed. W. Austin and S. Worchel. Monterey, Calif.: Brooks/Cole.

Apple, M. 1982. *Cultural and economic reproduction in education.* Boston: Routledge and Kegan Paul.

Arafat, I., and Cotton, W. 1974. Masturbation practices of males and females. *Journal of Sex Research* 10, no. 4:293–307.

Aronowitz, S. 1988. *Science as power.* Minneapolis: University of Minnesota Press.

Aronowitz, S., and Giroux, H. 1985. *Education under siege*. South Hadley, Mass.: Bergin and Garvey.

Asch, A. 1984. The experience of disability: A challenge for psychology. *American Psychologist* 39, no. 5:529–36.

———. 1986a. Will populism empower disabled people? In *The new populism: The politics of empowerment*, ed. H. C. Boyte and F. Riessman. Philadelphia: Temple University Press.

———. 1986b. Real moral dilemmas. *Christianity and Crisis* 46, no. 10:237–40.

———. 1986c. On the question of Baby Doe. *Health / PAC Bulletin* 16, no. 6:6–10.

Asch, A., and Fine, M. 1988. Shared dreams: A left perspective on disability rights and reproductive rights. In *Women with disabilities: Essays in psychology, culture, and politics*, ed. M. Fine and A. Asch, 297–305. Philadelphia: Temple University Press.

Asch, A., and Sacks, L. 1983. Lives without, lives within: The autobiographies of blind women and men. *Journal of Visual Impairment and Blindness* 77, no. 6:242–47.

Aspira. 1983. Racial and ethnic high school dropout rates in New York City: A summary report. New York.

Asrael, W. 1982. An approach to motherhood for disabled women. *Rehabilitation Literature* 43, nos. 7–8:214–18.

Austin, R. 1989. Sapphire bound! *Wisconsin Law Review*, no. 3:539–78.

Baruch, G. K.; Biener, L.; and Barnett, R. C. 1987. Women and gender in research on work and family stress. *American Psychologist* 42:130–36.

Bastian, A. 1989. *Unwrapping the package: Some thoughts on school choice*. New York: New World Foundation.

Bastian, A.; Fruchter, N.; Gittell, M.; Greer, C.; and Haskins, K. 1986. *Choosing equality: The case for democratic schooling*. Philadelphia, Pa.: Temple University Press.

Bauer, G. 1986. *The family: Preserving America's future*. Washington, D.C.: U.S. Department of Education.

Becker, G. 1980. *Growing old in silence*. Berkeley: University of California Press.

Becker, H. 1986. *Writing for social scientists: How to start and finish your thesis, book, or article*. Chicago: University of Chicago Press.

Belenky, M. F.; Clinchy, B. M.; Goldberger, N. R.; and Tarule, J. M. 1986. *Women's ways of knowing: The development of self, voice, and mind*. New York: Basic Books.

Bell, D. 1987. *And we are not yet saved: The elusive quest for racial justice*. New York: Basic Books.

Bell, L. 1989. Something's wrong here and it's not me: Challenging the dilemmas that block girls' success. *Journal for the Education of the Gifted* 12, no. 2:118–30.

Belle, D. 1984. *Attempting to comprehend the lives of poor women*. Paper presented at a meeting of the American Psychological Association, Toronto, Canada, August.

———. 1990. Poverty and women's mental health. *American Psychologist* 45, no. 3:385–89.

Bellone, E., and Waxman, B. 1983. *Sexual assault and women with disabilities: An overview.* Monograph. Los Angeles: Planned Parenthood.

Belsey, C. 1980. *Critical practice.* New York: Methuen.

Bem, S. 1974. The measurement of psychological androgyny. *Journal of Clinical and Consulting Psychology* 42, no. 2:155–62.

Benedetto, R. 1987. AIDS studies become part of curricula. *USA Today,* January 23, D1.

Benjamin, J. 1983. Master and slave: The fantasy of erotic domination. In *Powers of desire,* ed. A. Snitow, C. Stansell, and S. Thompson, 280–99. New York: Monthly Review Press.

Bennett, W. 1987. Why Johnny can't abstain. *National Review,* July 3, 36–38, 56.

Bernstein, M. D., and Russo, N. F. 1974. The history of psychology revisited: Or, up with our foremothers. *American Psychologist* 29, no. 2:130–34.

Berscheid, E., and Walster, E. 1972. Beauty and the beast. *Psychology Today,* March, 42–46, 74.

Bhaba, H. 1983. The other question—the stereotype and colonial discourse. *Screen* 24:18–36.

Bigelow, M. 1921. *Sex education.* New York: Macmillan.

Blackman, J. 1986. Potential uses for expert testimony: Ideas toward the representation of battered women who kill. *Women's Rights Law Reporter* 9:227–38.

———. 1989. *Intimate violence.* New York: Columbia University Press.

Blackwell-Stratton, M.; Breslin, M. L.; Mayerson, A. B.; and Bailey, S. 1988. Smashing icons: Disabled women and the disability rights and women's movements. In *Women with disabilities: Essays in psychology, culture, and politics,* ed. M. Fine and A. Asch, 306–32. Philadelphia: Temple University Press.

Boffey, P. 1987. Reagan to back AIDS plan urging youths to avoid sex. *New York Times,* February 27, A14.

Bogart, K., and Stein, N. 1987. Breaking the silence: Sexual harassment in education. *Peabody Journal of Education* 64, no.4:146–63.

Bonwich, E. 1985. Sex role attitudes and role reorganization in spinal cord injured women. In *Women in disability: The double handicap,* ed. M. J. Deegan and N. A. Brooks, 56–67. New Brunswick, N.J.: Transaction Books.

Bookman, A. and Morgen, S., eds. 1988. *Women and the politics of empowerment.* Philadelphia: Temple University Press.

Bordo, S. 1990. Reading the slender body. In *Body/politics: Women and the discourses of science,* ed. M. Jacobus, E. Fox Keller, and S. Shuttleworth, 31–53. New York: Routledge.

Boston Lesbian Psychologies Collective, eds. 1987. *Lesbian psychologies: Explorations and challenges.* Urbana: University of Illinois Press.

Boston Women's Health Book Collective. 1985. *The new our bodies, ourselves.* 2d rev. ed. New York: Simon and Schuster.

Bourdieu, P. 1977. Cultural reproduction and social reproduction. In *Power and ideology in education,* ed. A. H. Halsey and J. Karabel, 487–551. New York: Oxford University Press.

Bowe, F. 1980. *Rehabilitating America.* New York: Harper and Row.

———. 1981. *Comeback: Six remarkable people who triumphed over disability.* New York: Harper and Row.

———. 1984. *Disabled women in America.* Washington, D.C.: President's Committee on Employment of the Handicapped.

Brickman, P.; Rabinowitz, V.; Karuza, J.; Coates, D.; Cohn, E.; and Kidder, L. 1982. Models of helping and coping. *American Psychologist* 37, no. 4:368–84.

Brightman, A. J., ed. 1984. *Ordinary moments: The disabled experience.* Baltimore: University Park Press.

Brodkey, L. 1988. *Academic writing as social practice.* Philadelphia: Temple University Press.

———. 1989. On the subjects of class and gender. In *The literacy letters. College English* 51, no. 2:125–41.

Brodkey, L., and Fine, M. 1988. Presence of body, absence of mind. *Journal of Education* 170, no. 3:84–99.

Broverman, I.; Vogel, S.; Broverman, D.; Clarkson, F.; and Rosenkrantz, P. 1972. Sex-role stereotypes: A current appraisal. *Journal of Social Issues* 28, no. 2:59–78.

Brown, L. 1989. New voices, new visions: Toward a lesbian/gay paradigm for psychology. *Psychology of Women Quarterly* 13, no. 4:445–58.

Brown, L. S. 1987. Lesbians, weight, and eating: New analyses and perspectives. In *Lesbian psychologies: Explorations and challenges,* ed. Boston Lesbian Psychologies Collective, 294–310. Urbana: University of Illinois Press.

Brown, P. 1983. The Swedish approach to sex education and adolescent pregnancy: Some impressions. *Family Planning Perspectives,* 15, no. 2:92–95.

Browne, A. 1987. *When battered women kill.* New York: Macmillan / Free Press.

Browne, S.; Connors, D.; and Stern, N., eds. 1985. *With the power of each breath.* Pittsburgh: Cleis Press.

Brownmiller, S. 1984. *Femininity.* New York: Simon and Schuster.

Brumberg, J. 1989. *Fasting girls: The history of anorexia nervosa.* New York: New American Library.

Burgess, A., and Holstrom, L. 1976. Coping behavior of the rape victim. *American Journal of Psychiatry* 133, no. 4:413–18.

Burke, C. 1980. Introduction to Luce Irigaray, When our lips speak together. *Signs: Journal of Women in Culture and Society* 6, no. 1:66–68.

Burt, M.; Kimmich, M.; Goldmuntz, J.; and Sonnenstein, F. 1984. *Helping pregnant adolescents: Outcomes and costs of service delivery.* Final report on the evaluation of adolescent pregnancy programs. Washington, D.C.: Urban Institute.

Buss, A., 1979. *Psychology in social context.* New York: Irvington Publishers.

Cagan, E. 1978. Individualism, collectivism, and radical educational reform. *Harvard Educational Review* 48, no. 2:227–66.

Campling, J., ed. 1981. *Images of ourselves: Disabled women talking*. Boston: Routledge and Kegan Paul.

Caplan, C. 1986. *Sea changes: Essays on culture and feminism*. London: Verso.

Caplan, P. 1989. *Don't blame mother*. New York: Harper and Row.

Caplan, P. J., and Hall-McCorquodale, I. 1985. Mother-blaming in major clinical journals. *American Journal of Orthopsychiatry* 55, no. 3:345–53.

Carnegie Forum on Education and the Economy. 1986. *A nation prepared: Teachers for the twenty-first century*. New York: Carnegie Foundation.

Carnoy, M., and Levin, H. 1985. *Schooling and work in the democratic state*. Stanford: Stanford University Press.

Cartoof, V., and Klerman, L. 1986. Parental consent for abortion: Impact on the Massachusetts law. *American Journal of Public Health* 76:397–400.

Census study reports one in five adults suffers from disability. 1986. *New York Times*, December 23, B7.

Chesler, P. 1972. *Women and madness*. New York: Doubleday.

Chicago school clinic is sued over birth control materials. 1986. *New York Times*, October 16, A24.

Childers, M., and hooks, b. 1990. A conversation about race and class. In *Conflicts in feminism*, ed. M. Hirsch and E. F. Keller, 60–81. New York: Routledge.

Children's Defense Fund. 1986. *Preventing adolescent pregnancy: What schools can do*. Washington, D.C.: Children's Defense Fund.

———. 1987. *Adolescent pregnancy: An anatomy of a social problem in search of comprehensive solutions*. Washington, D.C.: Children's Defense Fund.

Chodorow, N. J. 1978. *The reproduction of mothering: Psychoanalysis and the sociology of gender*. Berkeley: University of California Press.

Cixous, H. 1981. Castration or decapitation? *Signs: Journal of Women in Culture and Society* 7, no. 1:41–55.

Clark, M. 1990. The difficulty of saying "I": Identifying, analyzing, and critiquing voices of self, difference, and discourse in college students' reading and writing about literature. (Ph.D. diss., University of Pennsylvania, 1990). Also see *Dissertation abstracts, international*.

Cobb, S., and Kasl, S. 1977. *Termination: The consequences of job loss*. Pub. #LR77-224, Department of Health, Education and Welfare, Washington, D.C.

Cole, J. B., ed. 1986. *All American women: Lines that divide, ties that bind*. New York: Free Press.

Colen, S. 1986. "With respect and feelings": Voices of West Indian child care and domestic workers in New York City. In *All American women: Lines that divide, ties that bind*, ed. J. B. Cole, 46–70. New York: Free Press.

Collins, G. 1983. The success story of a disabled mother. *New York Times*, October 12, c.1–2.

Collins, P. 1988. *Black feminist thought*. Paper presented at the Penn Mid-Atlantic Women's Studies Seminar. University of Pennsylvania, Philadelphia.

Comer, J. 1980. *School power: Implications of an intervention project*. New York: Free Press.

Condor, S. 1986. Sex role beliefs and "traditional" women: Feminist and inter-group perspectives. In *Feminist social psychology: Developing theory and practice,* ed. S. Wilkinson, 97–118. Philadelphia: Open University Press.

Conneli, R.; Ashenden, D.; Kessler, S.; and Dawsett, G. 1982. *Making the difference.* Sydney, Australia: George Allen and Unwin.

Corbett, K. 1989. The role of sexuality and sex equity in the education of disabled women. *Peabody Journal of Education* 64, no. 4:198–212.

Cox, S., ed. 1981. *Female psychology: The emerging self.* New York: St. Martin's Press.

Crawford, M. 1989. Agreeing to differ: Feminist epistemologies and women's ways of knowing. In *Gender and thought: Psychological perspectives,* ed. M. Crawford and M. Gentry, 128–45. New York: Springer-Verlag.

Crawford, M., and Gentry, M. 1989. *Gender and thought: Psychological perspectives.* New York: Springer-Verlag.

Crawford, M., and Marecek, J. 1988. Psychology reconstructs the female: 1971–1988. Presented at Nags Head conference on sex and gender. Nags Head, North Carolina.

———. 1989a. Feminist theory, feminist psychology: A bibliography of epistemology, critical analysis, and applications. *Psychology of Women Quarterly,* 13, no. 4:477–92.

———. 1989b. Psychology reconstructs the female, 1968–1988. *Psychology of Women Quarterly* 13, no. 2:147–66.

Crenshaw, K. 1989. Demarginalizing the intersection of race and sex: A black feminist critique of antidiscrimination doctrine, feminist theory, and antiracist politics. *University of Chicago Legal Forum,* 139–67.

Crewe, N., and Zola, I. K., eds. 1983. *Independent living for physically disabled people.* San Francisco: Jossey-Bass.

Crosby, F.; Pufall, A; Snyder, R. C.; O'Connell, M.; and Walen, P. 1989. Gender and thought: The role of the self-concept. In *Gender and thought: Psychological perspectives,* ed. M. Crawford and M. Gentry, 100–127. New York: Springer-Verlag.

Cummins, J. 1986. Empowering minority studies: A framework for intervention. *Harvard Education Review* 56, no. 1:18–36.

Darling, R. B. 1979. *Families against society: A study of reactions to children with birth defects.* Beverly Hills, Calif.: Sage.

Darling-Hammond, L. 1988. On teaching as a profession: A conversation with Linda Darling-Hammond. *Educational Leadership* (November): #46, 11–15.

Davis, F. 1961. Deviance disavowal: The management of strained interaction by the visibly handicapped. *Social Problems* 9, no. 2:120–32.

———. 1963. *Passage through crisis: Polio victims and their families.* Bloomington, Ind.: Bobbs-Merrill.

Dawson, D. 1986. The effects of sex education on adolescent behavior. *Family Planning Perspectives* 18, no. 4:162–70.

Deaux, K. 1984. From individual differences to social categories. *American Psychologist* 39, no. 2:105–16.

Deaux, K., and Major, B. 1987. Putting gender into context: An interactive model of gender-related behavior. *Psychological Review* 94, no. 3:369–89.

———. 1990. A social-psychological model of gender. In *Theoretical perspectives on sexual difference*, ed. D. L. Rhode, 89–99. New Haven, Conn.: Yale University Press.

deCani, J.; Fine, M.; Sagi, P.; and Stern, M. 1985. *Report of the committee to survey harassment at the University of Pennsylvania. Almanac* 32 (September 24); 2–12.

Deegan, M. J., and Brooks, N. A., eds. 1985. *Women and disability: The double handicap.* New Brunswick, N.J.: Transaction.

de Lauretis, T. 1987. *Technologies of gender: Essays on theory, film, and fiction.* Bloomington: Indiana University Press.

Delacoste, F., and Alexander, P., eds. 1988. *Sex work: Writings by women in the sex industry.* Pittsburgh: Cleis Press.

Delpit, L. 1988. The silenced dialogue. *Harvard Educational Review* 58, no. 3: 280–98.

DePaulo, B. 1980. Social psychological processes in informal help seeking. In *Basic processes in helping relationships*, ed. T. Wills. New York: Academic Press.

Dill, B. T. 1987. The dialectics of black womanhood. In *Feminism and methodology: Social science issues*, ed. S. Harding, 97–108. Bloomington: Indiana University Press.

Dinnerstein, D. 1976. *The mermaid and the minotaur: Sexual arrangements and human malaise.* New York: Harper and Row.

Disability Rag. 1984. Special issue. June.

———. 1986. *Care that kills* 7, no 6:9–10.

Dobie, K. 1988. Black women, white kids. *Village Voice*, January 12, 20–27.

Dowd, M. 1986. Bid to update sex education confronts resistance in city. *New York Times*, April 16, A1.

Dryfoos, J. 1985a. A time for new thinking about teenage pregnancy. *American Journal of Public Health* 75:13–14.

———. 1985b. School based health clinics: A new approach to preventing adolescent pregnancy? *Family Planning Perspectives* 17, no 2:70–75.

Duffy, Y. 1981. . . . *All things are possible.* Ann Arbor, Mich.: A. J. Garvin Associates.

Dweck, C., and Licht, B. 1980. Learned helplessness and intellectual achievement. In *Human helplessness*, ed. J. Garber and M. Seligman. New York: Academic Press.

Eagleton, T. 1991. *Ideology: An Introduction.* New York: Verso.

Echols, A. 1989. *Daring to be bad: Radical feminism in America, 1967–1975.* Minneapolis: University of Minnesota Press.

Ehrenreich, B. 1989. *Fear of falling: The inner life of the middle class.* New York: Pantheon.

Ehrenreich, B.; Hess, E.; and Jacobs, G. 1986. *Remaking love: The feminization of sex.* Garden City, N.Y.: Anchor Press.

Eichenbaum, L., and Orbach, S. 1983. *Understanding women: A psychoanalytic approach.* New York: Basic Books.

Eisenstein, H. 1983. *Contemporary feminist thought.* Boston: G. K. Hall.

Eisenstein, H. and Jardine, A., eds. 1985. *The future of difference.* New Brunswick, N.J.: Rutgers University Press.

Eisenstein, Z. 1984. *Feminism and sexual equality: Crisis in liberal America.* New York: Monthly Review Press.

Elliott, D.; Voss, H.; and Wendling, A. 1966. Capable dropouts and the social milieu of high school. *Journal of Educational Research* 60, no 4:180–86.

Espin, O. 1984. Cultural and historical influences on sexuality in Hispanic/Latina women: Implications for psychotherapy. In *Pleasure and danger,* ed. C. Vance, 149–64. Boston: Routledge and Kegan Paul.

———. 1987. Issues of identity in the psychology of Latina lesbians. In *Lesbian psychologies: Explorations and challenges,* ed. Boston Lesbian Psychologies Collective, 35–55. Urbana: University of Illinois Press.

Evans, M. 1991. *A good school: Life at a girls' grammar school in the 1950's.* London: Women's Press.

Felice, L. 1981. Black student dropout behaviors: Disengagement from school rejection and racial discrimination. *Journal of Negro Education* 50, no. 4:415–24.

Fine, M. 1979. Options to injustice: Seeing other lights. *Representative Research in Social Psychology* 10, nos. 1 and 2:61–76.

———. 1980. Options to injustice. Unpublished diss., Columbia University, Teachers' College.

———. 1982. When nonvictims derogate: Powerlessness in the helping professions. *Personality and Social Psychology Bulletin* 8, no. 4:637–43.

———. 1983a. Expert testimony delivered in *Newberg v. Board of Public Education.* Philadelphia.

———. 1983b. Perspectives on inequality: Voices from urban schools. In *Applied Social Psychology Annual IV,* ed. L. Bickman, 217–46. Beverly Hills, Calif.: Sage.

———. 1983c. The social context and a sense of injustice: The option to challenge. *Representative Research in Social Psychology* 13, no. 1:15–33.

———. 1984. Coping with rape: Critical perspectives on consciousness. *Imagination, Cognition and Personality: The Scientific Study of Consciousness* 3, no. 3:249–67.

———. 1985a. Dropping out of high school: An inside look. *Social Policy* 16:43–50.

———. 1985b. Reflections on a feminist psychology of women: Paradoxes and prospects. *Psychology of Women Quarterly* 9, no. 2:167–83.

———. 1986a. Contextualizing the study of social injustice. In *Advances in applied social psychology,* vol. 3, ed. M. Saks and L. Saxe, Hillsdale, N.J.: Lawrence Erlbaum.

———. 1986b. Why urban adolescents drop into and out of public high school. *Teachers College Record* 87, no. 3:393–409.

———. 1987a. Expert report for *Board of Education of the Borough of Englewood*

Cliffs v. Board of Education of the City of Englewood v. Board of Education of the Borough of Tenafly, Newark, N.J.

————. 1987b. Silencing in public school. *Language Arts* 64, no. 2:157–74.

————. 1991. *Framing dropouts: Notes on the politics of an urban high school.* Albany: SUNY Press.

Fine, M., and Asch, A. 1981. Disabled women: Sexism without the pedestal. *Journal of Sociology and Social Welfare* 8, no. 2:233–48.

————. 1982. The question of disability: No easy answers for the women's movement. *Reproductive Rights Newsletters* 4, no. 3:19–20.

————, eds. 1988. *Women with disabilities: Essays in psychology, culture and politics.* Philadelphia: Temple University Press.

Fine, M., and Gordon, S. 1989. Feminist transformations of/despite psychology. In *Gender and thought: Psychological perspectives,* ed. M. Crawford and M. Gentry, 146–74. New York: Springer-Verlag.

Fine, M., and Rosenberg, P. 1983. Dropping out of high school: The ideology of school and work. *Journal of Education* 165, no. 3:257–72.

Fine, M., and Vanderslice, V. 1992. Qualitative activist research: Reflections on politics and methods. In *Methodological issues in applied social psychology,* ed. E. Posavac, New York: Plenum.

Fine, M., and Wade, J. 1986. Evaluation of domestic violence programs in Tennessee. San Francisco: Hilton Foundation.

Fine, M., and Zane, N. 1989. On bein' wrapped tight: When low income females drop out of high school. In *Dropouts in schools: Issues, dilemmas, and solutions,* ed. L. Weis, Albany: SUNY Press.

Finger, A. 1983. Disability and reproductive rights. *off our backs* 13, no. 9.

————. 1984. Claiming all of our bodies: Reproductive rights and disabilities. In *Test-tube women: What future for motherhood?* ed. R. Arditti, R. Duelli-Kelin, and S. Minden, 298–312. Boston: Pandora.

Fisher, B., and Galler, M. J. 1988. Friendship and fairness: How disability affects friendship between women. In *Women with disabilities: Essays in psychology, culture, and politics,* ed. M. Fine and A. Asch, 172–94. Philadelphia: Temple University Press.

Fisher, W. E.; Byrne, D.; and White, L. 1983. Emotional barriers to contraception. In *Adolescents, sex, and contraception,* ed. D. Byrne and W. Fisher, 207–39. Hillsdale, N.J.: Lawrence Erlbaum.

Flax, J. 1987. Postmodernism and gender relations in feminist theory. *Signs: Journal of Women in Culture and Society* 12:621–43.

————. 1990. *Thinking fragments: Psychoanalyses, feminism, and post-modernism in the contemporary west.* Berkeley: University of California Press.

Fordham, S. 1988. Racelessness as a factor in Black students' school success: Pragmatic strategy or pyrrhic victory? *Harvard Educational Review* 58, no. 1:54–84.

Foucault, M. 1972. Intellectuals and power. *TELOS* 16:103–9.

————. 1980. *The history of sexuality,* vol. 1. New York: Vintage Books.

Fox-Genovese, E. 1991. *Feminism without illusions: A critique of individualism.* Chapel Hill: University of North Carolina Press.

Frank, G. 1981. *Venus on wheels: The life history of a congenital amputee.* (Ph.D. diss., Anthropology Department, University of California, Los Angeles).

———. 1988. On embodiment: A case study of congenital limb deficiency in American culture. In *Women with disabilities: Essays in psychology, culture, and politics,* ed. M. Fine and A. Asch, 41–71. Philadelphia: Temple University Press.

Franklin, P. 1977. Impact of disability on the family structure. *Social Security Bulletin* 40, no. 5:3–18.

Freeman, J., ed. 1984. *Women: A feminist perspective.* Palo Alto, Calif.: Mayfield.

Freire, P. 1985. *The politics of education.* South Hadley, Mass.: Bergin and Garvey.

Freudenberg, N. 1987. The politics of sex education. *HealthPAC Bulletin.* New York: HealthPAC.

Friedman, G. 1980. The mother-daughter bond. *Contemporary Psychoanalysis* 16, no. 1:90–97.

Funk, R. 1987. Disability rights: From caste to class in the context of civil rights. In *Images of the disabled: Disabling images,* ed. A. Gartner and T. Joe, 7–30. New York: Praeger.

Furby, L. 1979. Individualistic bias in studies of locus of control. In *Psychology in social context,* ed. A. Buss, 169–90. New York: Irvington.

Gaertner, S. L., and Dovidio, J. F. 1981. Racism among the well intentioned. In *Pluralism, racism, and public policy: The search for equality,* ed. E. Clausen and J. Bermingham, 208–20. New York: G. K. Hall.

Galler, R. 1984. The myth of the perfect body. In *Pleasure and danger,* ed. C. S. Vance, 165–72. Boston: Routledge and Kegan Paul.

Gaventa, J. 1980. *Power and powerlessness: Quiescence and rebellion in an Appalachian valley.* Urbana: University of Illinois Press.

Gaylin, W.; Glasser, I.; Marcus, S.; and Rothman, D. 1978. *Doing good: The limits of benevolence.* New York: Pantheon Books.

Genovese, E. 1972. *Roll, Jordan, roll: The world the slaves made.* New York: Vintage.

Gergen, M. 1988. *Feminist thought and the structure of knowledge.* New York: New York University Press.

Giddings, P. 1984. *When and where I enter: The impact of Black women on race and sex in America.* New York: Bantam.

Gilbert, L. L. 1980. Feminist therapy. In *Women and psychotherapy: An assessment of research and practice,* ed. A. M. Brodsky and R. T. Hare-Mustin, 245–65. New York: Guilford Press.

Gilkes, C. 1988. Building in many places: Multiple commitments and ideologies in black women's community work. In *Women and the politics of empowerment,* ed. A. Bookman and S. Morgan, 53–76. Philadelphia: Temple University Press.

Gillespie, P., and Fink, A. 1974. The influence of sexism on the education of handicapped children. *Exceptional Children* 5, no. 3:155–62.

Gilligan, C. 1982. *In a different voice: Psychological theory and women's development*. Cambridge, Mass.: Harvard Univeristy Press.

———. 1990. *Joining the resistance: Psychology, politics, girls, and women*. Essay presented as the Tanner lecture on human values, University of Michigan, Ann Arbor.

Gilligan, C.; Wards, J; and Taylor, J. 1988. *Mapping the moral domain*. Cambridge, Mass.: Harvard University Press.

Giroux, H. 1982. *Theory and resistance: A pedagogy for opposition*. South Hadley, Mass: Bergin and Garvey.

———. 1988. *Schooling and the struggle for public life: Critical pedagogy in the modern age*. Minneapolis: University of Minnesota Press.

Giroux, H. and McLaren, P., eds. 1989. *Critical pedagogy, the state, and cultural struggle*. Albany: State University of New York Press.

Gitlin, A.; Siegel, M.; and Boru, K. 1988. *Purpose and method: Rethinking the use of ethnography by the educational left*. Paper presented at the meeting of the American Psychological Association, New Orleans.

———. 1989. The politics of method: From leftist ethnography to educative research. *Qualitative Studies in Education* 2:237–53.

Gliedman, J., and Roth, W. 1980. *The unexpected minority: Handicapped children in America*, New York: Harcourt Brace Jovanovich.

Goertz, M. E. 1982. *Dissemination of school finance services in urban school districts*. Princeton, N.J.: Education Policy Research Institute, Educational Testing Service.

Goffman, E. 1963. *Stigma: Notes on the management of spoiled identity*. Englewood Cliffs, N.J.: Prentice-Hall.

Gold, S. 1985. A year of accomplishment: Sharon Gold reports to the blind of California. *Braille Monitor* (November): 629–40.

Golden, C. 1984. Diversity and variability in lesbian identities. Paper presented at lesbian psychologies conference of the association of women in psychology.

———. 1987. Diversity and variability in women's sexual identities. In *Lesbian psychologies: Explorations and challenges*, ed. Boston Lesbian Psychologies Collective, 18–34. Urbana: University of Illinois Press.

Goodlad, J. 1984. *A place called school: Prospects for the future*. New York: McGraw-Hill.

Gordon, S. 1988. *Evolution of a research proposal: The personal becomes methodological*. Unpub. ms., Graduate School of Education, University of Pennsylvania, Philadelphia.

Grady, K. E. 1981. Sex bias in research design. *Psychology of Women Quarterly* 5, no. 4:628–36.

Gramsci, A. 1971. *Selections from prison notebooks*. New York: International Publishers.

———. 1973. *Letters from prison*. New York: Harper and Row.

Green, P. 1981. *The pursuit of inequality*. New York: Pantheon.

Greene, M. 1986. In search of a critical pedagogy. *Harvard Educational Review* 56, no. 4:427–41.

Greenspan, M. 1983. *A new approach to women and therapy.* New York: McGraw-Hill.

Gurin, P.; Gurin, G.; Lao, R.; and Beattie, M. 1969. Internal-external control in the motivational dynamics of Negro youth. *Journal of Social Issues* 25, no. 3:29–53.

Haber, L., and McNeil J. 1983. *Methodological questions in the estimation of disability prevalence.* Population Division, Bureau of the Census. Washington, D.C.: Government Printing Office.

Hahn, H. 1983a. *"The good parts":* Interpersonal relationships in the auto-biographies of physical disabled persons. Wenner-Gren Foundation Working Papers in Anthropology, December, 1–38.

———. 1983b. Paternalism and public policy. *Society,* March–April, 36–44.

———. 1987. Civil rights for disabled Americans: The foundation of a political agenda. In *Images of the disabled: Disabling images,* ed. A Gartner and T. Joe. New York: Praeger.

Hall, G. S. 1914. Education and the social hygiene movement. *Social Hygiene* no. 1 (December):29–35.

Halson, J. 1990. Young women, sexual harassment and heterosexuality: Violence, power relations and mixed sex schooling. In *Gender, sexuality and power,* ed. P. Abbott and C. Wallace. London: Macmillan.

Hanna, W. J., and Rogovsky, B. 1986. *Women and disability: Stigma and "the third factor."* Unpub. ms., Department of Family and Community Development, College of Human Ecology, University of Maryland, College Park.

Hannaford, S. 1985. *Living outside inside: a disabled woman's experience.* Berkeley, Calif.: Canterbury Press.

Hansot, E., and Tyack, D. 1988. Gender in American public schools: Thinking institutionally. *Signs: Journal of Women in Culture and Society* 13, no. 4:741–60.

Haraway, D. 1988. Situated knowledges: The science question in feminism and the privilege of partial perspective. *Feminist Studies* 14:575–99.

———. 1989. *Primate visions: Gender, race, and nature in the world of modern science.* New York: Routledge.

Harding, S. 1986. *The science question in feminism.* Ithaca, N.Y.: Cornell University Press.

———, ed. 1987. *Feminism and methodology: Social science issues.* Bloomington: Indiana University Press.

———. 1991. *Whose science? Whose knowledge?* Ithaca, N.Y.: Cornell University Press.

Hare-Mustin, R. 1991. Sex, lies, and headaches: The problem is power. In *Women and power: Perspectives for therapy,* ed. T. J. Goodrich, 63–85. New York: Norton.

Hare-Mustin, R., and Marecek, J. 1987. *The meaning of difference: Gender theory, postmodernism, and psychology.* Paper partially presented at the meeting of the American Psychological Association, New York.

———. 1990a. *Making a difference: Psychology and the construction of gender.* New Haven, Conn.: Yale University Press.

———. 1990b. *Toward a feminist post-structural psychology: The modern self and the post-modern subject.* Paper presented at the meeting of the American Psychological Association, Boston.

Harris, A. 1990. Race and essentialism feminist legal theory. *Stanford Law Review* 42, no. 3:581–616.

Harris, A., and Wideman, D. 1988. The construction of gender and disability in early attatchment. In *Women with disabilities: Essays in psychology, culture, and politics*, ed. M. Fine and A. Asch, Philadelphia: Temple University Press.

Harris, L., and Associates. 1985. *Public attitudes about sex educatoin, family planning, and abortion in the United States.* New York: Louis Harris and Associates.

Harrison, B. W. 1986. Feminist realism. *Christianity and Crisis* 46, no. 10:233–36.

Hartmann, H. 1981. The unhappy marriage of Marxism and feminism: Towards a more progressive union. In *Women and revolution: A discussion of the unhappy marriage of Marxism and feminism*, ed. L. Sargent, 1–42. Boston: South End Press.

Hartsock, N. 1985. *Money, sex, and power.* Boston: Northeastern University Press.

———. 1987. The feminist standpoint: Developing the ground for a specifically feminist historical materialism. In *Feminism and methodology: Social science issues*, ed. S. Harding, 157–80. Bloomington: Indiana University Press.

Haug, F. 1987. *Female sexualization: A collective work of memory.* London: Verso.

Heinrich, E., and Kriegel, L. 1961. *Experiments in survival.* New York: Association for the Aid of Crippled Children.

Henley, N. M. 1985. Psychology and gender. *Signs: Journal of Women in Culture and Society* 11, no. 1:101–19.

———. 1989. Molehill or mountain? What we know and don't know about sex bias in language. In *Gender and thought: Psychological perspectives*, ed. M. Crawford and M. Gentry, 59–78. New York: Spinger-Verlag.

Hey, V. 1987. *"The company she keeps": The social and interpersonal construction of girls' same sex friendships.* Ph.D. diss., University of Kent, Canterbury, England.

Higgins, P. 1980. *Outsiders in a hearing world.* Beverly Hills, Calif.: Sage.

Hill, N.; Mehnert T.; Taylor, H.; Kagey, M.; and Leizhenko, S.; et al. 1986. *The ICD survey of disabled Americans: Bringing disabled Americans into the mainstream.* Study #854009. New York: International Center for the Disabled.

Hill, N.; Mehnert, T.; Boyd, M.; Taylor, H.; and Leizhenko, S.; et al. 1987. *The ICD survey, vol. 2: Employing disabled Americans.* Study #864009. New York: International Center for the Disabled.

Hilliard, A. G., III. 1988. Public support for successful instructional practices for at risk students. In *School success for students at risk*, ed. Council of Chief State School Officers, 195–208. New York: Harcourt Brace Jovanovich.

Hispanic Policy Development Project. 1987. 1980 high school sophomores from poverty backgrounds: Whites, blacks, Hispanics look at school and adult responsibilities. *Hispanic Policy Development Project* (New York) 1, no. 2.

Hobbs, N. 1975. *The futures of children: Categories, labels, and their consequences.* San Francisco: Jossey-Bass.

Holmes Group. 1986. *Tomorrow's teachers.* East Lansing, Mich.: Holmes Group.

Holtz, A. 1989. Central High: An ethnographic study of court-ordered female integration at a prestigious public high school. Ph.D. diss., University of Pennsylvania.

hooks, b. 1981. *Ain't I a woman: Black women and feminism.* Boston: South End Press.

———. 1984. *Feminist theory from margin to center.* Boston: South End Press.

———. 1990. *Yearning: Race, gender, and cultural politics.* Boston: South End Press.

Hottois, J., and Milner, N. 1975. *The sex education controversy.* Lexington, Mass.: Lexington Books.

Huddy, B., and Goodchilds, J. 1985. *Older women in action: The influence of personal interests on collective action.* Paper presented at the annual meeting of the American Psychological Association, Los Angeles.

Hudson, B. 1984. Femininity and adolescence. In *Gender and generation,* ed. A. McRobbie and M. Nava, 31–53. London: Macmillan.

Imber, M. 1984. Towards a theory of educational origins: The genesis of sex education. *Education Theory* 34, no. 3:275–86.

Irigaray, L. 1980. When our lips speak together. *Signs: Journal of Women in Culture and Society* 6, no. 1:69.

Janoff-Bulman, R. 1979. Characterological versus behavioral self-blame: Inquiries into depression and rape. *Journal of Personality and Social Psychology* 37, no. 10:1798–1809.

Janoff-Bulman, R., and Marshall, G. 1982. Mortality, well-being and control: A study of a population of institutionalized aged. *Personality and Social Psychology Bulletin* 8, no. 4:691–98.

Janoff-Bulman, R., and Wortman, C. 1977. Attributions of blame and coping in the "real world": Severe accident victims react to their lot. *Journal of Personality and Social Psychology* 35, no. 5:351–63.

Johnson, M. 1987. Emotion and pride. *Disability Rag* 8, no. 1:1, 4–6.

Jones, E.; Forrest, J.; Goldman, N.; Henshaw, S.; Lincoln, R.; Rosoff, J.; Westoff, C.; and Wulf, D. 1985. Teenage pregnancy in developed countries. *Family Planning Perspectives* 17, no. 1:55–63.

Joseph, G. 1981. The incompatible ménage à trois: Marxism, feminism, and racism. In *Women and revolution: A discussion of the unhappy marriage of Marxism and feminism,* ed. L. Sargent, 91–108. Boston: South End Press.

Joseph, G., and Lewis, J. 1981. *Common differences: Conflicts in black and white feminist perspectives.* Boston: South End Press.

Journal of Sociology and Social Welfare 8, no. 2. 1981. *Women and disability: The double handicap.* Special issue.

Journal of Visual Impairment and Blindness 77, no. 6. 1983. *Being blind, being a woman*. Special issue.

Kahn, A., and Yoder, J. 1990. *Domination, subordination and the psychology of women: A theoretical framework*. Paper presented at the meeting of the American Psychological Association, Boston.

Kaminstein, D. 1988. *The rhetoric of science and toxic waste dumps: A study of community quiescence*. Unpublished MS, Graduate School of Education, University of Pennsylvania, Philadelphia.

Kantrowitz, B.; Hager, M.; Wingert, S.; Carroll, G.; Raine, G.; Witherspoon, D.; Huck, J.; and Doherty, S. 1987. Kids and contraceptives. *Newsweek*, February 16, 54–65.

Keller, E. F. 1982. Feminism and science. *Signs: Journal of Women in Culture and Society* 7, no. 3:589–602.

Kelly, E. 1988. *Surviving sexual violence*. London: Basil Blackwell.

Kelly, G. 1986. *Learning about sex*. Woodbury, N.Y.: Barron's Educational Series.

Kidder, L., and Fine, M. 1982. *The justice of rights versus needs*. Paper presented at the meeting of the International Society for Political Psychology, Washington, D.C.

Kirby, D. 1985. *School-based health clinics: An emerging approach to improving adolescent health and addressing teenage pregnancy*. Washington, D.C.: Center for Population Options.

Kirby, D., and Scales, P. 1981. An analysis of state guidelines for sex education instruction in public schools. *Family Relations* (April): 229–37.

Kirchner, C. 1987. Assessing the effects of vocational rehabilitation on disadvantaged persons: Theoretical perspectives and issues for research. In *Proceedings of the Annual Meeting of the Society for the Study of Chronic Illness, Impairment, and Disability, 1984–1985*. Salem, Ore.: Willamette University Press.

Kirschner, D. A., and Kirschner, S. 1986. *Comprehensive family therapy: An integration of systemic and psychodynamic treatment models*. New York: Brunner/Mazel.

Kitzinger, C. 1988. "Its not fair on girls": Young women's accounts of unfairness in school. Paper presented at the annual conference of British Psychological Society, University of Leeds.

———. 1991. Feminism, psychology, and the paradox of power. *Feminism and Psychology* 1, no. 1:111–30.

Kolodny, A. 1988. Dancing between left and right: Feminism and the academic minefield in the 1980s. *Feminist Studies* 14:453–66.

Koop, C. E. 1986. *Surgeon general's report on acquired immune deficiency syndrome*. Washington, D.C.: Office of the Surgeon General.

Koop's AIDS stand assailed. 1987. *New York Times*, March 15, A25.

Kurz, D. 1988. Unpublished raw data presented to research seminar in social methods at the University of Pennsylvania, Graduate School of Education, Philadelphia.

Kutner, N. G. 1985. Gender, social class, and social support to disabled persons.

Paper delivered at the meeting of the Society for the Study of Social Problems, American Sociological Association, Washington, D.C.

Kutner, N. G., and Gray, H. L. 1985. Women and chronic renal failure: Some neglected issues. In *Women and disability: The double handicap*, ed. M. J. Deegan and N. A. Brooks, 105–16. New Brunswick, N.J.: Transaction.

Ladner, J. 1972. *Tomorrow's tomorrow: The black woman*. Garden City, N.Y.: Doubleday.

———. 1987. Black teenage pregnancy: A challenge for educators. *Journal of Negro Education* 56, no. 1: 236–44.

Lakoff, R., and Scherr, R. L. 1984. *Face value: The politics of beauty*. Boston: Routledge and Kegan Paul.

Lather, P. 1986. Research as praxis. *Harvard Educational Review* 56, no. 3:257–77.

———. 1990. Staying dumb? Student resistance to liberatory curriculum. Paper presented at the annual conference of the American Educational Research Association, Boston.

———. 1991. *Getting smart: Feminist research and pedagogy within the postmodern*. New York: Routledge.

Laufer, M. (1982). Female masturbation in adolescence and the development of the relationship to the body. *International Journal of Psycho-Analysis* 63, no. 3:295–302.

Lawrence, M. 1987. *Fed up and hungry*. Minneapolis: University of Minnesota Press.

Lefcourt, H. 1980. Personality and locus of control. In *Human Helplessness*, ed. J. Gerber and M. Seligman. New York: Academic Press.

Legalized kidnapping: State takes child away from blind mother. 1986. *Braille Monitor*, August–September, 432–35.

Leo, J. 1986. Sex and schools. *Time* (November 24): 54–63.

Lerman, H. 1986. *A mote in Freud's eye: From psychoanalysis to the psychology of women*. New York: Springer-Verlag.

Lesko, N. 1988. The curriculum of the body: Lessons from a Catholic high school. In *Becoming feminine: The politics of popular culture*, ed. L. Roman, 123–42. Philadelphia: Falmer Press.

Levin, H. 1989. Financing the education of at-risk students. Paper presented to Public/Private Ventures, Philadelphia, Pa.

Lewin, K. 1948. *Resolving social conflicts: Selected papers on group dynamics*. New York: Harper.

Lewis, M., and Simon, R. 1986. A discourse not intended for her: Learning and teaching within patriarchy. *Harvard Educational Review* 56, no. 4:459–72.

Lieberman, A. 1988. *Building a professional culture in school*. New York: Teachers' College Press.

Lightfoot, S. 1978. *Worlds apart*. New York: Basic Books.

Linton, R., and Whitham, M. 1982. With mourning, rage, empowerment, and defiance: The 1981 women's pentagon action. *Socialist Review* 12, nos. 3–4:11–36.

Lorde, A. 1980a. *The cancer journals*. Argyle, N.Y.: Spinsters, Ink.

———. 1980b. *Uses of the erotic: The erotic as power*. Paper presented at the Fourth Berkshire Conference on the History of Women, Mount Holyoke College.

Lott, B. 1985. The potential enrichment of social/personality psychology through feminist research and vice versa. *American Psychologist* 40, no. 2:155–64.

Lykes, M. B. 1986. *The will to resist: Preservation of self and culture in Guatemala*. Paper presented at the meeting of the Latin American Studies Association, Boston.

———. 1989. Dialogue with Guatemalan Indian women: Critical perspectives on constructing collaborative research. In *Representations: Social constructions of gender*, ed. R. Unger, 167–84. Amityville, N.Y.: Baywood Publishing Co.

Lykes, M. B., and Stewart, A. J. 1986. Evaluating the feminist challenge to research in personality and social psychology: 1963–1983. *Psychology of Women Quarterly* 10, no. 4:393–412.

McDade, L. 1988. *Ethnography and journalism: The critical difference*. Paper presented at the Urban Ethnography Forum, University of Pennsylvania.

McHugh, M. C.; Koeske, R. D.; and Frieze, I. H. 1986. Issues to consider in conducting nonsexist psychological research: A guide for researchers. *American Psychologist* 41, no. 8:879–90.

McIntosh, P. 1983. *Interactive phases of curricular re-vision: A feminist perspective*. Monograph. Wellesley College.

———. 1990. *Interactive phases of curricular and personal revision with regard to race*. Working paper no. 219. Wellesley, Mass.: Wellesley College, Center for Research on Women.

MacKinnon, C. 1983. Complicity: An Introduction to Andrea Dworkin's "Abortion," chap. 3; "Right-wing women." *Law and Inequality* 1, no. 1:89–94.

Macklin, R., and Gaylin, W. 1981. *Mental retardation and sterilization: A problem of competency and paternalism*. New York: Plenum.

McNeil, L. 1981. Negotiating classroom knowledge: Beyond achievement and socialization. *Curriculum Studies* 13:313–28.

Majors, B.; Cozzarelli, C.; Sciacchitano, A.; and Cooper, M. 1990. Perceived social support, self-efficacy and adjustment to abortion. *Journal of Personality and Social Psychology* 59, no. 3:452–63.

Marsiglio, W., and Mott, F. 1986. The impact of sex education on sexual activity, contraceptive use, and premarital pregnancy among American teenagers. *Family Planning Perspectives* 18, no. 4:151–62.

Mascia-Lees, F. E.; Sharpe, P.; and Ballerino Cohen, C. 1989. The postmodernist turn in anthropology: Caution from a feminist perspective. *Signs: Journal of Women in Culture and Society* 15, no. 1:7–33.

Matthews, G. F. 1983. *Voices from the shadows: Women with disabilities speak out*. Toronto: Women's Educational Press.

Mayo, C. 1982. Training for positive marginality. *Applied Social Psychology Annual* 3:57–73.

Mead, G. H. 1934. *Mind, self, and society*. Chicago: University of Chicago Press.

Meier, D. 1987. Central Park East: An alternative story. *Phi Delta Kappan* 68 (June): 753–57.

Melling, L. 1984. Wife abuse in the deaf community. *Response to Family Violence and Sexual Assault* 9, no. 1:1–2, 12.

Melton, G. B., and Russo, N. 1987. Adolescent abortion: Psychological perspectives on public policy. *American Psychologist* 42, no. 1:69–72.

Militarism Resource Project. 1985. High school military recruiting: Recent developments. Philadelphia.

Miller, A. 1970. Role of physical attractiveness in impression formation. *Psychonomic Science* 19:241–43.

Miller, J. B. 1976. *Toward a new psychology of women*. Boston: Beacon Press.

Miner, V., and Longino, H. E. 1987. *Competition: A feminist taboo?* New York: The Feminist Press at CUNY.

Mishler, E. 1979. Meaning in context: Is there any other kind? *Harvard Educational Review* 49, no. 1:1–19.

Mohanty, C. 1987. Feminist encounters: Locating the politics of experience. *Copyright* 1:39.

Morawski, J. 1990. Toward the unimagined: Feminism and epistemology in psychology. In *Making a difference: Psychology and the construction of gender*, ed. R. Hare-Mustin and J. Marecek, 159–83. New Haven, Conn.: Yale University Press.

Moser, P. 1989. Double vision. *Self* (January):51–52.

Mudrick, N. R. 1983. Disabled women. *Society* (March): 51–55.

Mytelka, A., and Trachtenberg, P. 1987. Legal brief for *Board of Education of the Borough of Englewood Cliffs v. Board of Education of the City of Englewood v. Board of Education of the Borough of Tenafly*. Newark, N.J.

Nagi, S. 1969. *Disability and rehabilitation*. Columbus: Ohio University Press.

National Council on Alcoholism. 1980. *Facts on alcoholism and women*. New York: Affiliate.

National Research Council. 1987. *Risking the future: Adolescent sexuality, pregnancy, and childbearing*, vol. 1. Washington, D.C.: National Academy Press.

Nestle, J. 1983. My mother liked to fuck. In *Powers of desire: The politics of sexuality*, ed. A. Snitow, C. Stansell, and S. Thompson, 468–70. New York: Monthly Review Press.

New York City Board of Education. 1984. *Family living curriculum including sex education: Grades K through 12*. Division of Curriculum and Instruction.

New York State Department of Education. 1985. Memo from Dennis Hughes, state administrator on high school equivalency programs, December 4, Albany, N.Y.

Noble v. Massachusetts Institute of Technology. 1986. Memorandum of decision and order on defendants' motion for summary judgment. Commonwealth of Massachusetts, Middlesex, ss. Superior Court Civil Action, 86-5669.

Noddings, N. 1986. Fidelity in teaching, teacher education, and research for teaching. *Harvard Educational Review* 56, no. 4:496–510.

Ogbu, J. 1978. *Minority education and caste: The American system in cross-cultural perspective*. New York: Academic Press.

off our backs 11, no. 5 (1981). *Women with disabilities*. Special issue.

Omolade, B. 1983. Hearts of darkness. In *Powers of desire: The politics of sexuality,* ed. A. Snitow, C. Stansell, and S. Thompson, 350–67. New York: Monthly Review Press.

———. 1985; 1981. Black women and feminism. In *The future of difference,* ed. H. Eisenstein and A. Jardine. New Brunswick, N.J.: Rutgers University Press.

Opotow, S. 1990. Moral exclusion and injustice: An introduction. *Journal of Social Issues* 46, no. 1:1–20.

Orbach, S. 1986. *Hunger strike: The anorectic's struggle as a metaphor for our age.* New York: Norton.

Packer, J. 1983. Sex stereotyping in vocational counseling of blind/visually impaired persons: A national study of counselor choices. *Journal of Visual Impairment and Blindness* 77, no. 6:261–68.

Panel details "abusive conditions" in California care facilities. 1984. *New York Times,* January 16, B11.

Parlee, M. 1979. Psychology and women. *Signs: Journal of Women in Culture and Society* 5, no. 1:121–33.

———. 1981. Appropriate control groups in feminist research. *Psychology of Women Quarterly* 5, no. 4:637–44.

———. 1990. Psychology of menstruation and premenstrual syndrome. Unpublished MS, Graduate School and University Center, City University of New York.

———. 1991. Happy birthday to feminism and psychology. *Feminism and Psychology* no. 1, 1:39–48.

Payne, M. 1991. Canon: The new testament to Derrida. *College Literature* 18, no. 2:5–21.

Payton, C. 1984. Who must do the hard things? *American Psychologist* 39:391–97.

Peiss, K.; Schwarz, J.; and Simmons, C. eds. 1989. *Passion and power: Sexuality in history.* Philadelphia: Temple University Press.

Penn Harassment Survey. 1985. Office of the vice provost for research, University of Pennsylvania.

Peplau, L. A., and Conrad, E. 1989. Beyond nonsexist research: The perils of feminist methods in psychology. *Psychology of Women Quarterly* 13, no. 4:379–400.

Perlez, J. 1986a. On teaching about sex. *New York Times,* June 24, C1.

———. 1986b. School chief to ask for mandatory sex education. *New York Times,* September 24, A36.

Person, E. S. 1982. Women working: Fears of failure, deviance, and success. *Journal of the American Academy of Psychoanalysis* 10, no. 1:67–84.

Petchesky, R. 1984. *Abortion and woman's choice.* New York: Longman.

Peterson, C.; Schwartz, S.; and Seligman, M. 1981. Self-blame and depressive symptoms. *Journal of Personality and Social Psychology* 41, no. 2:253–59.

Philadelphia School District. 1986. *Sex education curriculum.* Draft.

Polit, D.; Kahn, J.; and Stevens, D. 1985. *Final impacts from Project Redirection.* New York: Manpower Development Research Center.

Poovey, M. 1988. Feminism and deconstruction. *Feminist Studies* 14:51–65.

————. 1990. Speaking of the body: Mid-Victorian constructions of female desire. In *Body politics: Women, literature, and discourses of science,* ed. M. Jacobus, E. Keller, and S. Shuttleworth, 29–46. New York: Routledge.

Pratt, M. 1985. Scratches on the face of the country: Or, what Mr. Barrow saw in the land of Bushmen. In *"Race," writing, and difference,* ed. H. L. Gates, Jr., 138–62. Chicago: University of Chicago Press.

Public/Private Ventures. 1987. *Summer training and education program.* Philadelphia: Public/Private Ventures.

Rapp, R. 1984. XYLO: A true story. In *Test-tube women: What future for motherhood?* ed. R. Arditti, R. Duelli-Klein, and R. S. Minden. Boston: Pandora Press.

————. 1987. Chromosomes and communication: The discourse of genetic counseling. *Medical Anthropology Quarterly.*

Raskin, M. G. 1986. *The common good: Its politics, policies, and philosophy.* New York: Routledge and Kegan Paul.

Rehab Group. 1979. *Digest of data on persons with disabilities.* Falls Church, Va.: May.

Reinharz, S. 1988. *The concept of voice.* Paper presented at meeting of Human Diversity, Perspectives on People context. University of Maryland, College Park.

Reproductive Freedom Project. 1986. Parental consent laws on abortion: Their catastrophic impact on teenagers. New York: American Civil Liberties Union.

Rich, A. 1979. *On Lies, Secrets, and Silence.* New York: Norton.

————. 1980. Compulsory heterosexuality and lesbian existence. *Signs: Journal of Women in Culture and Society* 5, no. 4:631–60.

Robertson, C.; Dyer, C. E.; and Campbell, D. 1988. Campus harassment: Sexual harassment policies and procedures at institutions of higher learning. *Signs: Journal of Women in Culture and Society* 13:792–812.

Robinson, L. 1989. What culture should mean. *Nation,* September, 319–21.

Robinson, T., and Ward, J. V. 1991. "A belief in self far greater than anyone's disbelief": Cultivating resistance among African-American female adolescents. *Women and Therapy* 2, nos. 3–4.

Rodgers-Rose, R., ed. 1980. *The black woman.* Beverly Hills: Sage.

Rohter, L. 1985. School workers shown AIDS film. *New York Times,* October 29, B3.

Rollins, J. 1985. *Between women: Domestics and their employers.* Philadelphia: Temple University Press.

Roman, L. G. 1988. Intimacy, labor and class: Ideologies of feminine sexuality in punk slam dance. In *Becoming feminine: The politics of popular culture,* ed. L. G. Roman, L. K. Christian-Smith, and E. Ellsworth, 143–84. Philadelphia: Falmer Press.

Roman, L. G.; Christian-Smith, L. K.; and Ellsworth, E.; eds. 1988. *Becoming feminine: The politics of popular culture.* Philadelphia: Falmer Press.

Rosaldo, R. 1989. *Culture and truth: The remaking of social analysis.* Boston: Beacon Press.

Rose, P. 1984. Hers. *New York Times,* April 5, C2.

Rosewater, L. B., and Walker, L. E. A., eds. 1985. *Handbook of feminist therapy: Women's issues in psychotherapy*. New York: Springer-Verlag.

Roskies, E. 1972. *Abnormality and normality: The mothering of thalidomide children*. Ithaca, N.Y.: Cornell University Press.

Roth, W. 1981. *The handicapped speak*. Jefferson, N.C.: McFarland and Co.

———. 1983. Handicap as a social construct. *Society* (March–April): 56–61.

Rothman, B. K. 1986. On the question of Baby Doe. *Heath / PAC Bulletin* 16, no. 6:7, 11–13.

Rousso, H. 1984. Fostering healthy self-esteem. *Exceptional Parent* (December): 9–14.

———. 1987. Positive images for disabled women. Presented at the conference Moving Up and Out Together: Women and Disability, Southern Connecticut State University, New Haven.

Rubin, G. 1984. Thinking sex: Notes for a radical theory of the politics of sexuality. In *Pleasure and danger: Exploring female sexuality*, ed. C. S. Vance, 267–319. Boston: Routledge and Kegan Paul.

Rubin, L. B. 1976. *Worlds of pain: Life in the working-class family*. New York: Basic Books.

Ruddick, S. 1980. Maternal thinking. *Feminist Studies* 6, no. 3:343–67.

Russo, N. 1984. *Women in the American Psychological Assocation*. Washington, D.C.: American Psychological Association.

Ryan, W. 1981. *Equality*. New York: Pantheon Books.

Safilios-Rothschild, C. 1977. Discrimination against disabled women. *International Rehabilitation Review* (February): 4.

St. Paul Maternity and Infant Care Project. 1985. Health services project description. St. Paul, Minn.

Sampson, E. 1981. Cognitive psychology as ideology. *American Psychologist* 36, no. 7:730–43.

Sargent, L. 1981. *Women and revolution: A discussion of the unhappy marriage of Marxism and feminism*. Boston: South End Press.

Saxton, M. 1984. Born and unborn: The implications of reproductive technologies for people with disabilities. In *Test-tube women: What future for motherhood?*, ed. R. Arditti, R. Duelli-Klein, and S. Minden, 143–84. Boston: Pandora.

Saxton, M., and Howe, F., eds. 1987. *With wings: An anthology of literature by and about women with disabilities*. New York: The Feminist Press at CUNY.

Scales, P. 1981. Sex education and the prevention of teenage pregnancy: An overview of policies and programs in the United States. In *Teenage pregnancy in a family context: Implications for policy*, ed. T. Ooms, 213–53. Philadelphia: Temple University Press.

Schechter, S. 1982. *Women and male violence: The visions and struggles of the battered women's movement*. Boston: South End Press.

Schlafly, P. 1986. Presentation on women's issues. American dreams symposium, Indiana University of Pennsylvania.

Schorr, D., and Rodin, J. 1982. The role of perceived control in practitioner-patient relationships. In *Basic processes in helping relationships*, ed. T. Wills, New York: Academic Press.

Schutz, R. 1976. Effects of control and predictability on the physical and psychological well-being of the institutionalized aged. *Journal of Personality and Social Psychology* 33, no. 5:563–73.

Scotch, R. K. 1984. *From goodwill to civil rights: Transforming federal disability policy*. Philadelphia: Temple University Press.

Scott, J. 1985. Is gender a useful category of historical analysis? Paper presented at the meeting of the American Historical Association, New York.

———. 1991. Deconstructing equality-versus-difference: Or the uses of post-structuralist theory for feminism. In *Conflicts in Feminism*, ed. M. Hirsch and E. Keller, 134–48. N.Y.: Routledge.

Sears, D. O. 1986. College sophomores in the laboratory: Influences of a narrow data base on social psychology's view of human nature. *Journal of Personality and Social Psychology* 51, no. 3:515–30.

Selected group to see original AIDS tape. 1987. *New York Times*, January 29, B4.

Seligman, M. 1975. *Helplessness: On depression, development, and death*. San Francisco: W. H. Freeman.

Semin, G., and Gergen, K. 1990. *Everyday understanding: Social and scientific implications*. London: Sage.

Sennett, R. 1980. *Authority*. New York: Vantage Books.

Sheehy, L. 1984. Women and disability. Master's thesis, Columbia University Law School.

Sherif, C. W. 1987. *Bias in psychology*. In *Feminism and methodology: Social science issues*, ed. S. Harding, 37–56. Bloomington: Indiana University Press.

Shields, S. 1975. Functionalism, Darwinism, and the psychology of women. *American Psychologist* 30, no. 7:739–54.

Shor, I. 1980. *Critical teaching and everyday life*. Boston: South End Press.

Siller, J.; Ferguson, L.; Vann, D. H.; and Holland, B. 1976. *Structure of attitudes toward the physically disabled*. New York: New York University School of Education.

Silver, R., and Wortman, C. 1980. Coping with undesirable life events. In *Human helplessness*, ed. J. Garber and M. Seligman. New York: Academic Press.

Simon, B. L. 1988. Never-married old women and disability: A majority experience. In *Women with disabilities: Essays in psychology, culture, and politics*, ed. M. Fine and A. Asch, 215–25. Philadelphia: Temple University Press.

Sizer, T. 1984. *Horace's compromise—the dilemma of the American high school*. The first report from a study of high schools, cosponsored by the National Association of Secondary School Principals and the Commission on Educational Issues of the National Association of Independent Schools. Boston: Houghton-Mifflin.

Smith, A., and Stewart, A. J. 1983. Approaches to studying racism and sexism in black women's lives. *Journal of Social Issues* 39, no. 3:1–15.

Smith, D. 1987. *The everyday world as problematic: A feminist sociology*. Boston: Northeastern University Press.

———. 1988. Femininity as discourse. In *Becoming feminine: The politics of popular culture*, ed. L. Roman, L. Christian-Smith, and E. Ellsworth, 37–59. London: Falmer Press.

Smith, D. E. 1987. Women's perspective as a radical critique of sociology. In *Feminism and methodology: Social science issues*, ed. S. Harding, 84–96. Bloomington: Indiana University Press.

Smith, V. 1991. Split affinities: The case of interracial rape. In *Conflicts in Feminism*, ed. M. Hirsch and E. Keller, 271–87. New York: Routledge.

Smith-Rosenberg, C. 1978. Sex as symbol in Victorian purity: An ethnohistorical analysis of Jacksonian America. *American Journal of Sociology* 84:212–47.

Snitow, A.; Stansell, C.; and Thompson, S., eds. 1983. *Powers of desire: The politics of sexuality*. New York: Monthly Review Press.

Solano, C.; Batten, P.; and Parish, E. 1982. Loneliness and patterns of self-disclosure. *Journal of Personality and Social Psychology* 43, no. 3:524–31.

Sonnenstein, F., and Pittman, K. 1984. The availability of sex education in large city school districts. *Family Planning Perspectives* 16, no. 1:19–25.

Spelman, E. 1988. *Inessential woman*. Boston: Beacon Press.

Stacey, J. 1988. Can there be a feminist ethnography? *Women's Studies International Forum* 11, no. 1:21–27.

Stacey, J., and Thorne, B. 1984. The missing feminist revolution in sociology. Paper presented at the annual meeting of the American Sociological Association, San Antonio, Tex.

Stack, C. 1975. *All our kin: Strategies for survival in a black community*. New York: Harper and Row.

Steiner,-Adair, C. 1986. The body politic: Normal female adolescent development and the development of eating disorders. *Journal of the American Academy of Psychoanalysis* 14, no. 1:95–114.

Stewart, A., and Healy, J. 1986. Longitudinal studies of psychological consequences of life changes in children and adults. *Journal of Personality and Social Psychology* 50, no. 1:143–51.

———. 1989. Linking individual development with social changes. *American Psychologist* 44, no. 1:30–42.

Stone, D. 1986. Policy case: Selecting clients for rehabilitation. Paper presented at the Hastings Center for Society, Ethics, and the Life Sciences, Hastings-on-Hudson, N.Y.

Strong, B. 1972. Idea of the early sex education movement in America, 1890–1920. *History of Education Quarterly* 12, no. 2:129–61.

Sullivan, M. 1990. *The male role in teenage pregnancy and parenting*. New York: Vara Institute of Justice.

Swenson, C. 1981. Using natural helping networks to promote competence. In *Promoting competence in clients*, ed. A. N. Maluccio, 125–51. New York: Free Press.

Symonds, M. 1980. The second injury to victims. Special issue of *Evaluation and Change*, 36–38.

Taylor, S.; Wood, J. V.; and Lichtman, R. R. 1983. "It could be worse": Selective education as a response to victimization. *Journal of Social Issues* 39, no. 2:19–40.

Thompson, S. 1983. Search for tomorrow: On feminism and the reconstruction of teen romance. In *Powers of desire: The politics of sexuality*, ed. A. Snitow, C. Stansell and S. Thompson, 367–84. New York: Monthly Review Press.

———. 1990. Putting a big thing in a little hole: Teenage girls' accounts of sexual initiation. *Journal of Sex Research* 27, no. 3:341–61.

Tiefer, L. 1987. Social constructionism and the study of human sexuality. In *Sex and gender*, ed. P. Shaver and C. Hendrick, 70–94. Beverly Hills, Calif.: Sage.

———. 1990. Gender and meaning in DSM-III (and III-R) sexual dysfunctions. Paper presented at the Meeting of American Psychological Association, Boston.

Titley, R., and Viney, W. 1969. Expression of aggression toward the physically handicapped. *Perceptual and Motor Skills* 29, no. 1:51–56.

Tobier, E. 1984. *The changing face of poverty: Trends in New York City's population in poverty, 1960–1990*. New York: Community Service Society.

Tolman, D. 1990. Discourses of adolescent girls' sexual desire in developmental psychology and feminist scholarship. Unpublished MS, Graduate School of Education, Harvard University.

Torres, A., and Forrest, J. 1985. Family planning clinic services in the United States, 1983. *Family Planning Perspectives* 17, no. 1:30–35.

Unger, R. 1982. Controlling out the obvious: Power, status and social psychology. Paper presented at the meeting of the American Psychological Association, Washington, D.C.

———. 1983. Expert testimony delivered at *Newberg v. Board of Public Education*, Philadelphia.

———. 1985. Personal appearance and social control. In *Women's worlds: From the new scholarship*, ed. M. Safire, M. Mednick, D. Izrael, and J. Bernard, 142–51. New York: Praeger.

———. 1987. The social construction of gender: Contradictions and conundrums. Paper presented at the meeting of the American Psychological Association, New York.

———, ed. 1989a. *Representations: Social constructions of gender*. Amityville, N.Y.: Baywood.

———. 1989b. Sex, gender and epistemology. In *Gender and thought: Psychological perspectives*, ed. M. Crawford and M. Gentry, 17–35. New York: Springer-Verlag.

———. 1990. Sources of variability: A feminist analysis. Paper presented at the meeting of the American Psychological Association, Boston.

Unger, R.; Hilderbrand, M.; and Mardor, T. 1982. Physical attractiveness and assumptions about social deviance: Some sex-by-sex comparison. *Personality and Social Psychology Bulletin* 8, no. 2:293–301.

U.S. Census Bureau. 1983. Labor force status and other characteristics of persons with a work disability: 1982. *Current Population Reports*, ser. P-23, no. 127. Washington, D.C.: Government Printing Office.

U.S. Commission on Civil Rights. 1982. *Unemployment and underemployment among blacks, Hispanics, and women*. Washington, D.C.: Government Printing Office.

———. 1983. *Accommodating the spectrum of individual abilities*. Washington, D.C.: Government Printing Office.

U.S. Department of Education. 1987. *Ninth annual report to Congress on the implementation of the Education of the Handicapped Act.* Washington, D.C.: U.S. Department of Education.

U.S. Department of Health, Education and Welfare. 1975. *Report of a comprehensive service needs study.* Contract #100-74-03-09. Washington, D.C.: Government Printing Office.

U.S. Department of Labor. 1983. *Time of change: 1983 handbook of women workers.* Washington, D.C.: Government Printing Office.

U.S. Department of Labor, Employment Standards Administration. 1982. *A study of accommodations provided to handicapped employees by federal contractors.* Washington, D.C.: Government Printing Office.

Vance, C. 1984. *Pleasure and danger.* Boston: Routledge and Kegan Paul.

Vanderslice, V. J. 1988. Separating leadership from leaders: An assessment of the effect of leader and follower roles in organizations. *Human Relations* 41, no. 9:677-96.

Vash, C. 1982a. Employment issues for women with disabilities. *Rehabilitation Literature* 43, nos. 7-8:198-207.

———. 1982b. Women and employment. In *Women and rehabilitation of disabled persons,* ed. L. Perlman and K. Arnseon, Report of the sixth Mary Switzer memorial seminar. Washington, D.C.: National Rehabilitation Association.

Walker, L. E. 1984. *The battered woman syndrome.* New York: Springer-Verlag.

Walkerdine, V. 1984. Some day my prince will come: Young girls and the preparation for adolescent sexuality. In *Gender and generation,* ed. A. McRobbie and M. Nava, 162-84. London: Macmillan.

———. 1986. Post-stimulated theory and everyday social practices: The family and the school. In *Feminist social psychology: Developing theory and practice,* ed. V. Wilkinson, 57-76. Philadelphia: Open University Press.

———. 1990. *School-girl fictions.* New York: Verso.

Wallston, B. S. 1981. What are the questions in psychology of women? A feminist approach to research. *Psychology of Women Quarterly* 5, no. 4:597-617.

Walsh, M. R., ed. 1987. *The psychology of women: Ongoing debates.* New Haven, Conn.: Yale University Press.

Weeks, J. 1985. *Sexuality and its discontents.* London: Routledge and Kegan Paul.

Weinberg, N. 1976. The effect of physical disability on self-perception. *Rehabilitation Counseling Bulletin* (September): 15-20.

Weis, L. 1990a. *Without work: High school students in a de-industrializing economy.* New York: Routledge.

———. 1990b. *Working class without work: Adolescence in deindustrializing America.* New York: Routledge.

Weitz, R. 1984. What price independence? Social reactions to lesbians, spinsters, widows, and nuns. In *Women: A feminist perspective,* ed. J. Freeman, 3d ed., 105-44. Palo Alto, Calif.: Mayfield.

Werner, L. 1987. U.S. report asserts administration halted liberal "anti-family agenda." *New York Times,* November 14, A12.

West, C., and Zimmerman, D. H. 1987. Doing gender. *Gender and Society* 1:125–51.

Wexler, P. 1983. *Critical social psychology.* Boston: Routledge and Kegan Paul.

Wilkinson, S. 1986. *Feminist social psychology: Developing theory and practice.* Philadelphia: Open University Press.

Willis, P. 1981. *Learning to labour: How working-class kids get working-class jobs.* Aldershot, Eng.: Gower.

Wittig, M. A. 1985. Metatheoretical dilemmas in the psychology of gender. *American Psychologist* 40, no. 7:800–811.

Women and Disability Awareness Project. 1984. *Building community: A manual exploring issues of women and disability.* New York: Educational Equity Concepts.

Wortman, C., and Brehm, J. 1975. Responses to uncontrollable outcomes: An integration of reactance theory and the learned helplessness model. In *Advances in experimental social psychology,* ed. L. Berkowitz, 8:278–336. New York: Academic Press.

Wright, B. A. 1960. *Physical disability: A psychological approach.* New York: Harper and Row.

———. 1983. *Physical disability: A psycho-social approach.* New York: Harper and Row.

Young, A. 1983. *Youth labor force marked turning point in 1982.* U.S. Department of Labor, Bureau of Labor Statistics. Washington, D.C.: Government Printing Office.

Young, M. 1985. New monthly data series on school age youth. *Monthly Labor Review* 108, no. 7 (July): 49–50.

Zabin, K.; Hirsch, M.; Smith, E.; Streett, R.; and Hardy, J. 1986. Evaluation of a pregnancy prevention program on urban teenagers. *Family Planning Perspectives* 18, no. 3:191–26.

Zelnik, M., and Kim, Y. 1982. Sex education and its association with teenage sexual activity, pregnancy, and contraceptive use. *Family Planning Perspectives* 14, no. 3:117–26.

Zorn, J. 1983. Possible sources of culture bias in the variation of ETS language texts. Paper presented at conference on Callipe Composition and Communication. Detroit, Michigan.

Index